D1202179

FOUR STRONG WINDS

FOUR STRONG WINDS
IAN & SYLVIA

JOHN EINARSON
with IAN TYSON & SYLVIA TYSON

McCLELLAND & STEWART

Library and Archives Canada Cataloguing in Publication

Einarson, John, 1952-
Four strong winds : Ian and Sylvia / John Einarson with Ian Tyson and Sylvia Tyson.

ISBN 978-0-7710-3038-3

1. Ian & Sylvia. 2. Tyson, Ian, 1933-. 3. Tyson, Sylvia, 1940-. 4. Folk
singers--Canada--Biography. I. Tyson, Ian, 1933- II. Tyson, Sylvia, 1940-
III. Title.

ML421.T977E35 2011   782.421620092   c2011-901989-2

We acknowledge the financial support of the Government of Canada through the Book
Publishing Industry Development Program and that of the Government of Ontario
through the Ontario Media Development Corporation's Ontario Book Initiative. We
further acknowledge the support of the Canada Council for the Arts and the Ontario
Arts Council for our publishing program.

Every effort has been made to trace copyright holders and to obtain their permission
for the use of copyright material. The publisher apologizes for any errors or omissions
in the above list and would be grateful if notified of any corrections that should be
incorporated in future reprints or editions of this book.

Published simultaneously in the United States of America by
McClelland & Stewart Ltd., P.O. Box 1030, Plattsburgh, New York 12901

Library of Congress Control Number: 2011930066

Typeset in Van Dijk by M&S, Toronto
Printed and bound in Canada

ANCIENT FOREST
FRIENDLY

This book was produced using ancient-forest friendly papers.

McClelland & Stewart Ltd.
75 Sherbourne Street
Toronto, Ontario
M5A 2P9
www.mcclelland.com

1   2   3   4   5   15   14   13   12   11

CONTENTS

INTRODUCTION: FOUR STRONG WINDS

New York's fabled Town Hall, at 123 West 43rd Street between Sixth Avenue and Broadway, is, like Carnegie Hall (the city's other renowned performance venue), more than just a concert location or another stop on a tour itinerary. A Town Hall engagement is a milestone in any artist's career, a pinnacle, a measure of success, and a sign that you have, indeed, arrived. Spearheaded by the League for Political Education, a suffragette movement determined to create a utilitarian meeting hall, and opened in 1921, the venerable 1,500-seat venue is known for its superb acoustics. Folk artists were especially fond of performing at Town Hall because of its unique sound qualities that lent themselves to acoustic folk music. The Clancy Brothers and Tommy Makem, Bob Dylan, Phil Ochs, and Joan Baez had all graced the Town Hall stage. Now it was Ian & Sylvia's turn.

On the evening of February 27, 1965, the Canadian folk duo, the darlings of the North American folk music circuit and heroes back home, performed to a sold-out Town Hall audience. It was a significant moment in their upward career trajectory from arriving in New York as unknowns from Toronto just three years earlier. "This was our first solo concert at a major New York City venue," recalls Sylvia, noting that while the Canadian duo may have played Town Hall previously on a multi-artist folk bill,* this was their unofficial coming-out event for New York audiences. "It was a big moment for us."

Having gone just about as far as one could on the largely scattered Canadian folk music scene by early 1962, Ian & Sylvia headed south to New York's folk music mecca, Greenwich Village. With no contacts or connections and armed only with their own confidence and a list of the key folk music impresarios located in the Big Apple, the two managed to charm their way into the big leagues within a matter of days. Theirs was no Cinderella story, however; Ian Tyson and Sylvia Fricker had put in countless hours perfecting their distinctive vocal blend – Ian's rich baritone combined with Sylvia's signature vibrato and gift for idiosyncratic harmonies – before dazzling folk patrons in Toronto coffeehouses and headlining the inaugural Mariposa Folk Festival. Their repertoire, drawn from obscure traditional sources, was the envy of their contemporaries, Bob Dylan among them. In short order the duo had become a top draw on the lucrative American college circuit and were regarded in folk music circles as on par with the likes of Dylan, Baez, and Peter, Paul & Mary. Now here they were at Town Hall.

"They brought so much dignity to our genre of music," acknowledges Carolyn Hester, a contemporary on the folk music scene back in the 1960s. "They kind of represented the Toronto folk scene and that gave them a bit more importance to the rest

---

* Ian & Sylvia appeared bottom of the bill at Town Hall on October 5, 1962, alongside Sandy Bull, Judy Collins, John Lee Hooker, and Bob Dylan.

of us. They didn't come down here and just become Americanized folksingers, which could have happened. And as a result a lot more of us went up to Canada to perform because of them." Adds veteran American singer/songwriter Tom Paxton, "Ian & Sylvia became as much a part of the American folk music community as Peter, Paul & Mary or the Kingston Trio or anybody. I just thought they were fantastic. It was their voices that impressed me. They both sang so beautifully."

"Everybody in the [Greenwich] Village loved them," recalls banjo player extraordinaire Eric "Dueling Banjos" Weissberg, a member of the folk group the Tarriers at the time. "They were so good and it was so refreshing to hear that music done so well; great songs, great harmonies. They were regarded as being at the top of the folk music food chain." As Suze Rotolo, Bob Dylan's girlfriend at the time (pictured on the cover of his *The Freewheelin' Bob Dylan* album), points out, "There was something about Ian & Sylvia that was so compelling. Their look, their voices, and their choice of songs were unique. They had this natural charisma. Bob liked Ian & Sylvia a lot. He and Ian were good friends. And Bob thought Sylvia was gorgeous. He really admired her and thought she had a wonderful voice. There weren't a lot of folk duos at the time; so many came after them."

Having released three critically acclaimed albums and penned three bona fide folk music standards – "Four Strong Winds," "You Were On My Mind," and "Someday Soon" – Ian & Sylvia stood poised at the top of their game. As they strode onto the Town Hall stage to a rapturous response – Ian, matinee-idol handsome in a well-tailored suit, guitar in hand, and Sylvia, slender and radiant in an iridescent shift dress, her long dark hair poker-straight, clutching her autoharp – each paused briefly to acknowledge the adulation and drink in the moment before

3

turning to face one another. Exchanging quick glances, they opened their set singing a cappella the traditional Elizabethan ballad "The Greenwood Sidie (The Cruel Mother)," one of the many songs Sylvia had researched from her books of old English ballads. With its extraordinary parallel fifth harmonies, the opening number proved, as if it were necessary, that Ian & Sylvia were in a league all their own.

"We had a mystique being from Canada," Ian suggests. "That was a bit of a novelty. I had the whole package because I was a cowboy from the west, not like the cowboy I became much later. And Sylvia had the look back then with the long straight hair. It was like a script writer had written the whole thing."

For the next seventy-five minutes, Ian & Sylvia, accompanied by American guitarist Monte Dunn, presented a mesmerizing mix of traditional and original folk music, from two-hundred-year-old French Canadian ballads and Mississippi chain gang wails to cowboy laments and Appalachian bluegrass, all delivered in their inimitable harmonic blend. Interspersed with the traditional folk numbers was a growing cache of original songs, including Sylvia's "You Were On My Mind" (a pop hit later that year for We Five) and Ian's cowboy-themed "Four Rode By," inspired by the true story of the notorious Canadian outlaws the McLean brothers. Ian handled the between-song patter, jokes, and introductions while Sylvia, beguilingly shy, stood quietly at his side. Having recently completed recording sessions for their yet-to-be-released fourth album, the two debuted songs by then-unknown writers Gordon Lightfoot (the album's title track "Early Morning Rain," as well as "For Loving Me") and Steve Gillette ("Darcy Farrow"). Sylvia's funky "Maude's Blues" brought the house down, while "Come In, Stranger" was Ian's tip of the cowboy hat to friend and fellow traveller Johnny Cash.

4

By the time the duo closed their set with Ian's evocative "Four Strong Winds," its Western Canadian imagery harkening back to simpler times, there was little doubt that Ian & Sylvia had achieved a level of critical and commercial success, along with peer respect, that few Canadian performers before them had attained. When they returned for a rousing encore (in the days when an encore was earned, not pre-programmed) of "Nova Scotia Farewell," it was clear that despite all they had achieved in the North American popular music pantheon, the two remained steadfastly rooted in their Canadian homeland.

That close bond with their roots would ultimately earn Ian & Sylvia iconic status, multiple awards, and accolades in Canada in later years, long after breaking up to pursue separate careers, as their groundbreaking achievements were acknowledged (Order of Canada, Canadian Music Hall of Fame, Canadian Country Music Hall of Honour, Prairie Music Hall of Fame, Mariposa Hall of Fame, Governor General's Award, and honorary doctorates). In 2005, CBC radio listeners overwhelming voted "Four Strong Winds" the most essential Canadian song of all time. Writer Bob Mersereau's *The Top 100 Canadian Singles* (Goose Lane, 2010) ranked the song at number 9. Beloved CBC broadcaster Peter Gzowski once declared "Four Strong Winds" Canada's unofficial national anthem. "'Four Strong Winds' is the foundation of modern day songwriting in Canada," states veteran music journalist and former *Billboard* Canadian bureau chief Larry LeBlanc. "There's nothing like it that has stood the test of time."

"'Four Strong Winds' is an anthem," says fellow Canadian folk performer Bonnie Dobson. "Ian & Sylvia, along with Gordon Lightfoot, really set the scene for Canadian singer/songwriters. I love Ian & Sylvia's music. Even after they split up I continued to follow their music." As folk music legend Oscar Brand points out,

"Between the two of them Ian & Sylvia carried a lot of beauty. They were very special people who had great songs and performed them beautifully, which is something you couldn't say about all folksingers back then. They commented on the Canadian highways and byways to the world. They carried the banner for Canada. Ian wrote some of the greatest Canadian songs."

Whether together or individually, the two continue to inspire a whole new generation of singer/songwriters. "No woman in the music industry can say they haven't in some way been influenced by Sylvia Tyson," notes Alana Levandoski, part of a new wave of young Canadian musicians drawing attention beyond our borders. "With discipline, grace, and humour she has touched the generations." Singer/songwriter John Hiatt observes, "Ian writes great songs. He's a great lyricist and always has a good story to tell. That's my idea of a good lyric. The thing about songs is that they're really not poetry. A lot of it is the melody and the delivery and Ian knows that. He has that all put together." Dallas Good of respected roots-rock renegades the Sadies adds, "Of all people, Ian Tyson could give a rat's ass about what I think, which is something I love about the man. This is a kiss-ass business (I'm doing it now). That said, Ian never kissed an ass he didn't like (to my knowledge) and it shows in his uncompromising, stellar career. And Sylvia is a goddess. The Great Speckled Tysons made some perfect records and I thank them for it."

As for Ian & Sylvia's signature song, rock music icon and fellow Canadian Neil Young remains a fervent fan. "I've always loved it," says Neil of "Four Strong Winds." "It was the most beautiful record I heard in my life and I could not get enough of it." Muses Sylvia, "For so many people it was the first truly Canadian song that they heard that they could identify with as being a Canadian song. It's become a standard. Some people even think of it as a traditional song." Adds Blue Rodeo's Jim Cuddy, "I remember being a young person and hearing the singles, 'You Were On My Mind' and, of course, 'Four Strong Winds' and being more than a bit proud that those were Canadian songs."

"'Four Strong Winds' was before my time," notes multi-award winning Western Canadian alternative country singer/songwriter Corb Lund, "but it's definitely one of the iconic Canadian songs. I remember as a kid at camp when we'd all be sitting around the campfire singing 'Kumbaya' and 'Michael Rowed the Boat Ashore' someone would always start singing 'Four Strong Winds' and everyone would join in. Someone would write down the chords for me and we'd all do it. I didn't even know it was written by a Western Canadian. It was probably the first Canadian song I'd ever heard. It's just one of those songs in the campfire library that everybody knows." In recent years, Corb and Ian have developed a close friendship, with the latter serving as mentor to the young artist. "I tend to forget about his status when I'm around him," says Corb, "because even though he's from a different age bracket than me he's just like any one of my musician buddies. It doesn't feel any different hanging out with Ian. But every once in awhile I'll look over and see his Order of Canada medal on his dresser and I'll remember he's a legendary figure. Earlier, when I was just starting to write this kind of music, Ian was the one who showed me that it was okay to write about Canada, to put Calgary in my songs instead of Houston, and to sing about the Rocky Mountains instead of Texas. And that's become very important to my music."

Few things are more quintessentially Canadian than Ian & Sylvia. "They are a part of the fabric of this country," stresses Gordon Lightfoot, whose own career received a major boost once Ian & Sylvia brought him to wider attention by championing his brilliant songwriting. "They left a legacy of a lot of hard work and a lot of great music. They opened the doors for a lot of people and were very generous with other people including myself. And they're both still at it. I still pay attention to whatever they're doing."

MARLBOROUGH STREET BLUES

If it's true that opposites attract then it was inevitability more than serendipity that brought Ian Tyson, born in Victoria, and Sylvia Fricker, from the sleepy Southern Ontario community of Chatham, together in Toronto in the fall of 1959. Theirs was a deceptively sweet and stirring harmonic vocal blend like no other, yet it was born of contradiction: Ian, the self-confident, gregarious, outspoken, private-schooled, art college graduate cum rodeo cowboy, matinee-idol handsome, with no shortage of female admirers; and Sylvia, the shy, quiet, waif-like public school graduate, church choir veteran, and bookworm seven years his junior. Where Ian was all Western Canadian bravado and braggadocio, a slap on the back with a hail-fellow-well-met, a good joke and a beer, Sylvia, on the other hand, was enigmatic, dark, and alluring, with an air of inscrutability. She was the yin to his yang.

"They were an unlikely duo if there ever was one," recalls close friend and one-time manager Edgar Cowan. "Sylvia was this wispy little thing doing a kind of Jean Ritchie [the pre-eminent female traditional American folk performer] impersonation. She was kind of ordinary but she had the most unusual and unique voice. And she knew her music, where Ian was more of a 'hit the guitar and sing' kind of performer. It was a most peculiar matching when she and Ian hooked up together. He was handsome, rugged, orderly, urbane, and clearly western and she was thin, fey, timid, folksy, and very definitely non-city." And yet there was no denying the unique chemistry their joining forces created. It was a case of one plus one equals three.

Born in England to a well-to-do Liverpool shipping magnate family, Ian's father, George Dawson Tyson, immigrated to Canada as a teenager in 1906, seeking adventure and fortune in the untamed west. Travelling by train from Montreal he arrived in the then-frontier cow-town of Calgary. "The barbed wire hadn't completely taken over Alberta yet," notes Ian, "and there was still a lot of open range." The horse industry was big business then, and George fell in love with horses. "It was real wide-open cowboy country and I guess a lot of those English kids were as green as a gorge but they could get work simply because it was all supply and demand and there were just too many jobs." George worked on a ranch near Innisfail north of Calgary and lived the cowboy life as best he could in Alberta, where real live six-shooters weren't allowed but a man could carry a rifle. After three years on the open range he pulled up stakes for Vancouver Island, settling on 160 acres just outside of Duncan. "Magic mountains caught him, never let him go," sang Ian in "Stories He'd Tell," a rumination on his early years with his father. When war broke out in 1914, George was among a number of young men from the vicinity who enlisted, ending up a British captain and the lone survivor from Duncan. "When the Canadians got over there it was apparent what was happening. They were being mowed down just like goddamn cannon fodder. So his father, my grandfather Edward Dawson Tyson, used his money to buy him a commission and he was transferred out of the Canadian army to the British army as a captain. Saved his life, that did." Twice earning the Military Cross, George was wounded several times, and also held prisoner. Shortly before the war ended he was repatriated back to England to convalesce before returning to Vancouver Island. Nonetheless, he never forgot his fallen comrades. "He never spoke much about the war, he was a selective raconteur, but I know it affected him," offers Ian. "On Armistice Day [Remembrance Day] we would get off our horses and stand for two minutes' silence. It was very ritualistic. I remember that very, very well."

Leaving his cowboy dreams unfulfilled and ever the pragmatist, George Tyson took a job as an insurance agent. "He wasn't much of a businessman – he was always fishing or riding horses – but he was a character," muses Ian. "A very colourful man and very well-liked." George's love of horses and the outdoors, however, continued throughout his life. "We used to buy Indian horses off the reservation and break them and Dad played polo. He never paid more than forty dollars for a horse in his life and that's how I got into it and started breaking horses for him. The first cowboys I saw when I was a kid growing up, I knew right away that's what I wanted to be. Polo was okay [Ian played polo as a youngster] but I wanted to be a bronc rider."

Not long after settling into a routine life, George met Margaret Gertrude Campbell, a second-generation British Columbian whose family had come out from Ontario in 1872 and established the first pharmacy on the West Coast. Margaret was among the well-heeled gentry on Vancouver Island and came from money. "They were kind of West Coast aristocrats," suggests Sylvia. "There was money on Ian's mother's side of the family, the Campbells. They owned properties in downtown Victoria. His mother's family was well placed in B.C. society. She had been a concert pianist who had studied in New York. Ian's uncle Don always called me 'Cynthia' in this very upper-crust tone."

"My mother was very much a Scots Presbyterian," Ian stresses, admitting he was never very close to her, unlike his relationship with his father. "She was a very kind of alone person. She wanted to be a pianist but didn't follow that route. I think the old man was more musical than she was. He'd sing Patti Page songs in the shower. Still, my mom was very proud of Ian & Sylvia and our success." Margaret Campbell Tyson was possessed of a far more dominant personality than George Tyson and wore her family wealth openly. As one writer recalled on meeting her, "I was gob-smacked meeting Ian's mother. They had real money. That house was something perched up on the top of the highest hill in Victoria. When she came to the door to meet me she was wearing enough jewellery to warrant having bodyguards. She then proceeded to tell me that her son would have me believe that he fell off a shit wagon but 'I'm here to show you that's not the friggin' case.'" She claimed that Ian left home at age seventeen after throwing the lieutenant-governor's son down the stairs at the Royal Victoria Yacht Club.

George Tyson had all the airs of a British aristocrat, if not the bank account. Ian refers to his father as "the remittance man," living off a modest Tyson family stipend in anticipation of the big pay-off that would come once the family fortune was dispersed. In the background there was always the expectation of a significant inheritance once George's father in the United Kingdom passed away. "Old Edward lived to a ripe old age and when the inheritance finally came down in the 1950s there wasn't much left after the British Government got it. It was okay but it wasn't what he thought it would be. But he lived out a pretty comfortable life after that." George and Margaret were married June 18, 1930, in Victoria, which was still very much a British city in tone. If he didn't necessarily have money at the time, George certainly married into money with the Campbell clan, British Columbia old-family landed-aristocracy. Ten months later, April 12, a daughter, Jean, was born, followed by Ian on September 25, 1933, at Victoria Hospital.

Very much his father's son, Ian was born with an adventurous spirit and a rough-and-tumble attitude. His fondest memories of his preschool youth are times with his father, whether on the nearby beach at Smuggler's Cove along with his sister, hunting for treasure his father would buy at the five-and-dime store and bury in advance, or being around horses. As he related to writer Colin Escott, "The first cowboy I ever saw was when the rodeo came to town and my dad took me. I was maybe four or five. I saw this Indian. He was dark as mahogany and he had a purple silk shirt. He lifted me up and stuck me on the saddle. I said, 'That's it.'" It was the beginning of a lifelong obsession.

Music wasn't a factor in his early years but everyone knew the lad could carry a tune. "When I was a boy my father took me to see the original Sons of the Pioneers [featuring ex-Winnipegger Bob Nolan, composer of "Tumbling Tumbleweeds" and "Cool Water"] with Tex Ritter as a guest," Ian remembers. "That left quite an impression on me." He would also tune his radio to the Grand Ole Opry on Saturday nights and read Will James's vivid accounts of life in the Old West.

In 1946, thirteen-year-old Ian was enrolled at Glenlyon, a private school for the sons of Victoria's elite. His mother's inheritance paid the tuition. He endured Glenlyon's rigorous sports and academic programs until graduation in 1951. "I never really applied myself at school or later at art school," he admits. "I just went any way the wind blew." From his mid teens onward, Ian and his father weren't seeing eye to eye. Perhaps George saw too much of himself as a young man in Ian's wanderlust and lack of commitment. His time at Glenlyon left Ian with a profound aversion to private schools. When, in the mid 1970s, Sylvia suggested that their son Clay attend an Ontario private school offering a more disciplined environment, Ian was adamantly opposed. As Sylvia explains, "Ian had been a private school boy and put his foot down, saying, 'No child of mine is ever going to a private school.' But at that point it might have been good for Clay. He needed that structure and discipline. But Ian wouldn't have anything to do with it, wouldn't countenance it, and wouldn't pay for it."

Although the music bug had yet to bite, Ian's dream of being a cowboy continued unabated. "I went to work for the forest service after I graduated and I would rodeo whenever I had time off. I was rodeoing in B.C. and in Alberta. I used to ride bareback horses, saddle broncs, and bareback broncs. I rode on the weekends like a semi-pro. Never full-time." When he was twenty-one, Ian entered the Vancouver School of Art's four-year degree program and completed the first three years before a rodeo accident near Cremona, Alberta, put him in hospital with a shattered ankle. "This bareback horse came out of the chute wrong and she bucked me off real high and I came down and landed on my feet, but as my foot hit the ground she stepped on my ankle, and my ankle, her foot, and the ground all met at one point. It was a real mess. I was on crutches for about four months." But the unfortunate accident did have an upside. "Eight or nine of us were in the broken-leg ward in Calgary and a kid in the next bed had a guitar which he couldn't play, and neither could I. You really had to work at it to learn because there weren't any books or records. I started just fooling around trying to learn how to tune it and that's how I began, actually." He proved to be a quick learner. Although left-handed by birth, he played guitar right-handed. "I didn't know any better. I didn't know there were left-handed guitars. But I don't think it made a lot of difference. One hand compensates for the other. You've either got a fast fretting hand or a fast picking hand. I wanted to be a flat picker and that's what I do to this day." Returning in the fall of 1957 on crutches for his final year of art school, Ian began playing some of the dives, honky-tonks, and juke joints in downtown Vancouver. "You could disappear from the school for periods of time," he remembers. "You could juggle different lives, which most of us did. Most of us had night jobs to work our way through. I was a waiter. But I always got back in time to make the school year."

Rock 'n' roll was already entering its original golden age by 1957, incorporating rural southern rockabilly and urban do-wop emanating from northern cities with significant black populations. Rockabilly was the most raucous and liberating of these influences, and as such regarded with a jaundiced eye by parents, preachers, and school principals. It was a jumped-up version of hillbilly country swing and black rhythm and blues played by young whites like Carl Perkins and Elvis Presley (originally known as "The Hillbilly Cat"). In August of that year, local radio CKWX deejay and music impresario Robert "Red" Robinson hosted a sell-out concert at Vancouver's Empire Stadium headlined by Elvis Presley, one of only three concerts The King ever played outside the United States (the others being Toronto and Ottawa earlier that year). Buddy Holly & the Crickets' recording "That'll Be the Day" was released that year, along with the Everly Brothers' "Wake Up Little Susie," while the wildest of the rockabilly performers, Jerry Lee Lewis from Ferriday, Louisiana, abandoned theology school for rockabilly, releasing "Whole Lotta Shakin' Goin' On" and "Great Balls of Fire" on Sun Records out of Memphis. In Canada, rock 'n' roll was beginning to challenge country and western and hit-parade pop (Patti Page, Perry Como, Rosemary Clooney, et al.) for air time on radio, although the live rock 'n' roll scene remained largely regional and isolated. Red Robinson is often credited with being the first to play rock 'n' roll recordings on Canadian radio, although there are likely several others who would challenge that claim. In the '50s Canadian recording was barely in its infancy, hastening the migration south-ward of the likes of the Crewcuts, Four Lads, the Diamonds, and a sixteen-year-old Ottawa kid, Paul Anka.

"I started playing rockabilly," states Ian, who, smitten with Elvis and Buddy Holly, joined a band called the Sensational Stripes. "I had a Hofner flattop guitar before getting a Hofner electric. I was a rockabilly guy playing down on Hastings and Main in Vancouver, right down in the tenderloin with the strippers and the black hookers and Indian junkies. Right around Chinatown. I was trying to sing a little rockabilly." The Sensational Stripes even played a concert alongside Buddy Holly, Eddie Cochran, and LaVern Baker. "Bill Haley's 'Rock Around the Clock,' Gene Vincent's 'Be-Bop-A-Lula,' Buddy Knox's 'Party Doll,' I loved all that stuff. Buddy Knox and I later became good friends [Knox eventually settled in Dominion City, Manitoba]. Then I joined a band with Gerry Fiender and we did a lot of the Red Robinson dances. Red was a huge deejay back then. But I got fired because the kid who was the Elvis clone, Jimmy Morrison, well, the girls liked me better than him. So I had to go. I was finishing art school and we were living hand to mouth. We were stealing peanut butter from the Chinese grocery store." Ian would also spend time with Taller O'Shea and his Pistol Packin' Rhythm western swing band playing the Indian reservation circuit, along with art school buddy Steve Cresta. "I was drifting towards country music even then," he later admitted. He also played with country music bands in the Port Alberni area. Folk music, however, was not yet on his radar.

That would all change in 1958 with an old North Carolina folk song inspired by the 1866 murder of a woman named Laura Foster and the hanging of her murderer. Originally sung as "Tom Dula," a California-based singing group called the Kingston Trio recorded the song as "Tom Dooley" on their self-titled debut album released in June 1958. Released as a 45 single featuring sparse accompaniment on banjo and acoustic guitar, by August the song was number 1 on the *Billboard* pop charts, and with that event what would later be known as the folk music boom or folk revival was born. Though traditional folk songs were being performed by the likes of the Weavers (with Pete Seeger), Burl Ives, Woody Guthrie, and Harry Belafonte, the Kingston Trio turned the fringe musical genre into a commercially viable pop entity. The genre's appeal was mainly to the young college crowd, whose numbers were swelling through the late 1950s to early '60s. Folk music spoke to that post-beatnik demographic more than did bebop jazz or rock 'n' roll. Jazz was too intellectual and exclusive; rock was too lower class, preoccupied with mindless teenage romance, aimed at the groin rather than the brain. Folk music addressed issues of inequality, poverty, civil rights, war, and the simple virtues found in an idyllic rural American past, topics on the minds of socially conscious college-age youth. The Kingston Trio had as much of an impact on guitar sales (and five-string banjos) as Elvis had a few years earlier.

"Quite simply, folk music is music of the folk, the common people, and it's music that discusses the conditions of, the protests coming from, and the aims and goals of the folk," offers Ruth Jones McVeigh, a leading light on the early Toronto folk scene. She and her husband Crawford "Casey" Jones spearheaded the first Mariposa Folk Festival in 1961. Indeed, folk music had a DIY (do-it-yourself) ethos from the get-go, which furthered its mass appeal. All you needed was to be able to play three chords and you were on your way. The other common characteristic of the early folk boom was that it was based on traditional songs, whether bluegrass, Appalachian, or Mississippi field hand chants – the older and grittier the better. The wisdom was you didn't *write* folk music, you *discovered* it. The most orthodox of the purists even recreated any mistakes in the original recordings, as if to tamper with the original was somehow sacrilegious. "Before I ever joined the Journeymen I was writing these banjo pieces, like extended banjo suites, in about 1959," claims Dick Weissman, banjo player in the Journeymen, along with John Phillips, and a contemporary of Ian & Sylvia, "and John Cohen from the New Lost City Ramblers said to me, 'You don't have the right to write folk songs.' Woody Guthrie can do that, Leadbelly can do that, but not me, a middle-class kid from Philadelphia. The prevailing attitude was that it was not acceptable or honourable for me to do that. I found that totally mystifying. Even in my folkiest days I was interested in extending the traditions, not duplicating them." The new decade would bring the divisions between the traditionalists and new folk revivalists into sharper focus and folkies would have to take sides.

"I remember clearly hearing 'Tom Dooley' on the radio in Toronto, as clear as I can remember when Jack Kennedy was assassinated," confirms Ian, recalling his arrival in Toronto in September 1958. "I thought, 'What the hell is that? It's not country. It's really cool.' And it was folk music. The Kingston Trio had their moment in the sun and they were huge. When Bob Shane left that kind of took the wind from behind them because he was the heart and soul of that group. But they were very influential. They were a real California deal, like the fathers of the Beach Boys." In their wake came innumerable folk ensembles pitched to the middle of the road, such as the Limeliters, the Travelers Three, the Brothers Four, the Clancy Brothers and Tommy Makem, the Chad Mitchell Trio, the Rooftop Singers, the Serendipity Singers, the New Christy Minstrels, the Tarriers, and Bud & Travis, as well as individual folk artists like Pete Seeger, Judy Collins, Bob Gibson, Theodore Bikel, Josh White, Len Chandler, Carolyn Hester, Oscar Brand, and the queen of all folkies, Joan Baez. Folk music was suddenly big business, especially on college campuses.

Ian had already been introduced to folk music in Vancouver prior to the Kingston Trio's breakthrough. "I didn't come from a rural folk background although I'd always loved country music on the radio in B.C. I can remember very distinctly as a young boy hearing the Grand Ole Opry on the radio for the first time. I don't know how it got all the way to B.C. but you could hear it. It had a tremendous impact on me. When I was going to art school in Vancouver around 1956 a fellow came to the school and was looking for someone to volunteer to design a poster for a series of singers who were coming to town. Pete Seeger was one of them, along with Odetta, who was just starting her career, and this was one of the very first concerts she did as a marvellous young folksinger. So we were asked to participate in designing these posters. I didn't know what folk music was. All I listened to was that terrible music on the radio like 'Tennessee Waltz' before Bill Haley & the Comets and rock 'n' roll started. They couldn't pay us for the posters but we got to go to the concerts. I did the Odetta poster and she sang in a little labour hall. Folk music in those days was closely associated with the socialist movement. It was this little labour hall on Pender Street and I was really knocked out by it. I was really impressed with it and really liked the music. I got very excited about it."

The year before Ian headed east to Toronto, Welsh émigré Roy Guest opened what Ian considers the first coffeehouse in Vancouver. Named the Heidelberg Café and located on Robson, it was modelled on the British coffeehouses that had been around since the early '50s. Here Roy would play guitar and sing traditional English folk songs. Ian met Roy in 1958. "He talked me into coming down and sitting in. I learned a couple of songs from him. I didn't know any songs so I just cribbed it from wherever I could. Roy Guest was really the one who got me started. Before that I was working at the odd job with country bands playing legions. You try to play two or three legion halls a week with a country band and make a living that way. I played with a guy called Gerry Fiender and we played rock 'n' roll and country. But Roy Guest had a strong impact on the few of us around at the time in Vancouver. About a year later he went back to England and became a very successful folk music concert promoter there. But by the time he left I had gone back to singing and playing rock 'n' roll and country and was working in Chinatown and there just wasn't the opportunity to do folk music. It's hard to remember it now, but very few people even knew what the term meant. People just didn't play guitars or banjos in those days. My God, when I left Vancouver hitchhiking east with my guitar I never had to wait more than ten minutes on the highway. People would stop to find out what that thing was I was carrying. Nowadays, of course, every kid has a guitar. It was different back then.

"Roy Guest was the instigator for me stylistically, and he laid down the pattern, a real English ballad pattern, which was basically what Sylvia and I followed for years. A lot of our style was based on that. I really liked what Roy was doing and really liked that kind of music. I knew folk music but I didn't *know* it was folk music. I was more taken with Roy's music than I was with Buddy Holly. I loved the band stuff, the Buddy Holly thing, but putting a band together was very difficult in those days. The band thing was kind of unreachable for me at that point. I was very much attracted to the fact that it was one man and one guitar. You didn't even need a sound system. We didn't even use microphones."

Every culture has its folk music, often referred to as ethnic music. What initially drew Ian, and ultimately Sylvia, to folk music were the old Elizabethan ballads that English immigrants brought over to North America and that remained part of the culture of the Appalachian Mountains and Atlantic Canada. "There's a lot of it down east," he notes. "That's where the tradition is. As far as Western Canadian folk music, I looked for it far and wide and finally decided that if there was ever going to be a Western Canadian folk tradition I'd better hurry up and start writing it, which is what I did. The cowboy thing, the real traditional cowboy songs in Alberta and Saskatchewan, came up the trail from Texas in the 1880s. Down in the Atlantic provinces, especially in Newfoundland, their ballads are exactly the same as Appalachian ballads. They're all Scots/Irish/English ballads; same songs, sometimes different variations from a later period and sung with different accents. It's amazing that the same songs that [ethno-musicologist] Cecil Sharp collected in the Appalachians in the 1912 to 1925 period have been collected by Helen Creighton and people like that in the Canadian Maritimes; exactly the same stuff. The Maritime versions tend to be more lyrical and prettier, though.

"The traditional Canadian instrument was pretty much the fiddle and that's it," Ian continues. "That's why there are so many great fiddlers in Canada. You didn't see the guitar back at the turn of the century. In the West there was all kinds of ethnic traditional music brought over from Europe and kept alive. For example, there's all kinds of folk music from the Ukraine all over the Prairies. That's a big part of it out in Western Canada, this ethnic music tradition."

In his third year at art school, Ian embarked on a star-crossed relationship with fellow art student Evinia Pulos from Vernon in the Okanagan Valley. "We were each other's first great love," he confesses. "She broke hearts from one end of the Okanagan Valley to the other, then, when she was seventeen, she came to art school where I met her. We each met our match. We had many loves after that but through it all we remained soul mates. She lives in Kelowna now and has been many times married. But we are soul mates. She was a great beauty of her time and a terrific person. She broke a lot of hearts, including mine, I guess. We've been lovers for fifty-five years. How many people can say that? We were in love. She was married to one of my best friends for awhile. She's a great woman." As Evinia recalls, "Ian was very good looking. We planned to go to Toronto to be artists together. We came close to marrying but never did. We thought we'd spend the rest of our lives together, but we didn't." All Ian will say is, "It got complicated." Evinia headed south to Los Angeles. Ian visited once but returned to Vancouver. The two maintained a distant relationship throughout the decades and Evinia, who still has Ian's letters to her, insists that "Four Strong Winds" was inspired by that relationship. "He still sees her," Sylvia remarks ruefully. "She was the third person in our marriage." Indeed, since his second divorce, Ian has reconnected with Evinia. "That was the spectre everyone who was involved with Ian has had to deal with, the spirit of Evinia Pulos, the great love of Ian's life."

Following graduation in June of 1958 Ian discovered there was little work for a commercial artist in Vancouver, nor for a budding folksinger, so after scuffling about for the summer, he determined there was little choice but to leave. He had no specific destination nor vocation in mind, just a single-minded urge to leave. "Jack Kerouac was a huge influence on me back in Vancouver days," he reveals. "I read *On the Road* and connected with that whole beat generation thing. Nancy Patterson, who won all the scholarships at art school and eventually moved to England and has never been heard from again, her boyfriend Gordie Cox, a disbarred jockey, was a real honest-to-God beatnik. He was the first kid on the block with a copy of *On the Road*. I loved that book. It had a very strong influence on me. So I became a beatnik cowboy." Kerouac's debut novel defined the beat generation, post-war teens and twenty-somethings who felt alienated from their parents' ideals and goals and who found their voice in bebop jazz and the poetry of the likes of Allen Ginsberg and Lawrence Ferlinghetti. For Kerouac, life was to be found out on the wide open road. Ian could relate to that concept. A friend, Tom Jones, drove Ian across the American border and dropped him along the highway. It was either south or east. "I decided to leave Vancouver on the advice of an old Vaudevillian comic who was working in this joint I was playing in. He thought I had possibilities of something and told me the best thing I could do was to get out. And so I did. I told my friend Tom I was going to hitchhike somewhere. I was going to get the hell out of Vancouver. I got picked up by a guy going east and I ended up in Chicago about a week later. I hitchhiked from there to Toronto. That's how I got to Toronto, and I was there for seventeen years." After a run in with the police outside Chicago, Ian took a bus to Windsor before sticking his thumb out and making his way to Toronto. "If the car had been going south I would have ended up in L.A. It was just by accident that I ended up in Toronto."

George Tyson was less than pleased with his wayward son's unsettled ways, fretting that following a career in either art or music offered little in the way of security and wanting him to go into something secure and steady, like insurance. "It's interesting because my father was a classic case of someone who had no concept of the leisure industry and its huge postwar growth and potential, of which music and entertainment was a major part," reflects Ian. "His generation had gone through the Great Depression, and if you didn't have a solid job like shoe salesman or doctor, lawyer, or car salesman you were giving yourself to a life of total poverty. He was from a different era where show business was an extremely tough life. He had no concept of the skiing industry or the television industry, anything involved with leisure, in combination with the arts. People had discretionary money after the war for leisure activities and the arts. He just didn't get it, even though he hated the nine-to-five grind. He was proud of me after I was successful, but he thought it was just luck. He didn't understand talent. He was always so worried I'd end up an artist or a cowboy or a musician, and I ended up doing all three."

When Ian arrived in Toronto in September 1958 he encountered a city more conservatively strait-laced than the one he'd fled. "Toronto the Good" earned its sobriquet for its sense of self-righteousness, moral superiority, and Victorian-era uptightness (all that would change with the new decade). Nonetheless, attitudes towards beatniks, folksingers, and cowboys were less than tolerant. "You had to be over twenty-one to buy beer or booze," notes Edgar Cowan. "There wasn't anywhere for younger people to gather and socialize, so coffeehouse clubs, some with memberships, opened up just to serve coffee, sandwiches, and desserts. In order to help pay for the entertainment some of the clubs had small weekend cover charges. These clubs attracted large numbers

of young high school and university students and old urban folkies. On the weekends, the young suburban crowd swelled the
coffeehouses."

The seminal Yorkville music scene that spawned the likes of
Murray McLauchlan, David Clayton Thomas, Joni Mitchell, the
Dirty Shames (featuring Amos Garrett), the Sparrow (later
Steppenwolf), and, briefly, Neil Young with the Mynah Birds, had
yet to blossom. In the mid '60s, that four-square-block area of
Victorian homes-turned-coffeehouses/nightclubs in the heart of
downtown Toronto (bounded by Bloor Avenue to the south and
Davenport to the north, and from east to west by Bay Street and
Avenue Road) would become a beacon for wannabe singer/song-
writers from across Canada, many drawn there by the success of
Ian & Sylvia. "We were already in New York by then," Ian points
out. "Neil Young and all those guys followed us into Yorkville after
we were gone. We had left Toronto by the time places like the
Riverboat opened."

"I arrived in Toronto before the first coffeehouse opened up,"
he maintains. "The First Floor club on Asquith Street one block
north of Bloor had been a black jazz club, bebop jazz. Then later
it started offering folk music, too. Initially the jazz guys resented
it. They didn't like it, but eventually it became so overwhelmingly
popular. The folk scene crowded out the jazz scene by the early
'60s. It's too bad, because it was apples and oranges. You don't
have to compare the two or say one's better than the other. It was
very competitive. After that all these other clubs started. And I
had a gig in every one of them. Back then, if you could play guitar
you got free beer and you got the girls. When I got to Toronto
the first wave of folksingers was just starting. I didn't know it at
the time, but there were all kinds of guys like me who were gravi-
tating towards Toronto, a lot of guys from England and Scotland.

It took awhile but by 1960 the coffeehouse scene was exploding. There were coffeehouses down in the village area and that's what started that whole Yorkville music scene. The folk music explosion hit Toronto so hard that at the time I think there were more folk music coffeehouses than folksingers. There was a nucleus of about ten singers and there were more coffeehouses than singers to perform in them. I find that amazing, but that's how quickly the coffeehouse thing took off. We'd work in a different coffeehouse each night. They had to share the folksingers, so we had a much easier time than the kids do now. Six months after I got to Toronto there was a whole scene happening. When I got to Toronto, you would go to the Colonial Tavern where they played jazz. Then Ronnie Hawkins came in and the rockabilly scene was big. He and I became buddies later on. There wasn't a national music scene then. You could be big in Vancouver but no one heard of you on the other side of the Rockies. Ian & Sylvia helped create a national music scene in Canada. We were a key ingredient in that."

In 1959 Arkansas-born rockabilly redneck Ronnie Hawkins arrived in Toronto. He quickly turned the city and Southern Ontario on its ear, with a raw, vibrant, and energetic sound. Fellow rockabilly artist Conway Twitty had tipped Ronnie off to the money he could make up in Southern Ontario. By the early 1960s only drummer Mark "Levon" Helm remained from Hawkins's southern contingent, and "The Hawk", always a larger than life character, found local replacements from various bands working the Ontario bar circuit. This nucleus of the Hawks would later become the Band, led by guitarist/songwriter Robbie Robertson. "There were two big scenes in Toronto," recalls Ian. "Down on the Yonge Street strip there was a big, big electric scene, rockabilly. It was a hell of a scene with Rockin' Ronnie Hawkins with Levon Helm on drums and a young punk kid from Cabbagetown on guitar, Robbie Robertson. Real exciting. But then up a few blocks north were all the coffeehouses. A couple of years later it all started merging and the music started blending together."

If the burgeoning coffeehouse scene offered steady work for the newly arrived Vancouverite, it didn't always provide a steady income, so Ian applied his art school degree to a series of jobs in commercial art. "I worked for Kenneth Smith Co. out in Leaside designing peanut butter jars and all that stuff. I worked briefly for the *Star Weekly* as a junior illustrator and had one *Star Weekly* illustration, for a detective story. I didn't last because I was late for work. But I didn't care because I was making $15 a night in the coffeehouses." Ian is also credited with designing the logo for Resdan, a popular dandruff shampoo. It was around this same time that Edgar Cowan met Ian. "I think I met him at a place called the Coffee House down on Gerrard Street run by John McHugh. He was performing. That would have been in late 1959. Then I met him at a party on McPherson Avenue, one of those parties where you drink a lot, play guitars, and sing songs throughout the night. I was at Ryerson Polytechnic and booking concerts there so I booked Ian to perform at Ryerson. This was before he met Sylvia. He was working a day gig at a tumbler glass manufacturing company, painting decals on glasses or designing pictures of cars, trucks, flowers, and whatever on kitschy kitchen glass sets. At night he'd play in the coffeehouses. He was doing the occasional evening gig at John Morley's the Village Corner club. He would also appear at John McHugh's Half Beat Coffeehouse or one of the two jazz clubs, the House of Hamburg or the First Floor club on Asquith, often appearing with actor/jazz singer Don Francks. Ian had had a rather comfortable, upper-middle-class life back in Victoria and worked a stint as a lumberjack, rodeo rider, and guitar picker. At the time he was sharing a house with Ron Roy, a potter, on Marlborough Street."

"I had a neat little place on Marlborough Street, a little dead-end street," confirms Ian. The house was later immortalized in the song "Marlborough Street Blues" on Ian & Sylvia's 1965 album *Early Morning Rain*. "They had these little shotgun houses built, I guess, for the railroad workers." Adds Edgar, "That's where the parties were, at Ian's on Marlborough. Later I shared an apartment with him in several places." Edgar would ultimately serve as an informal manager for Ian & Sylvia during their pre-Greenwich Village days.

"Ian could be a bit ornery at times," observed Edgar. "He always was trying to prove himself to his father. His mother was divine, a very grand woman. Ian related more in his head with his father and his history. His mother was a class act and a bit toney and Ian didn't like that. He was rebellious and didn't like that upper-crust aspect of his background and kind of hid it. She was private school–educated and so was Ian."

Not long after making his Toronto coffeehouse debut, Ian teamed up with singer/actor Don Francks. A legendary figure in Toronto folk and jazz circles and a notorious scenemaker, Vancouver-born Don arrived in Toronto a year before Ian. He is better remembered these days for his acting talents both on television and on Broadway. "Ian had only been in Toronto a very short time before we started working," Don recalls. "It wasn't somebody in the jazz scene, it was somebody in the folk scene, that introduced us, Vivian Stinson. I had been hanging out with [American folk and blues singer] Josh White. I had been interested in folk music since Vancouver, after attending a Pete Seeger concert on Pender Street. When I got to Toronto I was allowed to sing some folk songs at the First Floor club, which was basically a jazz club, but on Thursday night they would let folksingers come in and do their songs. I was very active in folksinging because I found

a connection between the old field songs and work songs, traditional Elizabethan songs and ballads, and folk songs. So I met Ian
and he looked like a movie star to me. I couldn't believe what I
was seeing. He was a very striking, handsome, tall young man and
a good singer. The room would literally stop when Ian walked in.
He commanded a sigh from all the ladies. So I asked him if he
wanted to sing with me. He was singing everything from 'Red
River Valley' to 'The Strawberry Roan,' cowboy songs, and I was
doing a lot of black songs, blues, field songs, and things like that.
I was also doing a lot of traditional English folk songs as well. I
knew a lot of the songs he knew so I'd do the harmony and let
him take the lead. And I would teach him some of the songs he
didn't know that I did and he'd sing with me. So we were able to
do a show together almost immediately. That was the fun. We
didn't have to rehearse for a month and a half. We would switch
back and forth like that so the audience got a real round of music.
And that became Ian & Don or Don & Ian. It wasn't long before
we were pretty well known in Toronto. We made very little money
but it helped both of us." Ian and Don also performed on some
local CBC television.

"Ian always had that cowboy aspect to him, and he was sincere
about it," reckons Don. "We would do those cowboy songs as honourably as we could. It wasn't just toying around with them. Ian
knew a lot of those songs. We had our own cowboy singing stars
right here in Canada, like Wilf Carter. They weren't called country singers back then, they were cowboy singers."

The two cut a dashing figure in Don's choice of vehicle. "Ian
and I were tooling around Toronto in a big, long-wheelbase Austin
Princess limousine, former Prime Minister Louis St. Laurent's old
car. I purchased it when he went out of office. It ended up back
at the Austin dealership here in Toronto and I saw it and just had

to have it. It was enormous and was gorgeous. We always had a good time together."

"Don Francks was a hugely influential and popular guy at that time," Ian points out. "The jazz guys idolized him. I worked with Don for a time. [jazz guitar great] Lenny Breau worked with Don, too, but I couldn't work with Lenny. He was too way out there. Don was very good to me and helped me a lot. Then he got the call to go to New York to be in this huge Broadway production [*Kelly*] and he was heading for the big time, but it closed after about the third night and he was never the same." Don was moving further in a free-form jazz direction, something that had less appeal to Ian, so they parted company amicably. Following the recording of a live jazz album at the Village Vanguard in Greenwich Village with his trio Three (comprised of Don, Lenny Breau, and bassist Eon Henstridge, father of actress Natasha Henstridge), Don would go on to a lengthy television and film career, beginning with NBC's *Jericho* in 1966 and a major role alongside Fred Astaire in the feature film *Finian's Rainbow* two years later. He ultimately fled Hollywood for the Red Feather Indian Reserve near North Battleford, Saskatchewan (where he took the name Iron Eagle) before returning to Toronto. He continues to work steadily in theatre, television, voice-overs, and movies. He even appeared in the 2007 Bob Dylan biopic *I'm Not There* as Hobo Joe, an ironic bit of casting since Don knew Dylan in the early '60s in Greenwich Village. "I would see Ian & Sylvia down in Greenwich Village when they were hanging out with Bobby Dylan," he recalls. "I was going around with Bob's girlfriend Suze Rotolo's sister Carla. She was the greatest, a wonderful girl." In the early '70s Ian invited Don to guest on his weekly CTV television series *The Ian Tyson Show*. "Ian called me on the reserve and invited me to be on his TV show in Toronto. I came with my autoharp and did a couple of songs. It was fun being with him again."

Gordon Lightfoot had already moved down from Orillia to Toronto and caught Ian and Don's act at the First Floor club and was suitably impressed. Working in a duo with Terry Whelan as the Tu-Tones, Gordon was also serving double duty playing drums and singing with local jazz player Jack Zaza. But he had his sights set on being a solo folk performer. Gordon had previously studied music composition at the Westlake College of Music in Hollywood, which he insists was "the best thing I ever did. I learned sight reading, melody, ear training, composing." He recalls his first time seeing Ian perform. "Ian hadn't been in Toronto all that long. His guitar playing was the first thing that really got me interested in him the very first time I heard him and Don Francks together. He had a very bluegrass-influenced style. Ian's a wonderful guitar player. When I saw him working with Don I got quite taken with his guitar playing, quite frankly. I said to myself, 'That's the way I want to play the guitar.' I wanted to get away from this Terry Whelan business and get out on my own. Ian inspired me through his guitar playing, his singing, and his repertoire. He had a whole stock of great songs that dated back into the cowboy era. That night I heard him sing 'Dark as a Dungeon' and I was so impressed I put it in my own repertoire. I actually learned a few songs from some of the guys who were around at the time, just to have enough material.

"The folk revival was taking place at that time," Gordon continues, "and there were a handful of clubs here in the city, including the Village Corner, the House of Hamburg, the First Floor club, the Bohemian Embassy, the Fifth Peg. I was still working with Terry at the same time I was playing guitar and singing in the folk clubs. I was also dancing and singing with the Singing

Swinging Eights on *Country Hoedown*. We would sing five backups a show, plus dance. I was doing the show on Friday night at 8:00, then hightailing it out to Orchard Park Tavern by the Woodbine racetrack to work with Jack, get in there by the skin of my teeth, drum and sing songs like 'A Foggy Day in London Town,' then dash out to sing folk music at the Village Corner club. I had a full schedule, so much so that by 1962 I was able to buy myself a new car. But Ian was a big influence on me, always. Not so much Sylvia, but I always think of the instrument, the guitar. Hearing Ian early on got me thinking a certain way in my career."

An early influence on both singer/songwriters was folk artist Bob Gibson. "He was our hero and influence and Gordie Lightfoot will tell you that, too," acknowledges Ian. "Bob's totally forgotten now but he was the king of the Chicago folk scene back then." Bob Gibson was a folk innovator who inspired many others, not just Ian and Gordon. Spotted by Chicago music impresario Albert Grossman in the late 1950s, Bob went on to become a fixture at Grossman's Gate of Horn club in Chicago and a mainstay on the folk and hootenanny circuit before being sidelined by drug addiction. "His twelve-string style was totally unique. We thought he was God. This was when I was in Toronto. That's when I started learning things from records. We were scrounging for songs absorbing that stuff like sponges. Dylan was doing the same thing down south."

Edgar Cowan laughs as he recalls the time CBC TV attempted to draw on Ian's movie-star good looks by having him sing "Bless Your Beautiful Hide" from *Seven Brides for Seven Brothers*. "That was very embarassing. He was mortified. They were trying to make him into somebody he wasn't. They were trying to turn Ian into a Robert Goulet-type singing, dancing, and acting feature player in their entertainment department. Fortunately, that

did not happen. He was so good looking and could sing, so someone at the CBC talked him into it.”

For a short time Ian teamed up with another singer, Noreen St.
Pierre, who was already a name on the Toronto scene. “It was quite
different than later with Sylvia,” notes Edgar. “Noreen was a very
sweet singer but not a folky. She was lovely and there was definitely an attraction there between them. I think they sang together
at the First Floor Club.” Unfortunately, Noreen’s vocal style was
ill-suited to Ian’s folk and cowboy sensibilities.

Soon after this, Ian was introduced to Sylvia Fricker. “That story
of her first singing to me over the phone is kind of an urban legend
and not exactly how it happened,” he stresses. “The guy that I
worked for in the glass factory was an Englishman, a really nice
guy. He was a swinger in a sophisticated way and he used to go
down to the Chatham area and party. Sylvia was at one of those
parties and he heard her sing. So he told me, ‘You’ve got to hear
this marvellous girl.’ He got her on the phone for me and I don’t
remember if she sang to me over the phone, I doubt it, but I told
her to come on up to Toronto. I was going to be singing at the First
Floor club and I said to her that we’d get her up to sing. She played
this weird mandocello or whatever the hell it was. It wasn’t like a
ukulele; it was this strange-looking instrument that she played in
this very unorthodox way.* And she was a weird-acting girl, a real
free spirit and very eccentric. She was a hippie before that term ever
existed; very eccentric, from eccentric parents. There always were
those kinds of ladies, it’s definitely a Canadian breed, loners and
distinctly outsiders. So she came up. She was nervous and she has
that vibrato already but when she’s nervous you could fill a diesel
truck with it. But she was very nice and that’s how it happened.”

---

* The instrument was an octophone, strung like a mandolin but larger in size,
  with four sets of octave strings.

Born September 19, 1940, in the rural town of Chatham, Ontario, some three and a half hours southwest of Toronto towards Windsor and the U.S. border, Sylvia Anne Fricker is the second oldest of four children. She and her sisters, Sonia and Valerie, and their brother, Brock (Sonia is three years Sylvia's senior; Valerie and Brock are seven and twelve years younger, respectively) were born to William and Phyllis Eleanor Fricker (nee Brock). Sylvia's mother, a Canadian, was born October 11, 1912, in the United States, allowing Sylvia to enjoy dual citizenship. Phyllis's family, most of whom were Great Lakes fishers, hailed from the Port Dover area of Ontario, and her father, Sylvia's grandfather, had lived a colourful life, which included stints as a chuck wagon cook in North Dakota, playing trumpet in the circus, and owning a shirt factory in Chicago. William, or "Bill," Sylvia's father, was born in Southampton, England, on April 17, 1898, but came to Canada as a youngster. He and his family lived in Mount Forest, Ontario. Bill served in both World Wars, the second as a gunnery instructor. "My father signed up for the First World War at the age of fifteen," notes Sylvia. "Family legend has it that my red-haired grandmother went down and attacked the recruiting sergeant with an umbrella. 'You can't take my Willie, he's too young.' But they eventually took him. That was in the First World War. After he came home he worked for the Heintzmann Piano Comany in Toronto. He even played piano for American evangelist Aimee Semple McPherson. He moved to London, Ontario where he met my mother when they were both working as piano sheet music demonstrators for the T. Eaton Co. in the early '30s. I remember, as a child during the Second World War, my mother being alone with two girls, my father being away in the air force, and my grandmother coming over to help out." After the war Bill took a job at the local T. Eaton Company department store in Chatham selling appliances, and he worked there till his retirement in the early 1970s. Unlike the Tysons, the Frickers had no upper-crust social status or old money but were instead an average Canadian middle-class working family. Sylvia's mother was a classically trained pianist and choir director who enlisted her daughter in the Holy Trinity Anglican Church choir at an early age. Phyllis Fricker also accompanied on the organ and taught Sunday School. "I sang alto in the church choir," notes Sylvia, "because we didn't have enough altos." As for being a choir member, "There was no way I could avoid it, although I did enjoy it. God knows, I had no choice but to be in the church choir. My older sister escaped it, as did my younger sister and brother. I was the one. I sang alto because I always had a fairly deep voice even as a kid, but if the tenor didn't show up I'd sing tenor. We only had one tenor. We always had more sopranos than we knew what to do with. I learned things about harmony from my choir experience. But my contention is that harmony singers are born, not made."

Living first on River Road (a place, now renamed River View Drive, that inspired one of her best-known solo compositions), Sylvia moved several times before the family finally settled on the Victoria Avenue extension. "It's very much in the city now but back then it was suburban. In fact, it was country living when I was growing up there. There were a lot of farms, creeks, and places to hike." She attended McKeough Public School, Sprucedale Public School and later Chatham Collegiate, from which she graduated in 1958.

For as long as she can remember, music was a part of Sylvia's life. "I always had an interest in music because both my parents were musical," she says. "My mother was an accredited music teacher and classically trained. Her speciality was Chopin. She had this huge collection of sheet music, all the popular songs of the

1920s, '30s, and '40s. She loved to play and sing them. She was also the church organist and choir leader. My father liked classical music; he liked Bach organ music and was very fond of Gilbert and Sullivan and ballet. He had a bit of piano training but he mainly played by ear. His love was the pipe organ. On weekends he went out in the country and repaired church organs. He actually bought a pump organ and hooked it up to a vacuum cleaner so he wouldn't have to pump it. We had that and a Heintzman upright piano in the house. I could play a little bit of piano and I could read music but I never really got into it that much. From the time I was about fourteen or fifteen I knew that's what I wanted to do, be a musician. Ian kind of came to it through the whole art school thing. He was more of a jazz and blues guy even when he came to Toronto. But I knew what I wanted to do, and that was music."

Besides the classical, church, and musical theatre music heard in her home, Sylvia also picked up on rhythm and blues. "I grew up sixty miles from Detroit so I listened to all the late-night R&B stations from there. My dad being in the appliance department, the minute someone traded in a radio we all had our own radios. I had a beauty made of mahogany and it stood several feet tall with a tiny dial. It was a piece of furniture and the cabinet gave it a really good sound. I tuned in all the late-night R&B stations or Rosalie Trembley's show out of Windsor. She was crucial to introducing so many people to a lot of great music. Little Willie John, Little Richard, Chuck Berry, Jerry Lee Lewis, I loved all of it. The local stations played some hit-parade pop but mostly country music because Chatham was still kind of a farming community. Hank Snow and Kitty Wells, they used to play a lot. I really wasn't into country music at the time. I think it was the western swing stuff that really turned me off, the Hawaiian-style steel guitar." It used to be true that there was a snobbery about enjoying country music, that it was a style regarded, in the eyes of many, as low class. "If you were really into it, that meant you were from a social level that was not great in the eyes of the average city dweller. When I was in high school you never would admit in a million years that you listened to country music because that meant you were right off the farm. And nice girls didn't go into places where country music was played. But all that's changed now." Live concerts were few and far between in Chatham. "There wasn't much going on in town," she remembers. "I used to go to the wrestling matches every Wednesday night."

At school Sylvia was very much a loner and an individual who marched to her own drumbeat in an era when conformity and peer pressure was paramount. "For one thing I was pretty shy and my interests in high school were not the same as most of the others," she admits. "I subsequently learned that there were in fact others with similar interests, only we didn't talk about them. I was pretty naive. It really was a fairly solitary kind of life in a lot of ways for me. I had a great family and I had friends, but really my interests were not the interests of my peers.

"My artiness didn't just extend to my music, it also extended to the way I dressed. I didn't conform to the standard Sandra Dee look that was popular for girls in the late '50s. I was dressing in black long before that became fashionable. We couldn't wear our jeans to school so I would have a black skirt and a black turtleneck sweater. Back then the big thing for girls was to wear three pairs of bobby socks, rolled around your ankles, with your penny loafers. I was wearing black knee socks and black ballet slippers. There was a bit of a kerfuffle at school because they weren't sure about allowing black knee socks because they were a little too close to black stockings. I always had long straight hair with bangs. But that was not stylish at that point. I guess what would have been thought at the time to be bohemian was the way I looked. But I didn't think about it one way or the other. That's just the way I dressed."

It was Sylvia's love for English literature that initially brought her in contact with traditional folk music. "I was always an avid reader," she states. "My parents belonged to the Book of the Month Club when it had amazing books. I still have some of them; classic books in classic bindings with illustrations. And I would read them probably when I was too young to even understand them. The turning point for me came in high school. We had a poetry textbook called *The Grass of Parnassus*, quite an interesting and varied collection of poetry. But one thing that was in it, it might have been 'Sir Patrick Spens,' where they included a line of music showing what the melody was. They had a few of these old English ballads. Up to that point you didn't think of them as songs. They were called ballads . . . That was an eye-opener for me and started me on a search for books of traditional ballads and music, old English music. Fortunately, we had a very enlightened librarian at the local library.

"I was able to pick out the melody to that old English song from the poetry book on the piano," Sylvia continues. "I really didn't play piano formally. My mother tried to teach me but it never works when your parent tries to teach you. She found me another piano teacher in town, an Englishman. His approach to teaching was less than appealing. It was the ruler on the knuckles thing, so that was a hindrance to playing with confidence. Finally I decided I wanted to play guitar, so my dad got me one from the Eaton's catalogue. It was a classic. I think it was made of plywood and had a picture of a cowboy lassoing a cow silk-screened on it and the word 'Stampede.' In rural Southern Ontario in the 1940s to early '50s there wasn't much folk music on the radio other than Allan Mills or Ed McCurdy. Other than that you just didn't hear folk music. The first American folk music record I heard was Joan Baez's first album and I was already in Toronto by then. Not that there weren't others around, I just didn't have access to them. That first Joan Baez album hit the folk world like a bombshell, the fact that one might actually make a record of that music. I had heard the occasional thing from Burl Ives and the Weavers' 'Kisses Sweeter Than Wine,' they did it before Jimmy Rodgers, but I hadn't heard Pete Seeger or anyone like that. All my songs I got out of books, which was kind of good when I hit Toronto because the songs I knew nobody else knew. So I always had a repertoire that sounded fresh. The little bit of folk music I had heard was on guitar, and the other thing was you could go anywhere with a guitar. It was something you could carry, unlike a piano. Even then I didn't play it the standard way. I had no one to teach me. I just tuned it to a chord and used a metal bar. I should have kept it up; I might have been a good slide player by now," she laughs. "Finally someone taught me how to tune it."

Following graduation, Sylvia took a job first at a local jewellers and later at a drycleaners, with the intention of saving up enough money to pull up stakes for Toronto in pursuit of her musical ambitions. After a year and a half she was ready to make her first tentative jab at the Toronto music scene. "My mother was very active in little theatre and so because of that I was involved in theatre, not as an actress but with the backstage stuff. But it introduced me to a lot of people who had interests outside of Chatham, Ontario. I had made a few trips to Toronto, mainly to see acting friends who had made the move to Toronto, all with the notion that I would ultimately move there. So I had a place to stay with friends at first. Peter Gzowski had been editor of the *Chatham Daily News* and had been involved in the local theatre group. I knew him then. He had moved on to Toronto by then so I knew him there, too." Peter would write the first major feature article on Ian & Sylvia for *Maclean's* magazine a few years later. "That was a result of him and me knowing each other from Chatham."

Unlike the Tysons, Sylvia's parents were surprisingly support- ive of their daughter's dreams. "My parents were remarkably lib- erated about the whole thing," she marvels. "Instead of saying, 'Oh horrors, you can't go to Toronto and try to be a folksinger,' their attitude was, 'Well, if it doesn't work out you can always come back home and get married.' The fact that they would let me go without making a big fuss about it was unusual for most parents in those days. I didn't know if I could make a living or do it as a full-time thing; I just knew that's what I wanted to do. But the pressure wasn't really on me the way it would have been for a boy because I could pretty much do as I pleased. And I knew I had to get out of Chatham. Toronto was the closest big city."

Then came the phone call from Ian in the fall of 1959. "I did one show before I actually moved to Toronto," explains Sylvia. "It was at the First Floor club with Ian but not performing as Ian & Sylvia. Ian was still working with Don Francks in a duo. The First Floor club was *the* jazz club. I think the show was called *Tonight in Person* on CBC. This was my first performance outside of Chatham. I had done the odd school or church performance in Chatham, maybe a song or two, but not a concert. Ian backed me on guitar as an accompanist but he didn't perform on his own. The place I came to stay at was way out in the West End, almost at the end of King Street, in that area along the lake. My landlady's second ex-husband was Ian's boss, where he was working as a commercial artist. She had a son through her second husband and Ian's boss would always come by and see his son. At one point he said there was this guy who works for him who sings and plays guitar. So it was actually John Miles, Ian's boss, who facilitated my meeting

Ian. We might have phoned each other, I don't remember. I do remember going to Ian's girlfriend Micki Boletto's place to rehearse and she was not happy to see me. There was nothing going on between Ian and me but she was not pleased when I showed up. I was fresh out of Chatham at that point. The whole time Ian and I are talking about songs and arrangements and exchanging musical ideas she's sitting right beside him playing with his ear or draping her leg over him. Very uptight."

And Sylvia's initial impressions of Ian? "Oh, I thought he was awfully good looking," she laughs. "But it was not love at first sight. I didn't think of us in terms of it becoming a relationship. I never did think that, actually. It was strictly a working relationship as far as I was concerned, because I came from a town where anyone who looked like him wouldn't have given me a second look. And he had a string of girlfriends. When I met him he was with another girl. But we got along well." And Ian's impression of her? "Sylvia was wearing one of those Ukrainian peasant blouses when I met her. I thought that was pretty interesting."

Initially the two performed separately, alternating sets at the Village Corner club. Sylvia also found a regular Thursday poetry night gig on her own at the Bohemian Embassy club on St. Nicholas just off Wellesley and Yonge. "I was sort of comedy relief between the terribly intense young poets from the University of Toronto who used to come in and read their poetry, swearing at their mothers and all that. There was a delightful young man named Padraig O'Brien who used to write these lovely gentle sort of Irish poems. And there was Margaret Atwood and Milton Acorn who was very sort of socialist and into the union thing."

The Village Corner club would ultimately become home base for Ian & Sylvia. Located up Avenue Road at Pears Street a block north of Davenport Road and a couple of blocks north of the

Yorkville district, the club was in a little brick house. Run by an Englishman, John Morley, it was, as Ian recalls, "the original folk place," only preceded by the First Floor club once it eschewed jazz for folk music. "It became our place," states Ian, "along with the First Floor club and later the Clef club [on Scollard Street just off Bay Street]." Toronto-born folksinger/songwriter Bonnie Dobson was already a name on the local folk circuit and about to establish herself in the United States more than a year before Ian & Sylvia ventured across the border. Her composition "Morning Dew" has become a folk music staple. "The Village Corner was a tiny little place but it had great atmosphere," she reminisces. "Being the first folk club it was kind of a refuge for like-minded people. Folk music was still very much on the fringe at that time. I remember when I was in high school in Toronto I was considered a real oddball because I was into folk music. Anyone who was into it was considered slightly odd. And the English chap who ran it was lovely, too." Bonnie recalls first seeing Ian at the Village Corner in 1959. "He was on his own I think, or maybe it was just because he was so gorgeous that I didn't take notice of anyone else with him," she laughs.

Despite the attention Ian was capable of drawing on his own he recognized something idiosyncratic in the wispy Chatham girl with the unusual vibrato and offbeat wardrobe. Her repertoire of songs was like nothing else on the folk circuit, steeped in history, and that caught his attention. Every folk performer was constantly scrounging for new material, either copping from folk albums or stealing from competitors' sets. "I came out of the country and western, rockabilly tradition," he states. "Sylvia came out of the books, the scholastic. She had collected the old ballad books – the Child ballads, Edith Fowke – and we became very involved with the Appalachian styles and sources. A lot of it was from those books."

"Sylvia was very well informed about a whole bunch of traditional music," acknowledges Gordon Lightfoot, "and she still is. She had a great interest in exploring those areas and finding a lot of those songs. For example, they did songs by Helen Creighton, a Maritimer, and a lot of old Scottish/Irish songs, lively stuff. Ian called it Celtic music."

"There was a musical connection between Ian and me right from the start," confirms Sylvia. "He had been working with Don [Francks] but his interests had gone beyond jazz, which was more Don's thing. He'd had a brief partnership with Noreen St. Pierre who was kind of a big deal in Toronto in those early days, but her voice was a little too operatic or too sweet for what Ian was looking for. One of the reasons Ian and I connected was that he had some background in country music and blues – he was a Big Bill Broonzy fan – and I was very interested in black music – blues, work songs, and spirituals, that sort of thing – mainly from books I'd taken out from the library. He was looking to do something new and interesting and my material was totally different from what anyone else was doing in Toronto at that time. I had a repertoire that was totally unknown. And I really liked the Appalachian stuff because it was related to the Elizabethan music I loved. What we did was unique. There were people who did blues and people who did the 'John Henry' standard folk repertoire but doing 'The Greenwood Sidie' in parallel fifths like we did was a little out there at that time."

After several forays, Sylvia Fricker, age nineteen, decided to take the plunge and move permanently up to Toronto in late 1959, only to discover that Ian had disappeared. "I had moved into the friend's place whose ex-husband was Ian's boss," she explains. "I tried to get hold of Ian at the various numbers I had but couldn't find him. Turns out he had gone back out west to visit the family.

He had that kind of lemming-like thing that a lot of West Coasters have, where they have to go home once a year. So I couldn't reach him. There I was in Toronto, kind of in limbo, because we had talked about getting together and now I couldn't find him. So I got a job in a jewellery store in the West End. I briefly had a job at a place on Yonge Street called Starlight Stores, which sold those kind of hookerish outfits. But I couldn't figure out how to work the cash register. Eventually Ian came back and we started putting our repertoire together."

"I wasn't looking to work with someone else," claims Ian. "I was doing okay on my own. I really don't know why I hooked up with Sylvia. I think [newspaper reporter and friend] Joe Taylor talked me into it. He and some others convinced me that the two of us singing had a very unique sound. And that became very apparent. I had this fiery Italian girlfriend who didn't like this going on at all. She was pretty possessive."

"It just came together," he continues. "We just sang and played. I had the beginnings of a distinctive guitar style, which has developed to what I do today, which is about as good as it's ever been. But it was our voices. We didn't plan anything. We just opened our mouths and sang. We didn't make any vocal adjustments stylistically or technically. We wouldn't have known how to do it anyway. She had a particular voice and I had a particular voice and when they came together and when we could hear what the hell we were doing it was very unique. It was completely natural because we didn't know any better. She had that vibrato thing and I had a fairly big baritone voice. Later on I got accused of not being as good a singer as Sylvia and all that shit. But under the right conditions, man, our voices could soar. That's what did it. You couldn't mistake that sound of Ian & Sylvia in those days." It was Sylvia who sang harmony to Ian's lead. "Any time I sang harmony I screwed it up," Ian admits. "Sylvia had that unique ability to come up with unusual harmonies." "I think he sang harmony once or twice," recalls Sylvia. "On 'You Were On My Mind' I actually sang the harmony."

After a period of solid rehearsal the duo debuted their new act at the Village Corner club. "We would rehearse together, which in those days was unheard of," Sylvia points out. "Back then everybody just fooled around on their own, or if they worked with somebody maybe got together for an hour or so before they went onstage. Ian and I would rehearse three or four days a week in the afternoon and get into songs. Nobody had ever done that before. Ian did the lead, I did the harmonies, and he played guitar. If Ian learned a song he'd sing it until I worked out a harmony that I thought was good. But we really didn't hang out together. We got along well. We didn't make any demands on each other during the early period of time we were working together. We didn't socialize that much. He had his social life. He was taking out a lot of different ladies." Sylvia soon moved in with one of Ian's female friends in an apartment on Avenue Road not far from the Village Corner club. "I don't think she was very happy about it," smiles Sylvia, "but I didn't have a place to live. Rents were very cheap then. That's what ultimately drew people to live around that area and around Yorkville, the cheap rents." Another early roommate was singer Sharon Trostin (later Sharon Hampson of popular children's entertainers Sharon, Lois & Bram). "For a short time Sylvia and I shared a place together in Toronto before she hooked up with Ian," states Sharon. "We were both on our own away from home. We lived near the Village Corner club. She was very quiet and innocent; very reserved, like she still is now. I remember Ian was the person who signed my application to join the musician's union. That got my career started."

Ian left his job as a commercial artist to focus exclusively on music. "It became clear to us that we could make a living doing this," he comments. "Sylvia had all the traditional folk music knowledge and all the songs books. I hadn't heard most of that material but I really came to like that stuff. I just knew the cowboy stuff. That's all I knew. We both liked bluegrass, especially me. When we started, our vocal sound was so all-pervasive and all-encompassing, it was a style all its own. That sound owned us, we didn't own it. At some point later it became a liability because we became trapped in it."

By early 1960, Ian Tyson and Sylvia Fricker, as they were billed, began performing as a duo. "There was no question that when they got together it created something special," states Edgar Cowan. "They each had their own distinctive style but together they created a third style and that really clicked with audiences. Ian provided the act with organization, energy, and musical drive. Sylvia brought to the duo solid traditional folk music substance, an interesting look and demeanour, a surprising and unusual singing style, repertoire, and a great ear for harmony: part Appalachia, part Blue Ridge, and part traditional English ballad singing."

With a heady mix of distinctive harmony, atypical repertoire, and physical attractiveness, the duo was an instant sensation. "The two of them together were such gorgeous people," recalls Ruth Jones McVeigh, "and their harmony was way beyond anything anyone else was trying at the time. That was mostly due to Sylvia. She did such astounding harmonies. Their harmony got right into the marrow of your bones and you didn't forget it. My brother had a tremendous crush on Sylvia and he wasn't alone." Mary Martin would go on to work in high-powered manager Albert Grossman's office in New York and is perhaps best remembered for suggesting that Ronnie Hawkins's former band the

Hawks back Bob Dylan in 1965. As a Toronto resident in 1960 she caught Ian Tyson and Sylvia Fricker at the Village Corner club. "I just thought they were perfect," she enthuses. "Their harmonies and their songs were magnificent. At that period in time, the music that was primarily in my house was classical music and I was looking for my own musical path. Folk music seemed to really speak to me. I loved Ian & Sylvia right away. They stood so tall and so secure on stage. I loved Sylvia's grace and Ian's ability to communicate with an audience. He was much taller than most people who took the stage and he had a real aura about him, an air of confidence, so that Sylvia could just be the waif. "

Contemporary Bonnie Dobson recalls, "When Sylvia got together with Ian it was this amazing transformation of both of them. She went from being this reedy and lovely girl to this stunning and elegant woman. The two of them onstage were just wonderful. And in their choice of material they always had great ears for songs. The fact that they picked up on Lightfoot early on says it all."

In short order Ian & Sylvia became the darlings of the nascent Toronto folk community. Their contemporaries included the Tu-Tones with Gordon Lightfoot, a young David Wiffen, Mary Jane and Winston Young, Jim McCarthy, and Bonnie Dobson. Despite a common appreciation for folk music, that community was in fact split between two camps, as Edgar Cowan observed. "One stream found its two homes at the downtown St. Christopher House/University Settlement House and the North Toronto YMCA. This particular stream was led in the north end by Sid Dolgay [of the Travellers] and in the south by Estelle Klein, a high-energy neighbourhood worker and important catalyst for what was to evolve in Canadian folk music in later years. The home of Estelle and her architect husband Jack would later become a kind of folk drop-in and welcome centre cum song salon where you could count on great food, stirring conversation, folk gossip, and great pickup music. This group sprung mainly from left-leaning socialist, mostly Jewish community activists, the left-wing Pete Seeger type folkies; the red-diaper babies kind of thing. Under the leadership of socialist counsellors and Zionist activists at various Ontario summer camps I was initially introduced to the folk songs of the Weavers, Josh White, Leadbelly, Pete Seeger, and Woody Guthrie. This faction's favourite house singers were Mary Jane and Winston Young, Merrick Jarrett, Bonnie Dobson, and, of course, the Travellers. The Travellers (Jerry Gray, Sid Dolgay, Helen Gray, Jerry Goodis, and Oscar Ross; later, Joe Hampson) were the Canadian Weavers, a carbon copy. Other Canadian red-diaper babies include the Lovin' Spoonful guitarist Zal Yanovsky and Sharon Trostin (Hampson).

"The other stream evolved quickly from the new 1960s' political movements and found its homes at the various Toronto folk clubs," Edgar continues. "This fresh stream tended to cluster around a small group of coffeehouse performers that included Ian Tyson and Sylvia Fricker, Klaus Van Graft, a gifted European singer, Israeli/Yugoslavian duo Malka & Joso, banjo-playing management consultant and sometime movie reviewer Ted Schafer, John Morley, owner operator of the Village Corner club, and myself. If there had been a right, left, and centre of folkies, Ian & Sylvia would have probably been right of centre. Oddly enough, the leaders of the two streams came together, when, in later years, Ian & Sylvia co-owned and co-occupied a duplex in Rosedale with their new friends the Kleins."

Never overtly political and avoiding taking sides, Ian & Sylvia were able to appeal to a broader audience who appreciated their traditional folk repertoire and not their politics. "All these political types like Pete Seeger never got over the Depression," grouses Ian. "They were all these socialist 'wobblies.' If you weren't a socialist you were suspect to some of those people. It was always politics with Pete Seeger. I never got into his politics. I don't know what his ultimate goal was, I still don't. I didn't get Woody Guthrie at all, I really didn't. It was all very trade union–oriented. I'd worked in that heavy trade union thing in B.C. and I always thought it was bullshit. The down-trodden workers? Christ, the trade unions screwed up B.C. It's never been the same."

"Ian's own politics," Edgar Cowan chuckles, "tended to be somewhere right of Genghis Khan."

Mary Martin remembers a convivial social atmosphere surrounding the local folk scene. "On rare occasions, being a folk music fan, one was invited to various people's places who would have gatherings on a Sunday in the early afternoon," she notes. "Several folksingers would be there and encouraged to share their new songs and what they had been working on. It was always pretty remarkable because you got to hear songs in the raw. So these were important little gatherings that I was fortunate to sometimes be a part of. And Ian & Sylvia would sometimes be there. This would have been around 1960. Estelle Klein was part and parcel of that scene and those get-togethers. She and her husband Jack were very much into Canadian folk music. At one point I became friendly with Ian & Sylvia, more so with Ian because he was a very attractive man. So for a period of about three or four months in Toronto he loaned me his twelve-string guitar." The guitar, a Gibson twelve-string acoustic, was stolen in New York a few years later. Ian never bought a replacement.

Much like with the jazz scene, soft drug use was prevalent among the folk community. "There was a lot of grass floating around in Toronto in those days," Edgar recalls. "It was beer and marijuana. But it wasn't what you'd consider a big drug scene going on, we were just smoking grass." Ian was among those partaking of marijuana; Sylvia did not drink or smoke. "I wasn't a drinker until I was already into my twenties and because I was never a smoker I never smoked pot. I certainly was around it a lot, though."

Bonnie Dobson had already been signed up by an American agent and had left on her first U.S. tour supporting Sonny Terry & Brownie McGhee. Her debut album had just been released when, back in Toronto, she met up with Ian & Sylvia. "It was at Estelle Klein's house," she remembers. "I'll never forget Sylvia listening to my album and pronouncing it 'a gas!' I thought that was a funny comment about my little folky record."

The rise of Ian & Sylvia's popularity on the budding Toronto folk scene went hand in hand with the expansion of that scene as more coffeehouses and clubs began springing up, offering further venues for them, including the Purple Onion at the corner of Avenue Road and Yorkville Avenue (later a mainstay for Joni Mitchell, and where Buffy Sainte-Marie wrote "Universal Soldier"), the Gate of Cleve further up Avenue Road, and the Fifth Peg club on Church Street, operated by another Toronto music impresario, Marty Onrot. Ian recalls performing at the Fifth Peg with up-and-coming comedian Bill Cosby as the opening act. Comedians often shared stages with folk artists. It was also at that club that American singer/songwriter Carolyn Hester first met Ian & Sylvia. Carolyn and Sylvia would go on to enjoy a close friendship after the duo moved to New York. Arriving in New York from Texas in 1960, Carolyn had already established herself on the New York folk scene[*] by the time she met Ian & Sylvia the following year. "It was an afternoon at the Fifth Peg in Toronto," she recalls,

---

[*] Carolyn would give a largely unknown Bob Dylan his first big recording studio experience in 1961 by inviting him to play harmonica on her third album.

"and Ian & Sylvia were there. There was some special reason why we were all there on a Sunday afternoon, some kind of activity that I can't quite remember, but I do recall when Ian & Sylvia came in. It was my first time meeting them and they were, of course, just gorgeous. I loved their singing and material without question and I became a big fan. After they performed, Sylvia walked up to me and, kind of looking down at me because she's taller than me, she said, 'I thought you would be taller.' That was the first thing she said to me," Carolyn laughs. "I didn't talk to Ian very much that day or other times, so I didn't know him as well as Sylvia. Other times when I'd be up in Toronto, Sylvia would invite me by their house on a Saturday or Sunday afternoon. She would make a big pot of chilli and we'd all get together and have fun. That was so sweet and hospitable of her. Being from Texas I loved that."

For Christmas 1960, Ian presented Sylvia with an autoharp. To that point she had been standing and singing alongside him and his guitar. They were not yet employing an accompanist. Even though Sylvia was versed in rudimentary guitar chording she chose not to play it onstage. "I was a competent rhythm guitar player," she admits, "but I'm not a picker like Ian. I didn't really play that much and I regret that, especially after we hired another guitar player. But a third guitar player onstage wasn't necessary." Instead she began playing the autoharp onstage and the appearance of an instrument closely associated with Appalachian mountain music gave Sylvia individually, and Ian & Sylvia collectively, not only a distinctive sound but a unique visual identity. The thirty-six-string instrument, a derivation of the German zither, includes at least fifteen preset chord bars – majors, minors, and dominant seventh chords – that one depresses while strumming. The instrument has a rich string sound that is unmistakable. The autoharp was popularized in the twentieth century by Mother Maybelle Carter of the Carter Family, regarded as one of the pioneers of country music. "I really admired Maybelle Carter and I think that's why Ian bought me the autoharp," Sylvia suggests. John Sebastian of '60s folk rock/pop group the Lovin' Spoonful played an autoharp on hits such as "Do You Believe in Magic" and "You Didn't Have to Be So Nice." Sebastian may have been influenced by Ian & Sylvia since he was a contemporary on the Greenwich Village music scene. "It's a unique-sounding instrument," Sylvia explains. "Every instrument you pick up has its intrinsic qualities that lend something to the music that no other instrument will. And that's true in terms of writing. I wrote things on the autoharp that I wouldn't have written on the guitar or piano. You have to be very inventive because its limitations are very challenging, which forces you to look for different chords because you can't vary them. So it makes it sound pretty interesting sometimes. It's a very literal instrument. 'You Were On My Mind' was written on the autoharp. But it was hell to keep in tune. It was a constant battle on the road keeping that thing in tune." Ian concurs. "Sylvia developed a unique autoharp style which mainly consisted of constantly tuning the damn thing."

By the spring of 1961, Ian Tyson and Sylvia Fricker were the top coffeehouse draw in Toronto. A measure of their notoriety came when Pete Seeger, the éminence grise of traditional folk music, invited the two onstage to sing a couple of songs during his sold-out Massey Hall concert, thus conferring on the duo a form of folk music legitimacy, as well as significant publicity beyond the folk community. It was not, however, the serendipitous moment it appeared to the audience to be. "I was organizing the concert," states Edgar Cowan, by now acting as manager for Ian & Sylvia. "I had become involved with film distributor and concert promoter Marty Bochner for a short period, helping him out with one of his Pete Seeger concerts. During the daytime round of the usual promotional interviews, I arranged a midday break for Pete at the apartment on Bloor Street that I shared with Ted Schafer. I arranged for Ian & Sylvia to be there and to meet, chat, exchange some songs and folk gossip with Pete. What I hoped would happen did. He listened to them and invited them up to do a song or two after half time at his concert that night at Massey Hall. It was an historic occasion for them, a seminal event in their early career, positioning Ian & Sylvia at the forefront of the Toronto folk scene."

From Sylvia's perspective, the duo had become like Roger Miller's "Kansas City Star" — big fish in the small pond of Toronto. "We were drawing big crowds by then and people were lined up around the block at the Village Corner club. But we'd played everywhere there was to play several times over. The Yorkville scene wasn't yet happening and it was all still very local. Recording in Toronto was out of the question because there just weren't the proper studios." New York was the centre of the music industry, with Greenwich Village, on the west side of Lower Manhattan, ground zero for the folk music scene in the United States. Folkies from across North America made the pilgrimage to the Village, acoustic guitars slung over fleece-lined jackets, hoping to be discovered in one of the dozen or so coffeehouses, basket joints (where performers passed a basket around for change following their set), and nightclubs centred around Bleecker and MacDougal Streets.

But before they could entertain thoughts of moving on, there was still the matter of the Mariposa Folk Festival. In the summer of 1959 the Newport Folk Festival debuted in Newport, Rhode Island, the brainchild of Newport Jazz Festival founder and East

Coast music impresario George Wein. George, along with fellow board members Theodore Bikel, Pete Seeger, Albert Grossman, and Canada's Oscar Brand, conceived of an event that encompassed a broad and eclectic definition of folk music and was held over three days of performances and workshops, July 30 to August 1. Everything from blues to bluegrass and field hollers to gospel and singalong was deemed worthy of inclusion, with the general caveat that the music be authentic, rootsy, and acoustic. Pete Seeger was among the headliners along with Leon Bibb, the Clancy Brothers and Tommy Makem, and Odetta. (The festival proved to be an enduring success and became the premiere annual folk event until finally folding in 1971 long after the folk boom was dead in the water. It was revived in 1985 and operates today as George Wein's Newport Folk Festival.) The success of Newport was not lost on the Toronto folk community, many of whom, including Edgar Cowan, had travelled down to Newport to witness the excitement. A contingent of enterprising young folk devotees decided to create a Canadian version in Stephen Leacock's fictional town of Mariposa, a.k.a. Orillia, Ontario, seventy miles northeast of Toronto.

The movers and shakers behind the inaugural Mariposa Folk Festival included Ruth and Crawford "Casey" Jones, Edgar Cowan, his friend Ted Schafer, Pete McGarvey, and Ian Tyson. As Edgar remembers it, "Ruth Jones and her husband, psychiatrist Dr. Crawford Jones, residents of Orillia, were regular weekend habitués of the Village Corner club, the weekend mecca for the Toronto folk music scene. The two Orillians, typical folk groupies of their era, introduced themselves to me and my three friends, Ted Schafer, Ian Tyson, and Sylvia Fricker, the latter two being the featured act at the club every weekend. We got to know Ruth and Casey from that point on. Then one night Ian & Sylvia were playing the First Floor club and afterwards we all went back to my apartment that I was sharing with Ted Schafer on Bloor, two floors above the Baroness, a wedding gown sweatshop, and opposite the University Theatre. It was 'party central' for the folk scene for a number of years. That's when we made the decision to do the first Mariposa Festival. I agreed to produce it. That was in late 1960 and I hadn't been working that long at the *Toronto Telegram*. It was decided that Ruth and Casey would be the Festival's founders. They, together with local Orillia broadcaster CFOR's Pete McGarvey, would arrange for the venue, raise the money, interface with town officials, and coordinate the volunteers and local media efforts. I would produce/direct the two-day folk event and coordinate the marketing and major media communication. Ted would be master of ceremonies, serving as ringmaster for the performances and producing any written copy. Ian would design the poster and sales brochure. Together we would decide on the program and participants. Mostly it was to be traditional folk music. Edith Fowke, the noted folklorist, even did a seminar one afternoon at the festival. What a glorious time we had, albeit incredibly naive. We had assembled a totally inexperienced group for what would turn out to be a large and complicated undertaking."

"We used to have meetings at Ted Schafer's apartment and Ian would be there," notes Ruth. "He was actively involved right from the start. But those meetings would tend to devolve into everyone doing skits from [BBC Radio's] *The Goons* show. We didn't necessarily get a lot of work done. Sylvia was involved, too, but quietly. My original goal was that the festival be strictly Canadian or at least mostly Canadian. It got away from that in later years long after I was gone but seems to be going back to that idea in recent years. I wanted to have small folk festivals across Canada and their winners come to perform at Mariposa. But organizing folkies was like trying to organize Jell-O, so it never happened."

Held over the weekend of August 18/19, the roster of performers for the inaugural festival reflected the best-known folk artists on the Toronto scene, besides casting a wider net across Canada. "They took the tiny burgeoning folk scene in Toronto to a stage up in Orillia," notes Ian. "All the folkies in Toronto were on it." The first Mariposa Folk Festival would be a watershed moment not only in Canadian folk music but also in the evolution of the national music scene. A kind of gathering of the tribes, it drew folk fans and aficionados from across the country who discovered to their delight that they were, indeed, not alone in their appreciation for this music. There were other like-minded souls out there. And it was held in a bucolic, serene backwater. What could be more idyllic or typically Canadian? Tickets were $2.00 for each of the evening concerts or $5.00 for all three. Friday and Saturday featured evening open-air concerts on a medieval-style tented platform designed by Ted Schafer's brother Larry, a set designer at the CBC. Friday's festivities concluded with a midnight "street jamboree" and dance. Saturday opened with a free children's concert that was followed in the afternoon by the second of the major concerts, this one billed as "Traditional Canadian Musicians." A symposium on Canadian folk music was next, moderated by Edith Fowke. The Saturday evening concert boasted the headliners and wrapped up with a hootenanny.

"The Festival's open-air holiday atmosphere was sublime from the opening 'licks' to the boisterous finale," gushes Edgar, "one of clear skies, golden sunshine, glorious summer picnics, and pure musical joy. Bright canvas deck chairs, sunburned folkies stretched out on blankets on the perimeter, babes in arms, colourful summer frocks, shorts and sandals, pickin' 'n' playin' and impromptu hootenannies all over town. It was part carnival fairground, country-dance, song swap, and Irish hooley, Massey Hall and Grand Ole Opry all rolled up into one. The Festival, which was all-Canadian, also managed to bring together, for the first time, the old-line, left-wing, socialist, Toronto folk song community, with national and regional folk legends, and the new, young, activist, songwriting folk performers. It was likened to a big Canadian folk music family reunion." The performers included the Travellers, who had enjoyed commercial success with Woody Guthrie's "This Land Is Your Land," adapted to name check Canadian locales; Montreal's Alan Mills; Newfoundlander Omar Blondahl; Bonnie Dobson; Merrick Jarrett; Mary Jane and Winston Young; Quebeckers Jean Carignan and Jacques Labreque; Finvola Redden from Nova Scotia; and Peter Wyborn and Alan McRae from Vancouver. Harpist Tom Kines, champion country fiddler Al Cherney, and the York County Boys' bluegrass band reflected the diverse folk fare. Ian Tyson and Sylvia Fricker were identified separately in the brochure, giving the impression to those not in the know that they would be two individual acts.

Bonnie Dobson debuted her anti-nuclear war song "Morning Dew" at the first Mariposa Festival. "I remember that Mariposa festival was very exciting, it being the first one," she states. "It was very collegial and fun. You felt like you were a part of something that was really burgeoning, particularly in Canada, because there was always that perception that you had to make it in the States first before you'd get recognized in Canada. But here were all these Canadian artists like Ian & Sylvia who were still in the homeland, even before they went to the U.S."

Gordon Lightfoot remembers hearing Ian & Sylvia together for the first time. "I was in the audience. It was a beautiful evening, a big crowd outdoors in the oval, and I was mesmerized. Ian &

Sylvia were fantastic, especially hearing them in that setting – it made me realize what it was that made it such a wonderful event. That's stayed with me all my life. Their harmony and their play-ing – Ian has absolute pitch on his guitar – the intonation of the tuning, the songs, it really stuck with me. The combination of the guitar and the autoharp was quite unique." The Tu-Tones, Gordon and partner Terry Whelan, auditioned only to be rejected for the festival bill. "They said we sounded too much like the Everly Brothers," he chuckles. "But Terry and I played the next one [1962] with Ian & Sylvia." Explains Ruth, "Gordon and Terry weren't really outstanding. They were average. I saw him years later and he came over and gave me a hug and asked, 'Ruth, wasn't I good enough back then?' As soon as he was on his own his talent became obvious."

"On the closing Saturday night concert under a blanket of an early Northern Lights display, the Festival packed over 3,000 people into the converted baseball park," notes Edgar. "With all the performers, planners, and workers on stage we finished with a rousing and nostalgic Canadian version of Woody Guthrie's 'This Land Is Your Land . . . from Bonavista to the Vancouver Islands.' It was a very emotional finale for all in attendance. As a final denouement, and much to the chagrin of the local constabu-lary, a number of well-oiled lads were apprehended at dawn Sunday morning serenading the statue of Samuel de Champlain in down-town Couchiching Park."

"It was pretty amazing how many people were there," states Ruth Jones McVeigh. "Nothing like it had happened before here. The pride I take is that in my naivety I didn't know it couldn't be done so I just did it. We had promotion right across the coun-try about the festival going to happen. That was amazing. We pretty much had a full house."

"When we came home from that festival," recalls Ruth, "we could hear a tremendous noise as we were coming onto Bay Street. We couldn't figure out what it was until we walked in the door. Our house was filled with folkies. It was a sea of people all over the house and spilling out onto the lawn. And they stayed for several days. They had tents pitched in the backyard. Ian & Sylvia were there and everyone was singing and jamming."

The Mariposa Folk Festival proved to be a pivotal moment for Ian & Sylvia's career. They had reached the top of the Toronto folk music food chain. Where else was there to go? The fragmented regional nature of the Canadian music industry meant that to achieve any measure of a national profile required tough slogging across Canada where the folk music community was largely isolated, scattered among a handful of coffeehouses like Harvey Glatt's Le Hibou in Ottawa; the Fourth Dimension chain of coffeehouses in Fort William (Thunder Bay), Winnipeg, and Regina; Saskatoon's Louis Riel; Calgary's Depression; and Vancouver's Bunkhouse. The university and college campus concert circuit had yet to open up. As much as Mariposa stitched together the folk music community across Canada, a singular event that united folk music fans from coast to coast, it was still slim pickings for work, few opportunities to record or get your records played, vast distances to travel, with little to show for it in the end. If you wanted to have a shot at a sustainable career and commercial success the reality was that you had to go south.

At that point, of the two, Sylvia was the more ambitious and career-focused. "She knew what she wanted and she wanted to be in New York," offers Ian. "As soon as she could she got a place in New York. I just wanted to chase the girls and I caught a lot of them. I think I wanted us to be famous, or at least myself. It was so much fun. For me, the first year we were together, before the big success, was special. We had these little apartments, every-body had them in that Davenport/Bloor area of Toronto, and Sylvia and I worked pretty hard. We'd have these afternoon rehearsals at either of our apartments. I was working at getting my guitar chops down. I was trying to take the guitar to another level. It took a long time but I worked hard at it."

As Sylvia remembers it, the two were entirely naive in their approach to the Big Apple. "We had no formal management nor even knew what real artist management was. We just had a friend booking us. So we decided, 'Well, we're so great we'll just drive down to New York and find ourselves a manager.' It just seemed that simple."

FAREWELL TO THE NORTH

"Greenwich Village was a very authentic place," Ian recalls. "It had a long history of artists and painters going way back, whereas Yorkville in Toronto wasn't really authentic. It was more of an explosion of the coffeehouse thing in the early '60s and the folkies that went with it. It didn't last very long. But Greenwich Village was the real thing, alright."

A bohemian artistic enclave in the heart of Manhattan, Greenwich Village, with its funky brownstone walkup apartments and Italian restaurants, had been home to painters, sculptors, and writers since the early twentieth century. By the 1950s the beat generation had taken the community over as its own, and with that, coffeehouses and nightclubs like the Village Vanguard and the Village Gate opened, offering jazz before folk music got its toe in the door by the end of the decade. The beacon for the folkies arriving from the far corners of the United States and later Canada was Washington Square, a public park, fountain (which everyone waded in), and Greenwich Village landmark. Sunday hootenannies in Washington Square drew thousands in the summers.

When the folk boom erupted in the late 1950s its heartbeat was the Village. Dave Van Ronk, Peter LaFarge, Fred Neil, Dylan, Phil Ochs, Ramblin' Jack Elliott, Eric Andersen, Tim Hardin, Tom Paxton, and Peter, Paul & Mary are all indelibly associated with Greenwich Village. "To think this all happened at the same time within a few blocks in a handful of clubs, bars, all-night coffeehouses, and apartments on only four streets in the Village," avers Eric Andersen, who came to the Village from San Francisco on the urging of singer/songwriter Tom Paxton. "West 3rd, West 4th, Bleecker, and MacDougal streets at places with names like Café Remo, the Figaro, Café Wha?, the Kettle of Fish, the Gaslight Café, the Night Owl, the Feenjon, and Gerde's Folk City. Those were heady times." For folkies it was a badge of honour to be associated with Greenwich Village. Bob Dylan had arrived there from Minnesota in January 1961 but was still scuffling when Ian & Sylvia hit town like a cool, fresh breeze from the north. The fortunes of both artists would be inextricably bound together in the early years of that decade.

It was early 1962 when, having accomplished all they possibly could in Toronto, Ian & Sylvia ventured southward to seek fame and fortune in New York. Accompanying them on the journey were newspaper reporter Joe Taylor (a big fan) and Edgar Cowan, though Edgar flew in while the other three drove down in Joe's Pontiac. "Dylan and Len Chandler, Tom Paxton, Buffy Sainte-Marie – we were all there that same summer, that must have been 1962," observes Ian. "We didn't know a soul." The Village was a magical spot unlike anywhere else. People migrated to the Village to be a part of what was happening. According to Edgar, "We only gave ourselves, and could only afford, three days. Ian & Sylvia were booked Thursday through Sunday at the clubs and had to be back in Toronto. I had to take three days of my holiday allotment from my then day gig at the *Toronto Telegram*."

Arriving Monday afternoon, the four had arranged to meet with Harold Leventhal, one of the leading folk luminaries on the East Coast. Besides managing a roster of folk elite, among them the political left wingers such as the Weavers, Woody Guthrie, Pete Seeger, Harry Belafonte, Oscar Brand, Judy Collins, and Joan Baez, Harold was also involved with Folkways Records, a significant player on the traditional folk music recording scene at the time. After listening to Ian & Sylvia (the duo contend they sang live while Edgar insists they had recorded a six-song acetate at CBC in Toronto and brought it along to the auditions), Harold deemed them not the right fit for Folkways. Besides, he was just too busy to take on another client. He did, however, suggest they knock on Albert Grossman's door instead.

Born in Chicago in 1926 of Russian Jewish immigrant parents, and a graduate of Roosevelt University with a degree in economics, Albert Bernard Grossman first entered the world of entertainment in 1956 when he opened the Gate of Horn folk club in the basement of Chicago's Rice Hotel. By 1959 he was managing several artists including folk performer Odetta and actress Lee Remick. That year he partnered with George Wein, one of the most powerful New York–based folk music managers, second only to Harold Leventhal. Together they launched the annual Newport Folk Festival. Never known to have an instinctive ear for the next big thing, Albert instead relied on the buzz from the street and the enlightened recommendations of others before signing an artist. Albert's angle was always the commercial rather than the artistic. With Albert in his or her corner, the artist could look after the creativity while he looked after the money. His biggest catch would be Bob Dylan, whom he managed until 1970 before an acrimonious split and the inevitable lawsuits. Examples of Albert's gruff, hard-nosed management style are best illustrated in the 1965 documentary *Don't Look Back*, during which he accompanied Dylan on his last acoustic tour of the U.K. Dylan observed in his *Chronicles: Volume One* autobiography that on first meeting Albert in 1962, "he looked like Sydney Greenstreet in *The Maltese Falcon*." He went on to describe Albert as possessing a commanding presence with a voice that was "loud like the booming of war drums. He didn't talk so much as growl."

"Albert Grossman was the king of Chicago," states Ian, "but I think the gangsters ran him out. When he arrived in New York he was living in George Wein's office. George was an established music impresario who had an apartment at 50 Central Park West. Albert was basically sleeping on George's couch. But it didn't take him long to get connected. He knew where the money was and that was with the record labels." In 1961 Albert made his first leap into the larger arena of popular music with Peter, Paul & Mary, a wholly contrived trio assembled by Albert around his friend Peter Yarrow. Paul was, in fact, Noel Stookey, and Mary was Mary Travers. The following year the freshly minted trio's debut album was released, and unlike their folk music contemporaries, Peter, Paul & Mary scored several pop chart single hits, including "If I Had a Hammer," "Lemon Tree," and "Puff the Magic Dragon," before turning their attention to newcomer Bob Dylan's catalogue. The success of Peter, Paul & Mary in the early years of the decade positioned Albert Grossman as a force to be reckoned with, a status that appealed to him. Albert always liked to negotiate from a position of power and intimidation.

Having struck out with Harold Leventhal, the next stop for Ian & Syliva was the office of George Wein where Albert Grossman held court. "It was late in the day and we were very down," recalls

Edgar. "Like fools we had hoped that everybody would fall over themselves for such a talented duo and this was definitely not happening. Already, on our first day, we had one turndown." As Sylvia remembers it, undeterred, the four arrived at George Wein's door. "The apartment had a huge two-story great room on the main floor — that was the reception area — with tiny cubbyhole offices off to the side. So we auditioned for Albert right in the middle of this great room with the high ceiling. Afterwards, what he said was something to the effect of, 'Well, I really like you but I've just signed this trio and I don't know how much time I'm going to have.' And that, of course, was Peter, Paul & Mary." Edgar describes Albert as a "Jabba the Hut–like character who turned out to be very courteous. George Wein was present as well. We put the demo on right there [or sang live in the great room], and we all sat and listened for the twenty or so minutes. It was agony. Fortunately, Albert liked what he heard and was very positive, but guarded. After an hour or so of talk, he invited us all out for some food and later to the famous Gerde's Folk City, where, we found out later, new acts were presented every Monday night. Before we left, Albert made a key phone call and then informed us that Ian & Sylvia had been invited to perform a short set that very Monday night at Gerde's. So, there they were getting ready to perform a set in a few hours at the centre of folk activity in the U.S., Greenwich Village."

Although tiny in square footage, Gerde's Folk City stood large in the folk community and in Greenwich Village lore. Located at 11 West 4th Street at Mercer, one block off Broadway, it had originally been Gerde's Bar and Restaurant until Izzy Young, owner of the Folklore Centre on MacDougal Street, and Mike Porco turned it into a folk club in 1959, retaining the Gerde's name. Charlie Rothschild would later manage the club. According to Suze Rotolo, then Bob Dylan's New York girlfriend, "If there were three people on stage at the same time, it was a crowd. Whoever came through the doors and signed up to play could perform at the Monday night hootenannies." Dylan had played Gerde's soon after his arrival in New York and often sat in on harmonica for the many blues acts that passed through.

Gerde's Folk City was the hub of the folk scene in the Village at that time. "You got to see and meet everyone there because they would have these Monday hoot nights and everyone would get up and play and sing," recalls Sylvia. "That's what we did, get up on hoot night and perform there." Albert kept a permanent table in one corner at Gerde's and was usually present on Mondays scouting the new talent. "Grossman was using this convenient venue as an opportunity to watch a live performance audition before an audience," Edgar insists. "That night, Ian and Sylvia were sensational, exuding confidence and energy, with a presence that was both fresh and interesting. However, it was when Sylvia tore into a big blues number that they brought the house down. That absolutely sewed it up for Albert and the next day the deal was done. It was amazing."

Singer/songwriter Tom Paxton ("The Last Thing on My Mind," "Bottle of Wine") was in the audience the night Ian & Sylvia made their New York debut. "I remember it very vividly," he states. "Albert Grossman brought them in to do a guest set and they blew the place down. They only did three songs, that's all you did in those days for a guest set, but they made an instant impact on me and everyone. I don't recall if they had an accompanist with them but I do remember they did 'Mary Anne,' which was one of my favourites." Did Tom see a star quality about them? "Without question. They were among the best at the time. And having Albert Grossman behind them didn't hurt at all."

Beyond their superb musical abilities, Albert saw in Ian & Sylvia a fresh, new, and appealing image that was easily marketable to young audiences: two good-looking young performers. According to Ian, "He signed us as much for our looks as the music. That's the fact. He definitely saw us as a big commercial folk act. He saw in us our clean-cut Canadian naivety." Charlie Rothschild was a friend of Albert's who would later come to work for him as road manager/agent for many of his artists, including Ian & Sylvia. As manager of Gerde's Folk City, Charlie was well respected in the Greenwich Village music fraternity. He had managed Carolyn Hester and later did the same for Judy Collins. Charlie was present the day the two Canadian singers auditioned for Albert. "When they first came to Albert's office they were like a young beautiful couple, charming, delightful, wonderful singers. A lovely couple. Ian could have been the Marlborough man. He had that rugged image, the cowboy hat and the good looks. And Sylvia was simply gorgeous. I think they had a beautiful sound and were winners. They took songs and made them into their own. They would be responsible for popularizing folk music."

The following day, Albert negotiated an exclusive management contract with a 15 per cent commission (not, as often stated, 25 per cent). A booking agent took another 15 per cent. "If there was a third party involved, David Braun, Albert's attorney, had put it into our contract that no more than 30 per cent could be taken in total and the three parties would have to work it out between themselves," confirms Ian. Edgar stepped aside as informal manager in return for a role booking the duo in Canada for club, small concert, and television appearances. "I became the Canadian surrogate for the Grossman office in Canada," states Edgar, "later taking charge of Peter, Paul & Mary concerts, publicity, promotion, and then on to Dylan, who was still a full year away from coming out with his first album." In later years Groscourt, the joint company formed by Albert and his partner John Court, would be responsible for a number of Canadian artists, including the Paupers, the Band, Gordon Lightfoot, and Ronnie Hawkins, besides Ian & Sylvia.

"Albert was a most interesting man," reflects Edgar. "A lot of people didn't like him but I did. I liked him an awful lot. He was always fair with Ian & Sylvia and fair with me because I was giving up Ian & Sylvia. I found Albert to be a fascinating guy; a very intellectual guy. I remember right after the 1963 civil rights March on Washington [where Dr. Martin Luther King made his famous 'I have a dream' speech]. I was in New York and Albert invited me over to his apartment at 6:00 in the evening. Now, he never left his office until at least 9:00 at night and would make the rounds of the clubs before going home. So I knew this was strange. I arrived at his place at 6:00 and he let me in. Sitting around a table were about seven or eight black guys. Albert says, 'I'm glad you came. Sit over there, if you don't mind.' What they were doing was dividing up the spoils from the March on Washington: the film rights, the television rights, the music, even the balloons and the novelties because it was such a big deal. And the guys around the table represented all the different black factions. I realized soon after why he had invited me over. As a Canadian I was trust-worthy and independent because I was an outsider. So if something needed adjudication I was there to do that. It never happened that they needed me to mediate but that was Albert. It was a huge event and the key was Peter, Paul & Mary, so everyone wanted a piece of it."

"Albert was a businessman," affirms Sylvia. "But because this was the era of peace and love, being a businessman was frowned upon. He was supposed to be doing it for the love of the music.

I think he did love the music but he was first and foremost a businessman and a very tough businessman and I'm very thankful for that. He certainly did us far more good than harm. He looked after our interests. Absolutely. Albert invested a lot in Peter, Paul & Mary and later in Janis Joplin but he didn't in Ian & Sylvia because we were pretty self-contained and low maintenance." To his credit, Albert stuck with Ian & Sylvia through their heyday and the lean times until the early '70s. Folk music contemporary and fellow Canadian Buffy Sainte-Marie* in hindsight acknowledges that having someone like Albert in her corner would have been an asset to her own career. "When I first went to Greenwich Village," states Buffy, "I had never met a businessman and never met a lawyer. I had no idea that it was about money. I thought it was about music and that it would last about five months and I'd have a great time, then that would be it. If Albert Grossman had been my manager, for instance, things might have been different. More wonderful, less wonderful, I don't know. But there would have been more structure, more thought, more guidance, more planning, more strategy."

It's extraordinary to find some artists from the '60s who do *not* insist they were ripped off by greedy managers and agents out to line their own pockets at the artists' expense. Ian & Sylvia are among that rare breed. "Ian & Sylvia were not ripped off," Charlie Rothschild insists. "Albert was a big believer in them and tried to do everything for them. If Albert was on your team then the opposition needed to worry. He never screwed his artists. He looked after them. Everything was in black and white. There was nothing hidden. It was a good team. There were no gonifs. Albert had the name and the mystique. He had the power to kill. His approach

---

* Ian admits to having a brief fling with the Saskatchewan-born singer/ songwriter in the early '60s.

to life was different: take the money and run." Adds Mary Martin, a fellow Torontonian who came to work for Albert soon after Ian & Sylvia were signed, "I also believe that Ian probably had a strong code of ethics that he would live or die by. And I think the ethics that both Ian and Sylvia stood for were to be admired and respected."

"We did socialize some with Albert and his wife Sally but not a lot," notes Sylvia. "Albert had a much closer relationship and understanding with his male artists than with his female clients. If Mary Travers were alive I'm sure she would agree with that. He related more to the guys. It was true with Butterfield and Dylan and [the Band's] Robbie Robertson. He was always closer to them and more involved with them. With Ian and me, whenever we ran into a problem with Albert, I was the one delegated to go in and talk with him because he didn't know how to deal with women. And therefore we got what we wanted. And there were times when I had to do that. He knew it was serious if I came in to see him. But Albert was always straight with us. He told us early on, 'You have to understand that in this business there are people who feel that much taller if they can stand on someone else's back and they will tell you anything they think you want to hear in order to achieve that.'" The two Canadians had much to learn about the music business. "We sure did but we had very good advice. Certainly Albert, in his wisdom, found us the right people. He found us a good lawyer [David Braun], a good accountant [Marshall Gelfand]. He saw to it that we were covered in pretty much every area we needed to be covered in." Confirms Ian, "We were very fortunate to have people around us with our best interests at heart. It was the correct, honourable Canadian way. That's the way we were."

"Albert was tough," Suze Rotolo agrees, "but Sylvia knew how to deal with him. She had the ability to understand what Albert was doing at a time when many artists didn't question or pay attention to their managers."

Albert shortened their stage name to a simple Ian & Sylvia and booked them for a six-week run, three sets a night, at the Gate of Horn in Chicago to tighten up their act. His target, however, was not clubs and coffeehouses, but the far more lucrative college circuit across the United States. The Kingston Trio were among the first folk acts to break into the colleges. "Albert got us a booking agency, ITA, International Talent Agency, which was founded on working with the Kingston Trio," notes Sylvia. "They were a big agency by then. You walked into their office and they had a map of North America on the wall with a red pin in it for every university and college the Kingston Trio had played. It was a mass of red pins. The Kingston Trio kind of opened the doors for everybody else because ITA had all those contacts. They pretty much had the whole ball of wax for many years. Later on ITA became GAC, General Artists, and we were with them for awhile, too. But ITA got us on that circuit quickly."

"It was always mind-boggling to me coming from Canada that there were literally thousands of these American colleges – not hundreds, but thousands – and every one of them had four, five, six, or eight concerts a year," boasts Ian. "For three or four years Sylvia and I would do two or three college concerts every weekend. Friday night would be in Maine and Saturday night might be on the West Coast. We'd fly to these goddamn places. I don't know how we never got killed like those rock 'n' rollers did."

"The very first job ITA got us was in Columbia, South Carolina, at Columbia Women's College," recalls Sylvia. "It was very bizarre because it was like going to a place that you had no relation to and was totally different from anything you've ever seen or experienced. It was a cotillion with ball gowns. Some of these gowns looked like antebellum dresses their grandmothers wore. And their escorts were from the nearby military school and they were all dressed in their uniforms. They were a very polite audience. What I found strange being a Canadian and having never been in the South was driving through that little town in South Carolina and seeing a public park divided in half, absolutely segregated, with a big fancy fountain, big trees, and flowers on one side, and a little drinking fountain and some scrubby bushes on the other side. All those experiences in the South of stopping at a late-night restaurant and seeing a pistol on the wall behind the cashier with a sign that read, 'We reserve the right to refuse service to anyone,' these were real eye-openers for us being Canadians. It was a major culture shock. Truth is I wasn't even aware of the kind of prejudice that existed in Chatham at that point because I seldom saw it. Black people did not live in Chatham. They lived in black communities. I went to high school with some black kids but they didn't go to the dances or any of that. But it was something I never noticed at that age."

Albert's next move was to secure the duo a recording contract and get an album out pronto. While the rock 'n' roll market was the domain of the pop hit 45 rpm single, folk music was largely album-driven (at least until Peter, Paul & Mary) and thus potentially more lucrative for an artist. Having already scored commercial success with Peter, Paul & Mary being signed to Warner Brothers records, a major player in the record business, Albert had an open door to bring his clients to that label, or to any label for that matter, given Peter, Paul & Mary's track record. Thus he suggested Ian & Sylvia sign with Warner. Elektra Records, an independent label, with a strong folk connection, operated out of New York by Jac Holzman, was also interested. "I spoke to Grossman about Ian &

Sylvia," recalls Jac Holzman, the label's founder and president, "but Grossman thought Elektra was small potatoes. I thought Vanguard was wrong for them but he got them on Vanguard, where Baez was. I never pursued it after Grossman brushed me off. I concentrated on the artists I had." Ian was determined to get what he wanted. "Ian really wanted to be on Vanguard Records," recalls Edgar Cowan. Sylvia was part of the decision-making progress and in agreement. "It was the prestige label in the folk world. They had Joan Baez and others. He really put the pressure on Albert to go with Vanguard even though Albert had an open book with Warner Brothers after Peter, Paul & Mary hit it big. They just told him to bring over anything he had. They were a much bigger company than Vanguard and had much greater distribution. But Ian resisted that. He wanted the classy label.* So Albert relented and went with that because that's what they wanted." Odetta, Albert's earliest client and an influential folk voice, had been signed to Vanguard, and Albert well knew the limitations of that label.

Founded in 1950 by brothers Maynard and Seymour Solomon, New York–based Vanguard Records began life as a boutique classical label before moving into jazz, blues, and, later, folk music, signing the Weavers, Joan Baez, the Rooftop Singers ("Walk Right In"), Ian & Sylvia, Patrick Sky, Mimi & Richard Fariña, Eric Andersen, and Buffy Sainte-Marie. "Classical music was their main bread and butter," notes Sylvia. "Seymour was in charge of the classical side of things and his young brother Maynard was allowed to record his folky things." The company released the Newport Folk Festival series of albums in the early 1960s. A brief foray into rock music later in the decade included psychedelic band Country Joe & the Fish. Today the label's back catalogue is owned by the

---

* The label's slogan on all its albums read "Vanguard Recordings For The Connoisseur."

Welk Music Group, founded by the late Lawrence Welk. "The Solomon brothers just bumbled their way into folk music," Ian insists. "They were early on the scene. It was Joan Baez who made them. Albert didn't want us to go with Vanguard. It was a prestigious label to be on because Baez was already on it but it wasn't where the big money was."

Despite being on the same label and travelling the same folk circuit, Sylvia admits she barely knew Joan Baez. "I was never really fond of her voice or her approach to the music. It always seemed to me a cold approach which seemed to be more about having a unique and strong voice than having anything to do with the lyrics. It was sort of an intellectual approach to the rawness of folk music. I preferred the raw side of it. Plus I never had the vocal instrument she had. She does have an amazing voice but it wasn't a voice that interested me." Adds Ian, "I was never friendly with her and the feeling was mutual. We were cordial but there wasn't anything there. Bob Dylan really used her and dumped her. She was very opinionated and hard to deal with. But she never grew with the music like many of the rest of us did. So she got left behind. Tell you the truth, I always thought she was a dyke, but then she fell hard for Dylan. She never liked me."

Mary Martin agrees that Vanguard was the wrong label for Ian & Sylvia. "If one checks the charts around that time you won't see too many Vanguard Records except maybe for Joan Baez; certainly not on the singles charts. Vanguard didn't know how to promote their records. Peter, Paul & Mary were on Warner's and Lightfoot later signed to United Artists. Look at the success Gordon Lightfoot and Peter, Paul & Mary had. Albert had a better offer from Warner's after Peter, Paul & Mary's success." Nevertheless, much to their manager's chagrin, the two Canadians held firm and he was forced to negotiate with the Solomons. "The only thing

Vanguard was capable of was the Rooftop Singers' 'Walk Right In' and a hit for Joan Baez," avers Charlie Rothschild. "They put out great music but they didn't know how to oil the wheels that made things happen for a recording artist. The Solomons were connoisseurs of classical music and Vanguard was a prestigious label but they didn't know how to market popular music for commercial success. If Ian & Sylvia had been on Columbia, where Dylan went, or Warner Brothers, they would have gotten a bigger shot. Even Elektra would have been better than Vanguard. Getting airplay was the key in generating record sales and making your artist into a bigger act. Jac Holzman knew that but the Solomon Brothers didn't. Peter, Paul & Mary got the hits because they had the big company machine behind them. Unlike them though, Ian & Sylvia was the genuine article. They weren't contrived."

"In many respects, Albert was quite right," reflects Sylvia. "We probably would have had a much more successful career if we had gone with Warner Brothers or Columbia. Vanguard's idea of promotion was buying an ad in *Evergreen Review*." Notes Charlie, "Vanguard Records was like a big weight dragging them down."

Vanguard's one ace in the hole was its recording process, seeking out venues that offered a natural acoustic sound rather than using a professional recording studio. Initially their choice was the Brooklyn Masonic Temple at 317 Clermont Avenue in Brooklyn. Later they switched to a converted ballroom in the once elegant old midtown Manhattan Towers hotel. "That's how they did it back then," Sylvia points out. "They would find a place with natural ambience, hang a couple of canvas drapes to dampen the sound a bit, hang a microphone from the ceiling, and record live from the floor. Our first album was recorded live off the floor at the Brooklyn Masonic Temple." Because of this basic approach the album has very much a live performance feel to it and the echo from the empty cavernous room and high ceiling gives the sound depth. Ian's guitar is not miked separately but is mixed in with the overall sound. Their voices blend beautifully, interweaving in and out around the melodies. The backing, guitarist John Herald of respected bluegrass outfit the Greenbriar Boys and bassist Bill Lee (father of film-maker Spike Lee), is also recorded live and is intentionally minimal, keeping the focus on the vocals and the live performance feel. There are no overdubs. Even Sylvia's autoharp is used sparingly. As for the material, it's all traditional, nothing original, with the exception of the arrangements, which were Ian & Sylvia's.

"Most of those songs on the first album would have been my choices of songs," Sylvia acknowledges. "That first album was largely our live repertoire. Ian may have had a choice in a couple of these songs but mainly it was stuff that I had dug up." Ian concurs. "Most of that stuff came from Sylvia and her songbooks. She knew all that folk stuff. 'Rocks and Gravel' we got from one of Alan Lomax's prison recordings, 'Mary Anne' we got from the Edith Fowke book. 'Old Blue' I got from Bob Gibson, as well as 'C.C. Rider.' 'En Canadien Errant' was from Marius Barbeau's book on French Canadien songs. 'Handsome Molly' was from Peggy Seeger. 'Pride of Petrovar' came from the Clancy Brothers. We hung out with the Clancy Brothers and Tommy Makem at the White Horse Tavern in New York. I had 'Rambler Gambler.' 'Got No More Home Than a Dog' and 'Live A-Humble' were also from one of Sylvia's songbooks. 'Down by the Willow Garden' was from the Child Collection of Appalachian Ballads." "That one's the Everly Brothers' arrangement," explains Sylvia. The Everlys had recorded the ballad on their 1959 album of traditional bluegrass and country music, *Songs Our Daddy Taught Us*. "I was a huge Everly Brothers fan," Sylvia admits. "Linda Ronstadt and I once joked that part of our learning harmony when we were younger involved adding a third part to every Everly Brothers song they ever did. And it was tricky because they would switch parts. We both had done that."

Most fans and record-buyers regarded Ian as the musical force behind the duo. He was the lead voice and the one who did the talking in concert. Sylvia remained the quiet shy one, uncomfortable in front of audiences.* "One of the things I often run into over the years is people assuming that I had very little to do with what Ian & Sylvia was," she avers. "That it was all Ian, mainly because he was the dominant character onstage. So there was the presumption that I had nothing to do with arrangements, the choice of songs, or hiring the musicians. That's a bit discouraging sometimes. I sort of understand why people think that (but I do run into that). And that's generally my fault too because I didn't put myself forward and say, 'Hey, I did that.' That just wasn't me. That perception put me in a bit of a spot years later when I embarked on my solo career, because people didn't know what it was I did." Notes Carolyn Hester, "I never saw Sylvia as not being an equal to Ian. Once she had you in the gaze of those big milky-brown eyes, I don't think you could forget her or her voice. The two of them were a team as far as I was concerned."

There was no doubting the fact that Ian & Sylvia's choice of material and the way they arranged that material set them apart from other folk artists of that period. "Absolutely," asserts Sylvia. "There were certain songs like 'When First Unto This Country,' that was definitely a New Lost City Ramblers song, but the way we did it was unique to our own sound. Nobody else was doing these songs. Vanguard never interfered with what we wanted to do musically. The song choices were all ours. I think those early

---

* Sylvia suffered debilitating bouts of stage fright and at one point consulted a hypnotist to help her overcome her anxiety.

Vanguard recordings still stand up, although their idea of stereo was to put me out of one speaker and Ian out of the other. That was a bit weird. But I once talked with someone who told me they liked that because they could learn all my parts by listening to one speaker."

While Albert was setting up Ian & Sylvia's music business contracts he also secured a deal for their song publishing with M. Witmark & Sons, a long established Tin Pan Alley publishing firm with a proven track record. By then Witmark had been purchased by Warner Music but the original name remained for several decades. Dylan and Gordon Lightfoot would also be signed to Witmark through Albert. It's believed that he had a deal with the publishers for a percentage of publishing earnings (the basis of lengthy litigation in the 1970s between Dylan and Albert).

For the uninitiated, which includes most 1950s to early '70s era songwriters who unwittingly signed over their publishing rights, publishing takes 50 percent of the money a song earns from four sources: performance income, including radio, television, film; synchronized licensing with film, television, or movies; print – sheet music; and mechanicals – record sales. The name "publishing" dates back to the days when sheet music was the principal source of income from songs, not record sales, performances, or radio airplay. Witmark was among the first companies to get in on the ground floor in the 1880s. The Beatles' long and sordid history of their own song publishing is a sobering lesson in the pitfalls of ownership of publishing. The fact that the late Michael Jackson owned the Beatles' publishing catalogue rankled Paul McCartney for years (although he still receives his half of writer's royalties, sharing it with John Lennon's estate). Some of the best-known songs of the last fifty years have been owned by someone other than the writer. Anyone can own a song's publishing rights. For many, it's the gift that keeps on giving. "The key to the music business is the publishing," notes Charlie Rothschild. "Performers only make the money as long as they're out there performing. The name of the game is publishing. If you have the publishing, you get money the rest of your life. Albert understood that."

By the late '60s many recording artists were becoming more savvy to publishing; however, most had neither the time nor the expertise to track down publishing money from a variety of sources. They would therefore license the right to "administer" – in other words, to monitor and collect monies owing – to an established publishing company, for a percentage. It's all very complex and the history of songwriting is littered with casualties.* "I didn't know what publishing was," Buffy Sainte-Marie admits. "I had only been in town for a very short time, a matter of weeks or months, I can't recall. I was singing at the Gaslight, and the Highwaymen were coming off a hit, 'Michael, Row the Boat Ashore.' I had gone down to Gerde's Folk City and sang there. Bob Dylan loved what I did and said, 'Go on down the street to the Gaslight.' So I went there and the Highwaymen heard 'Universal Soldier.' After my set I went and sat with them in the Gaslight and one of the people at the table said, 'Yeah, we're going to record that song. Who's the publisher?' And I said, 'What's that?' And Elmer Jared Gordon, damn his soul, spoke up right away and said, 'Oh, I can help with that. We'll have to do it legally though.' And he wrote up a contract right there and then and I signed it. There went 'Universal Soldier.' I sold it for $1. I just didn't know any better. A lot of musicians don't know about it. Who's gonna tell you? I only did it once, though. Never did it

---

* Randy Bachman and Burton Cummings of Canada's Guess Who fought a long- running litigation over control of their joint song-publishing rights before settling out of court. Currently Cummings owns the publishing on their post-1968 catalogue.

again because I learned from that experience. I bought that song back about ten years later for $25,000. I don't complain about the music business. I wish it wasn't they way it is because I think it fleeces artists in a terrible way. If only they would be honest about it. It's that plantation mentality and it's just awful."

Ian & Sylvia, on the other hand, were given sage advice. "David Braun, who was one of the main lawyers on Albert's team, he took care of us, bless his heart," acknowledges Ian. "He made sure we knew that after the mandatory twenty-eight year period we got our publishing back. When it came around, we got all of it, all our songs. We had a little piece of it before that but Albert had a lot more of it. He had a big piece of Dylan's publishing until Dylan figured that out pretty quickly. Us hicks from Canada, what did we know? We didn't know the difference between BMI and ASCAP."* Songs come up for renewal after twenty-eight years and if you don't serve notice to the publisher that you want to assert your rights then, they will revert to the publisher. Ian and Sylvia were aware of this because of their initial contract and took the proper steps to ensure they would get their publishing back from Warner Music. David also separated Ian and Sylvia's songwriting and publishing, which was very foresighted and beneficial to both in the long run. Today, Ian controls "Four Strong Winds" as well as "Some Day Soon" and the rest of his song catalogue, while Sylvia retains control of hers, including "You Were On My Mind." All three songs continue to generate a significant revenue stream.

Still, there were a few wrinkles that the two were unaware of

---

* While both essentially do the same thing, namely, collect royalties from a variety of formats including use by television, radio, Internet, ringtones, clubs, bars, hotels, and in live performances, BMI (Broadcast Music Inc.) is run by broadcasters, while ASCAP (American Society of Composers, Authors and Publishers) is a composers' organization. There are a number of ways that they differ in how they operate.

and as a result they lost out on some earnings. "A lot of the early material we recorded was traditional and not written by us," Sylvia points out. "It was never copyrighted for us as 'adapted or arranged by.' If you arrange or adapt traditional material you are supposed to get 25 percent of the publishing but if you don't assert that claim the money goes to the record company instead of you. So even though Vanguard keeps reissuing our recordings, our royalties are greatly reduced. And, of course, on compilations you get less than on the original. It's to their advantage to keep putting out compilations endlessly. Albert really had a problem with Vanguard taking the lion's share of the traditional material and said so right from the get-go. But we were starry-eyed. We just figured that since we didn't write it we weren't entitled to claim it." Adds Ian, "We were so green we didn't realize that Vanguard wanted us to record traditional material and they would get the money. We didn't know about publishing. Shit, we didn't make any publishing money off those first records but Vanguard made a fortune. Neither Sylvia nor I knew anything about publishing."

Released in the fall of 1962, *Ian & Sylvia* was a breath of fresh air in the increasingly crowded folk music market. It was well-received, garnering positive reviews. "Two young Canadian folk singers make an auspicious bow," declared *High Fidelity* magazine, going on to note "a tight-knit interplay of harmony and counterpoint. The duo shapes an exciting and unique vocal frame for each of their selections." The *Pittsburgh Press* stated, "By far the most pleasing folk record heard in the last five years." "Exciting singers," declared the *New York Times*. "Could be an influential new ensemble sound." Writing in *The Village Voice*, J. R. Goddard referred to Ian & Sylvia as "consummate musicians with intense feelings for their material. [The album] should serve well to introduce this exciting duo to a wide American audience."

And that it did. With their debut album released, Albert and ITA placed Ian & Sylvia on the more lucrative college circuit, eschewing the Greenwich Village coffeehouses, basket joints, and small clubs. Where most artists starting out on their careers had to play these venues low down on multi-act bills in hopes of catching the attention of a record label A&R (artist and repertoire) rep, Ian & Sylvia bypassed all that and made the leap straight to major clubs, and from there to the college circuit, in short order. "We were really hot in '63 and '64," notes Ian. "We played every college in the East and all those funny little mountain colleges in the Alleghenies and Appalachians and in New York state and Ohio. We played Harvard and Vassar, all the Ivy League colleges. The college music thing got started up pretty quickly and we played them all. Once it all started accelerating it really took off for us and was really happening. The big scene for us and our contemporaries was Boston – there was a big folk scene in Boston – New York in Greenwich Village, and in L.A. All the rest were secondary. But there were lots of places you could play in places like Oklahoma City, St. Louis, Fort Worth, and Dallas." While Peter, Paul & Mary may have sold more records, Ian & Sylvia were the darlings of the college folk scene. "We worked those southern colleges steadily," says Sylvia. Their good looks were an attraction for the young college crowd who identified with one or the other of them.

"That was pre-civil rights when we were playing all those southern colleges," adds Sylvia. "A real turning point for us was when we were booked to play Ole Miss. At that time as far as we knew Ole Miss was an integrated school because there had been so much in the newspapers about it. Two o'clock in the morning I got a phone call in my apartment in New York from Theo Bikel. We were set to leave the next morning to play that gig and he said to me, 'You can't play Old Miss. It's de facto segregation. There isn't one black student at Old Miss.' It was a real dilemma for us because we weren't political." In the end, Ian & Sylvia cancelled the gig and were later sued by the promoter. "I remember we were playing at a college in the South and we were being heckled and Ian had had enough and called the hecklers a bunch of pecker-woods. Suddenly the lights came up and there were these big black football players standing there at the back. I'm sure no one had ever called them peckerwoods before. There were black artists who played the same colleges as us in the Southern states, one group called the Hot Nuts who did mostly blues material. It was kind of a fraternity thing." At another concert in the South, following their set the two were confronted by a group of young girls who proceeded to berate them "for playing songs my grandmother sang," laughs Sylvia. "They wanted Kingston Trio songs, not all these old Appalachian ballads."

As Charlie Rothschild recalls, "I travelled on the road with Ian & Sylvia on occasion. They were a pleasure to work with and a lovely couple. It was much easier to travel in those days. Life was simpler. Everybody liked booking Ian & Sylvia and I could always get them back because they were great to work with, they enter-tained the audience, they delivered, and everything went well. It was a win-win situation. At the time I thought that we should do a direct mail out to the colleges to contact us about the acts. Then we would forward the information to the booking agents who would be coming to us for these acts. That way, by having the col-leges bypassing the agents and going directly to us, we could con-trol the bookings, which is what happened, and it worked." Initially the two travelled by car but as the bookings became further afield they would fly to a central location, rent a car, and drive from there. "Allegheny Airlines, holy shit, they'd break your guitar every time," avers Ian. "The guitar didn't have a chance with them. That was one of those 'by the seat of your pants' airlines." Back then flights were cheap. They would earn $400 a night and split it fifty-fifty. With the release of further albums their fee rose steadily up to $1,500 and $2,000. "We were making good money back then and our expenses were low," says Ian. The increased fees allowed them to take on an accompanist, guitar and banjo player Eric Hord, who was originally from San Diego (Eric would later join the Mamas & the Papas' touring band).

Back in Canada there were mutterings that the two had abandoned their homeland for the more lucrative pickings across the border. "People would sometimes say to us that we had gone off to New York and deserted Canada," muses Sylvia, "but there's such a thing as making a living. After you did six or seven clubs or universities across Canada that was just about the whole ball game back then." Winnipeg-born folk performer Oscar Brand had already carved out a career in the United States, while continuing to maintain a presence back home in Canada. His song "Something to Sing About (This Land of Ours)" was a Canadian folk music anthem. "I was in a unique position because I had one foot in Canada and one foot in the States," he notes. "I would do well in Canada and do well in the States." Oscar booked Ian & Sylvia on his CTV music program Let's Sing Out. "I knew they would do well. There was no question about it. They were very careful about their work and their performance. You might say that Ian & Sylvia were leading the procession for the folk people up in Canada when I first met them. The reality was that they had to go to the States where the business was happening. They needed that bigger platform and that was in the United States. The U.S. at the time was like a very large arena. It was like ancient Rome and you had to bang your way in and very often be carried out. But Ian & Sylvia succeeded.

They managed to maintain this combination of traditional and contemporary folk music and make it work. Here were these two people who were definitely not vagabonds, fascinating people – she was one of the most beautiful women on the continent and he was a good-looking, rugged masculine man – and between the two of them they carried a lot of beauty. I always wondered why Sylvia didn't make movies or become an actor. She was made for the stage and was so beautiful. Ian was a good writer and a good singer and a very prepossessing person in front of an audience. Each of them could have made something on their own but when they came together they really made something good happen. I envied them. I thought they were lovely."

Oscar also acknowledges the role Albert Grossman played in Ian & Sylvia's rise. "You had to have someone important representing you to the wider world. And when you have someone like an Albert Grossman, then you're fine. Unfortunately, when you don't have that clout behind you, you fall to the wayside, and in Canada we had plenty of people along that wayside. But Ian & Sylvia were able to rise above that. And they were damn good and wise with their work and were good musicians. So with the aid of a good manager they came out very well."

Ian & Sylvia toured the American South several times with folk trio the Journeymen, consisting of John Phillips (later the head Papa in the Mamas & the Papas), Scott McKenzie ("If You're Going to San Francisco"), and Dick Weissman. "I remember we were being driven through this town in the deep south," recalls Sylvia, "and the fellow driving took us through the shanty part of town and said, 'This is where those dirty, shiftless Negroes live.' Nobody said anything. So we drove on and he said, 'And this is a little better section of town.' Scott McKenzie was a funny guy and he replied, 'Oh, is this where the ambitious ones live?'"

"Doing college concerts at that time was like the world's easiest thing to do," says Dick Weissman. "You'd go out there and you'd get virtually a standing ovation for picking a string. We were darlings of the college concerts, too. In fact, our records didn't do that well but we were very popular with the college crowd. Ian & Sylvia were quite dynamic. Sylvia had quite an unusual voice and Ian was a good front man. It was the musicality they had, the blending of the harmonies that made them special. I remember there was a black chain-gang song they did ['Rocks and Gravel'] that I liked a lot. For me, it was an example of how you could take something traditional like that and make it pop or pop folk without making it sickening, so that you are actually extending the audience with this rather than dragging them along until it's no longer palatable. The other thing that made them unique was that there weren't very many male/female folk duos at that time.

"Sylvia always appeared to me as someone more comfortable performing in a living room than on a stage," continues Dick. "Yet she seemed to like being onstage. But I think she needed somebody as aggressive and assertive as Ian was at that point to be the front man to address the audience and answer the wisecracks. I don't remember Sylvia talking to the audience onstage at all back then. I almost felt like Sylvia was the real Joan Baez. I never thought that Joan Baez was who she was. She was acting out the role onstage. For a radical peacenik, Joan Baez was pretty damn competitive. And I never got that feeling from Sylvia. She just wasn't the kind of person to step on others to get ahead. Being who she was and being from Canada, I'm sure Sylvia was seen as a more fascinating figure. She was more exotic than these other people who drifted to Greenwich Village from Brooklyn."

Scott McKenzie (born Phillip Blondheim) has fond memories of his time with Ian. "We all found ourselves in Greenwich Village trying to play and sing and get jobs. That's when I met Ian, during that period, and I liked him immediately. We really hit it off. We enjoyed hanging out together and singing together and I loved listening to him. I remember Ian telling me how he loved to sing because it made him feel good. It was almost a sensual thing for him, a great sensation for him, he said. He would stand there almost with a proud look on his face because he got to do what he loved to do. Ian also had that kind of grin that gets guys in fights, that shit-eating grin. He loved to have fun. I remember one time on tour we checked into our hotel rooms late and this stuffy front desk manager told us the pool was closed and that we were not to use it. Next thing I know I hear this rebel yell and look out my window to see Ian diving off his balcony into the pool in the dark. We used to get drunk and he'd ride on the back of my BSA motorcycle. We laughed a lot. I'm sure we were both half crocked on that motorcycle. I tried to keep up with Ian but I couldn't do it." As for Ian and Journeyman leader John Phillips, the two were never close. "They were too much alike," Sylvia points out. "Too much ego between them."

Early on, Ian & Sylvia became a major draw in the Washington area and played there two and three times a year for several years. "Washington, D.C., was Ian & Sylvia's main market," confirms Charlie Rothschild. "The guy who ran the Cellar Door, Jack Boyle, was a huge fan of theirs and they became monsters in that area and could do no wrong. They were bigger in Washington, I would say at first, than they were in New York. Out of that generated colleges and other work. They were probably bigger than Peter, Paul & Mary in Washington. They managed to pack so many people into the Cellar Door. It was a one-story club but it was like they packed a second story's worth of people in because they loved Ian & Sylvia so much." Wayne Reichardt was a student in D.C.

who saw Ian & Sylvia often at the club. "The Cellar Door was a block away from Georgetown University but there were other universities and colleges in this area," notes Wayne. "Ian & Sylvia practically adopted Washington as kind of their home away from home down here." Located at the corner of 34th and M Street, the club had a side-door entrance. Inside was darkly lit with a semi-circular stage at the far end of the room as you walked in. Adjacent to the stage was a staircase up to the dressing rooms. "It was very cozy but when you were there, you were there to stay," adds Wayne. "Seating was first come first served and they packed as many people as they could into it when Ian & Sylvia were there." And what impressed Wayne the most about the duo? "They were always very well rehearsed and tight. It was the precision of the vocal arrangements that always knocked me out. I saw a lot of the folk acts of that time but none of them had the vocal harmonies that Ian & Sylvia had. They could reproduce their songs as if you were listening to the records. One time I remember Ian started the show and Sylvia descended the stairs singing and it brought the house down. What I recall most were the a cappella songs that were so precise. It was electrifying. And even though they always had great guitar players accompanying them, Ian's rhythm guitar carried it all. He had such a distinctive style and he was good at what he did beyond typical guitar players. His guitar was really the glue that kept it all together musically. He had a style all his own. Ian did all the talking during their sets."

"I was a good entertainer in the small clubs," Ian admits. "I was funny and I could talk to the audience and entertain quite well. But when we got into those big venues I'd stiffen up. A lot of times I'd clutch and it cost us. Sylvia would get nervous too but she didn't have to talk. But I did. A lot of those big shows we were not at our best like we would be in the Cellar Door in D.C. or at the Golden Bear in Huntington Beach because we were relaxed. Those big venues and big shows scared us."

Carolyn Hester ran into her two Canadian friends one time in Washington. "They had a gig at the Cellar Door and I was at the Shadows. Later that night they called me up at my hotel and asked if I wanted to get together with them. So we did and that was wonderful. That made me very happy because I really loved Sylvia and think she's a great woman, a real warrior woman. They were never 'show business' and I dislike that show business thing."

In February 1963, Ian & Sylvia taped an appearance at Brown University in Providence, Rhode Island, along with the Journeymen and other acts for ABC TV's quickie folk music cash-in television show *Hootenanny*. With folk music the flavour of the day in 1963, ABC sought to tap into that youth market with a half-hour "live" concert (although pre-taped and often spliced together from several different concerts) from a different campus location across the States each week. The popularity of the show's first thirteen-week run beginning in April 1963 led to a full hour in the second season, commencing that September. While folk purists reviled the homogenized folk fare the show offered, television critics deemed it a winner and early ratings bore that out. With the show's mixing of traditional folk artists like Theodore Bikel, Leon Bibb, Josh White Jr., Miriam Makeba, Bud & Travis, and the Greenbriar Boys with more pop-oriented folkies such as the Rooftop Singers, the Chad Mitchell Trio, Judy Collins, the Serendipity Singers, and the New Christy Minstrels, Ian & Sylvia fit right in, straddling both camps. Their attractive, photogenic image was perfect for television.*

---

* Ian & Sylvia had, in fact, done a number of television shows, including NBC's *The Bell Telephone Hour.* As Charlie Rothschild recalls, "They did a song on that show that had to be altered because the lyrics were considered too intimate for audience consumption. In today's world no one would probably notice it. But the censors said there was something in that song that they had to change."

"That *Hootenanny* show was pretty lame," comments Ian. Jack Linkletter, son of TV personality Art Linkletter, served as host although his opening bits were taped separately from the performances and edited in during post-production. Comedians were also included, such as Woody Allen, Bill Cosby, and Vaughn Meader (whose President Kennedy schtick was all but over on November 22, 1963). In its favour, the show did cross genres by introducing the likes of Johnny Cash, the Carter Family, Doc Watson, the Clara Ward Gospel Singers, Flatt & Scruggs, and even country crooner Eddy Arnold to folkies. It also helped spread Ian & Sylvia's name to a wider audience as their appearances on the show were always well-received and hardly hokey or pandering. Nonetheless, with the British Invasion of the Beatles in February 1964, *Hootenanny* became an instant anachronism and was cancelled at the end of season two. Such was the fickle nature of popular music crazes and cash-ins.*

Even before *Hootenanny* aired, a controversy raged over the show's non-political stance. Left-leaners like the Weavers and Pete Seeger were barred from appearing unless they signed a waiver revealing their associations with the Communist party. A boycott was organized in response but Seeger altruistically urged his fellow folk contemporaries to appear on the show and raise the profile of folk music in America. Joan Baez, Tom Paxton, and Ramblin' Jack Elliott all supported the boycott. The issue served to underscore the dividing lines in the folk community between not only the purists and contemporary folk artists but also between the political and non-political folkies. As the Journeymen's Dick Weissman explains, "At the time there was sort of a huge division between the pop people and the purists. To some extent it was

---

* *Shindig!*, *Shivaree*, *Hullabaloo*, and *A Go Go 66*, anyone?

Sylvia as a child at Government Beach (courtesy of Sylvia Tyson)

Ian, age 13, Vancouver Island (courtesy of Ian Tyson)

Sylvia as teenager, late 1950s
(courtesy of Sylvia Tyson)

Ian in Toronto, 1958
(courtesy of Ian Tyson)

Sylvia at first Mariposa Festival, 1961
(© Clive Webster; courtesy of Sylvia Tyson)

Sylvia and Ian backstage jamming with other musicians at the inaugural Mariposa Folk Festival, August 1961 (courtesy of Sylvia Tyson)

Brochure for inaugural Mariposa Folk Festival (courtesy of Peter O'Brien)

Globe and Mail newspaper photo: Sylvia and Ian circa 1962 (courtesy of Sylvia Tyson)

Handbill for October 1962 appearance at Town Hall, New York, alongside Bob Dylan (courtesy of Sylvia Tyson)

Ian & Sylvia taken in Vancouver, 1963 (© David Birley)

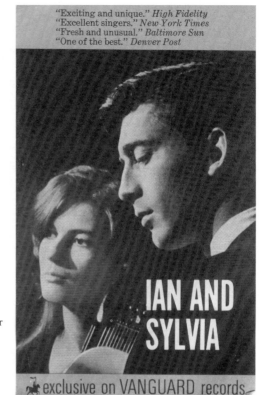

"Exciting and unique." *High Fidelity*
"Excellent singers." *New York Times*
"Fresh and unusual." *Baltimore Sun*
"One of the best." *Denver Post*

IAN AND SYLVIA

exclusive on VANGUARD records

Advertisement from Vanguard for
debut Ian & Sylvia album, 1963
(courtesy of Peter O'Brien)

Maclean's magazine,
1964 (courtesy of
Sylvia Tyson)

Wedding photo, June 26, 1964 (courtesy of Sylvia Tyson)

Brochure for UK Tour, 1966
(courtesy of Peter O'Brien)

Sylvia with Clay, circa 1969
(courtesy of Ian Tyson)

very humorous because Joan Baez was considered a purist but she was also the daughter of a nuclear physicist, so she had no connection personally to folk music in the sense of a Doc Watson or a Mississippi John Hurt. Where I was coming from, Joan Baez would have been considered a commercial folksinger. As for the people who hung out in Boston or in Greenwich Village, there were those who were considered cool and those who were considered uncool, the most extreme of those being the Brothers Four. They were seen as frat boys mining the folk music catalogue for pop hits. Ian & Sylvia were among maybe four or five artists who could appeal to both factions. Judy Collins was another one who appealed to both sides. We, on the other hand, who were not as denigrated as the Brothers Four, were considered pretty much in the pop vein."

The Journeymen began life as the Smoothies, a Virginia-area vocal group in the mould of the Four Freshmen or the Four Preps. When the folk boom hit, John Phillips and Scott McKenzie dove in and went in search of someone who could give them some folk credibility. Izzy Young at Greenwich Village's Folklore Center recommended Dick Weissman. Despite this, the Journeymen were still perceived as less than authentic folkies. "Peter, Paul & Mary managed to escape the pop folk stigma because of their association with Dylan and from that the civil rights movement, but we couldn't," states Dick. "Mary Travers came from the socialist end of folk music." Added to that perception was the non-political stance of the Journeymen, something they shared in common with Ian & Sylvia.

"It got really political in the Village," avers Ian. "If you weren't a socialist you were suspect to some of those people. It was always politics with Pete Seeger. There was pressure on us to be political. I never got into his politics. We didn't do any of those civil rights rallies. Dylan just idolized Woody Guthrie and used Woody.

Ramblin' Jack [Elliott] did that, too. But Jack wasn't political. That's why he and I were very tight. He wanted to be a cowboy. Albert [Grossman] was apolitical. He didn't pressure us to be political. He didn't like all that Pete Seeger stuff. He liked the money that he earned from Dylan's political songs. He could see way down the road. He had a sense of what worked." "I remember Sylvia saying that they didn't get involved much in the politics of the time because they were Canadians and it wouldn't be right," says Suze Rotolo. "I just thought it was because they were Canadians and too polite. They felt they shouldn't criticize their guest country. But not all artists in those days sang about politics. That wasn't the language of everyone's talent." Adds Dick Weissman,* "I had the sense that it was more of a Canadian thing. I remember we were on the *Hootenanny U.S.A.* tour in 1963 and Kennedy was assassinated while we were on this tour. We were asked not to play at the Jackson, Mississippi, city auditorium by the Student Non-Violent Coordinating Committee. Ian & Sylvia weren't on that tour but the Halifax Three [with Denny Doherty, later of the Mamas & the Papas] were. We took a vote of all the people on the tour whether we should play or not. We voted three to two not to play but the Halifax Three voted to play, except for their guitar player, Zal Yanovsky,† but he had no say. The other guys in the Halifax Three had the attitude that we as Americans were all into this stuff but as Canadians it wasn't their problem."

"We're the cousins of the Americans and I think that's how they look at us," suggests Gordon Lightfoot. "Their politics is so seriously involved that ours looks like child's play. I took some

---

* Dick Weissman has written extensively on the relationship between politics and music, including the book *Talkin' 'Bout a Revolution: Music and Social Change in America* (Milwaukee, MI: Backbeat Books, 2010).

† Originally from Toronto, Zal Yanovsky later founded the Lovin' Spoonful with John Sebastian.

shots for 'Black Day in July' because I was an outsider looking in. I admired Phil Ochs for his political stance." Nor was it any easier to tackle Canadian politics. "It's hard for a Canadian singer/song-writer to write about Canadian politics because no one else other than Canadians is really interested or knows about it," adds Gordon. "No one takes much interest in the Canadian Parliament so to have a Canadian singer/songwriter singing protest songs wouldn't make sense at all."

Protest songs tend to have a short shelf life. "I understand the purpose of topical songs and protest music making a point at that time," states Sylvia. "But that's just it, it's at that time, and at a certain point later it ceases to be relevant other than a little piece of history perhaps. So those kinds of songs were not the kind of music I was interested in. When we hung out in the Village with Dylan, Phil Ochs was a part of that scene. I think he was a very clever writer but that song 'Changes' was the only one of his songs we could do because he was very political.* I think 'Changes' was something that transcended that for Phil. He had found that niche as a topical songwriter – and he was very good with it – but it has affected his place in the history of that era. You can say profoundly political things in a way that makes them profoundly political. And Dylan got into that to some degree, too, but he was a little cleverer to be vague enough in his references. Dylan was perhaps a bit of a musical opportunist. That's what was going on at the time, political music, and he joined in with it. His association with that catapulted his career."

Despite their aversion to taking political sides, Ian & Sylvia were booked to play a garden party for the Kennedy family in mid 1963. "Ethel Kennedy had us booked to play that," Ian explains. "I'm

---

* Gordon Lightfoot also recorded Phil Och's "Changes" on his 1965 debut album.

sure all the Kennedy clan were there but I wouldn't have known any of them if I fell over them. I was a dumb farm boy from Canada. I didn't know shit. We were apolitical." Recalls Charlie Rothschild, "In Washington, they were everybody's sweethearts so it's no surprise that they would be booked for something like that. They were good guys." They also took part in a tour in support of Lyndon Johnson's presidential election bid in the fall of 1964, accompanying Lady Bird Johnson, Lyndon's wife, and a number of artists. As Sylvia remembers it, "We were whistle stopping with Lady Bird Johnson during the Johnson-Goldwater election. It seemed very important to us that Barry Goldwater not win. We had mixed feelings because we thought Goldwater was basically a decent guy but some of the people behind him were a bit scary. It was heavy duty at that time and it seemed important, not that Johnson was so great, but that Goldwater not get into the White House."

One of Ian & Sylvia's Greenwich Village contemporaries, Bob Dylan, was more inclined toward political issues and using his songwriting to espouse his views and those of his generation on civil rights, war, and social issues. Dylan (born Robert Zimmerman, from Hibbing, Minnesota) had arrived in Greenwich Village before Ian & Sylvia and was yet to be "discovered" when the duo signed up with Albert Grossman. The three would become close friends over the next couple of years, socializing together, sharing songs, inspiring and challenging each other, although you'd never know that from reading Dylan's autobiography *Chronicles, Volume 1* published in 2004. "I found it very odd that Ian & Sylvia were not mentioned in Bob's autobiography," muses Sylvia. "He liked our music, we were friends, we hung out together, Ian influenced the way Bob looked and dressed, yet it's somehow like we never existed in his world. Somehow we just weren't there. I'm not upset about it, I just found it odd, that's all. He's such a perverse bugger!"

Dylan had come to New York in early 1961 ostensibly to meet his folk music idol, Woody Guthrie, only to discover that Woody had been hospitalized for Huntington's disease. Bob's early presentation was liberally borrowed from his hero. Initially bitten by the rock 'n' roll bug (he briefly played piano behind Fargo, North Dakota's Bobby Vee), he switched his allegiance to folk music during a brief stint at university in Minneapolis. Recognizing that Bobby Zimmerman, son of a Jewish furniture salesman from Hibbing, Minnesota, had little in the way of cachet or mystique, he transformed himself into Bob Dylan, ex-rodeo rider and cowboy from way out west. While others may have bought the tall tale, Ian Tyson was having none of it. "A lot of those guys back then were a little leery around me because I was a little too authentic for them. I'd been there riding bucking horses and lived in the woods. Bob Dylan originally told me he was from Gallup, New Mexico, and I knew he was a lying son of a bitch. 'I'm from Gallup, New Mexico!' and I just thought to myself, 'I don't think so.' He claimed he used to rodeo but he had these little tiny arms. 'Uh, I don't know, Bob.'" Did Ian see Dylan as a bit of a charlatan? "Absolutely. We thought he was a total phoney. When Jack Elliott came back from England, Bob just absorbed everything from Jack – the look, the guitar playing – he just couldn't pull off the cowboy thing, though." Ian was initially not among Bob Dylan's early disciples. "I didn't get Dylan at first. I didn't get him until he was successful and making money. I loved [1966's] *Blonde on Blonde.*"

Suze Rotolo is not surprised that Bob Zimmerman would assume a new identity on arriving in New York. "Isn't that the purpose when you're young? You're leaving home and leaving all your baggage behind. You are who you are becoming and Dylan was no more guilty than anybody else of doing that, only he took it quite a few steps further. Because he became so famous it was more focused on. But Ramblin' Jack Elliott did the same thing. He was born in Brooklyn of doctor parents and was named Elliott Adnopoz. You would never have guessed that of him. People changed their names and who they were. It wasn't about where you were coming from but where you were going. Dave Van Ronk was from Queens and that was like coming from the outback, like this dirty secret. But Ian & Sylvia never hid where they came from, it just wasn't important. That wasn't the focus. To us they were just from Canada. But it didn't mean anything to us. I don't think it made any difference that Ian & Sylvia were from Canada and Jack Elliott was from Brooklyn. It wasn't part of anything. It was just accepted that we were in all this together. The conversation was about the music, not about where you came from or who your parents were. Back then that didn't matter. You were who you were."

Suze was born and raised in Queens, the daughter of communist Italian working-class immigrants. She met Bob Dylan in July 1961. She was seventeen years old; Bob was twenty and not yet a major presence on the folk scene. Suze would remain Bob's girlfriend until 1963.* She is pictured with Bob on his 1963 album *The Freewheelin' Bob Dylan*. As Suze recalls, "I think I met Ian with Bob and then later I met Sylvia. Everyone was kind of floating around and crossing paths. There was this family, the Baileys [Mell and Lillian], and they would have people over, all sorts of singers. They had a tape recorder and would record these parties and people singing. That's where I think I first met Sylvia. What struck me about her besides her being so extraordinarily beautiful was her

---

* For further insight into their relationship, Suze's autobiography, *A Freewheelin' Time: A Memoir of Greenwich Village in the Sixties* (New York: Broadway Books, 2008) is highly recommended.

voice, which was timeless and almost otherworldly, as if it came from the edge of time. And when they sang together, Sylvia's ethereal voice and Ian's baritone, it was just mesmerizing when they sang these traditional songs. The combination of their voices was incredible. Ian was very handsome and Sylvia was very beautiful. Together they had a glow about them."

Although Bob had arrived in Greenwich Village before Ian & Sylvia came down from Toronto, he was yet to be signed by Albert Grossman and Columbia Records, still scuffling for gigs and honing his craft. "I remember that Bob was always hitting on girls but it wasn't to sleep with them," laughs Sylvia. "It was because he had no place to sleep. A floor was fine." All the while Bob was absorbing everything around him as fodder for his own songwriting. "The thing most people don't realize about Bob Dylan," notes Sylvia, "is that he has a kind of photographic memory for things. He literally remembers everything he's ever heard or seen. I've had him recall to me conversations we had years earlier word for word. So he has a wealth of material to draw from in his songwriting. It's how he gleans from this, how he synthesizes all this, how he puts it together that is his real talent, I think. He was unique from the get-go. He was like a great big sponge. He absorbed everything and I don't even know how aware he was that he was doing it. He would come into the Kettle of Fish and say to us, 'I wrote this new song or at least I think I wrote it. Maybe I heard it somewhere.'" It took the concerted effort of several folkies to convince Albert to sign Bob as a client in August 1962. "It was a combination of Ian and me and Peter, Paul & Mary that got Albert to sign Bob," she insists. "Albert didn't 'hear' Bob but we did. He certainly didn't get Dylan at first. We told Albert to sign him, us, and Noel [Paul] Stookey. We convinced him that Bob was worth signing after he saw him at Gerde's. That fact that his stuff was original and he had an original sound was unmistakable. He was doing some traditional stuff and the Woody Guthrie stuff but the things he was making up, even his silly stuff, was all quite good. Even with Noel Stookey, Ian and me telling Albert he should sign this guy I don't think Albert really got it, until the Robert Shelton article in *The New York Times*."

As Charlie Rothschild remembers, "When Albert signed Ian & Sylvia, Bob Dylan only had a cult following. I ran Gerde's Folk City at the time and I hired Dylan to play there. Then Robert Shelton wrote about him in *The New York Times* that he was the greatest thing that ever happened. After that Dylan had a following. But was Dylan responsible for Albert becoming a kingpin or was it the reverse? Who came first, the chicken or the egg? I think they both benefitted from the relationship."

On a social level, Ian & Sylvia had quickly integrated into the Greenwich Village milieu. They were invited to all the parties and get-togethers in clubs and coffeehouses. "We were good friends with Len Chandler," Ian remembers. "Not Phil Ochs. But we were good friends with Eric Andersen and Tom Rush. Also Eric Weissberg, Johnny Herald. Scott McKenzie and I were very close. I never saw Scott after he became one of the flower power guys." Confirms Eric Weissberg, a member of the Tarriers, "Everybody in the Village loved Ian & Sylvia. They were regarded as being right at the top. They were so good and it was so refreshing to hear that music done so well. Great songs, great harmonies. And such nice people. I probably had a crush on Sylvia. I had a great time with them." Friends recall seeing Sylvia riding around Greenwich Village on the back of Eric's motorcycle.

"Everybody on the scene hung out at Gerde's, the Gaslight, or the Kettle of Fish," Ian recalls. "The Kettle of Fish was as much as or more of a hangout really than Gerde's. Bob Dylan, Dave Van

Ronk, the Greenbriar Boys, Simon & Garfunkel, Peter Yarrow and Mary Travers. Everybody hung out together and the music we played informally, which we did all the time, was predominantly bluegrass or old-time music. That was before the whole songwriting explosion. The bluegrass innovators of the early '60s really had a strong influence on the whole scene, especially in New York, which was the centre of the folk scene then. I loved bluegrass and so did Sylvia."

When not on the road, Ian and Sylvia often spent time with Suze and Bob. Suze recalls, "When they were in town they used to come over when Bob and I were living in this tiny apartment on West 4th Street. We were just like four friends. I'm sure Ian and Bob went out doing what they were doing then and Sylvia and I would hang out together. Whenever Sylvia was in town we saw each other. We had our own friendship apart from the two guys. We were very special friends and still are. When they would come over there would be this excitement about looking over new albums either Bob had or they would bring with them. And they would sing something they had recently worked out. There was this musical exchange and it was always fun. Ian and Bob would exchange songs together. It was so much harder to find new music back then than now. You really had to hunt. It was like a treasure hunt going from one person to another looking through record collections for new discoveries. Dave Van Ronk had an incredible knowledge of music and a big record collection and was a big influence on everyone. He doesn't get the recognition he deserves."

Suze noticed a genial competitiveness between Ian and Bob back then. "Both of them were ambitious. Bob was trying to do what Guthrie did and that was to write his own songs and in doing so unleashed this whole attitude of 'I can do that.' Oh God, everyone thought they were a songwriter after that." She also feels that

Bob admired Ian. "There were several guys in the Village who had been cowboys but Ian was certainly the most authentic. It's funny because it was a time when inventing personas was the thing and yet authenticity was highly prized. Ian was authentic, plus he looked great in his cowboy boots. Bob looked up to Ian. He was absorbing everything back then. Bob assimilated everything and it then evolved into what he became and he found his own voice and style. That was the artistic process and he was doing it right in front of our eyes."

"Bob was too afraid of Ian, like everybody else," admits Sylvia. "Ian never saw anybody as competition because he had such a strong sense of himself and his image and what he did. It was no surprise when after we arrived in New York in the folk community all the guys started wearing cowboy boots and not rolling their jeans up. Ian had a sense of style that others copied, including Bob." That wasn't the only instance where Ian influenced Bob Dylan. According to Suze, "The first memory I have of Ian is him introducing Bob to marijuana. There was such innocence back then even though marijuana was part of the beat generation and the jazz scene. I may have been pretty naive because I was younger than everyone else, but it seemed that that was the first time marijuana was introduced into our circle when Ian brought it over. At that point drugs were on the periphery. The cool image before that was a drink and a cigarette in your hand. It seems funny now thinking of this image of Ian, the dealer," says Suze with a laugh. "It seems so out of character with their image. Ian was cool back then. He was his own self back then."

Ian, too, is amused at the notion that he is perhaps ground zero for the entire drug subculture of the 1960s, given Bob Dylan's pervasive influence on popular culture and drug use. "Suze Rotolo claims in her book I was the Clark Gable of Greenwich Village," he smiles. "And you were, too," Sylvia replies. "You were a little too self-assured for many of the males in the Village." "None of our crowd was into serious drugs," admits Ian. "We were just beer-drinking country bumpkins."

As for Sylvia, Suze claims Bob admired her for her voice and her beauty but also admits, "I don't know if he ever thought about Sylvia's importance. I don't know if any of those guys thought about that. They would probably know it but not dwell on it. But how could you not when you heard them singing? It's not that they discounted Sylvia, it was just a given. In those days the guys were the kings and the women were there to serve them. If you were with some guy, that's who you belonged to. It was all about Ian because he was the male and Sylvia was seen as his partner onstage. That was probably the way it was seen by the public because of the male domination of the scene and the times. But to us it was always Ian & Sylvia. We all knew Sylvia's strengths. But Sylvia was more reserved. That was just her personality. Back then the women took the background role. It was still a time when you had one foot in the '50s slave woman way and another foot in the feminism that came out later in the '60s. That was the generation Sylvia and I came from. We followed the guy and were expected to do his bidding and you didn't question it. That's just the way it was. The guys got all the credit. It wasn't easy for women performers. But Sylvia could have done it on her own. She had the goods. It was just the climate of the times. In their case, maybe because Ian's song 'Four Strong Winds' was such a big hit nobody realized Sylvia was writing great songs, too. She didn't get the credit she deserved. She also had a strong business sense. She was a smart business woman. I admired her immensely.

"There weren't that many girlfriends around that you could hang out with in your own way," Suze concludes. "Sylvia was one of them. So she meant very much to me. We had that bond and the friendship continued even when we didn't see each other for many years." Following her breakup with Bob, Suze spent time in Italy before returning to New York. She avoided many of her folk music friends in her desire to establish a different identity for herself beyond the intense media glare that now engulfed her former beau. "I regret losing touch with some of these people like Sylvia but I built a wall to protect myself. She and I reconnected at the Dave Van Ronk memorial a few years ago."

So, if Bob Dylan and Ian & Sylvia were so tight back then, why no mention of them in his autobiography? Mutual friend Ramblin' Jack Elliott thinks he knows why. "In Ian's previous book, *I Never Sold My Saddle*, Ian was very critical of Bob.* I was proud to see that he would come out and say something critical because everyone else revered Bob and feared him so much that they wouldn't say anything negative. Ian was, I think, a little bit hurt by Bob's oftentimes rude behaviour back in the day, and he mentioned it in his book. Perhaps Bob resented that and repaid him by not mentioning him."

Even before the fame and godlike adulation, Bob Dylan was defying the folk music traditionalists by writing his own songs. Soon other folk acolytes would follow his lead, Ian & Sylvia included. As Ian remembers, "Dylan came running in one day in about 1962 and he said, 'Hey, you've got to hear this great song I've written,' and we said, 'Written? What do you mean written?' Everybody thought he was nuts. 'You don't write folk music.' I remember the day he wrote 'Blowin' in the Wind.' We were with him in the bar at the Kettle of Fish on MacDougal Street when he came running in after having probably stolen the pen and the

---

* Ian referred to Dylan as "an obnoxious little jerk . . . he got away with singing out of tune and playing out of tune."

paper that he wrote it on, he was so poor. But that was a mind-blower at that time. He started all that because before then the songs sung were all traditional songs, many American and Canadian. In the early '60s in New York it was all based on that traditional ballad style. Bob Dylan changed all that."

Hearing Bob Dylan perform "Blowin' in the Wind" hot off his typewriter would serve as a pivotal moment for Ian, spurring him on to begin writing his own songs. His first attempt would prove to be pure gold. "I've told so many fuckin' lies about 'Four Strong Winds' that I don't know what the truth is anymore!" he grumbles. "Actually, I do remember it very well. It was a rainy autumn afternoon at Albert Grossman's tiny little apartment in the east 50's. That was before Dylan was making the big dough. I had heard his 'Blowin' in the Wind' or one of his other early songs and just thought, 'Shit, how hard can this be? If that little shit can do it. . . . ' I didn't care that much for the melody because he just played rudimentary guitar but I started to get the imagery. I hadn't been writing before. I always thought the stuff I liked was written by people who knew something I didn't know. I liked Bob's imagery so I thought I'd write about my life and what I used to do. I wasn't a professional migratory farm worker or cowboy but I had done some of that stuff. You can't write a song like 'Summer Wages' unless you've done some of that stuff. It came very easy. It took maybe half an hour. It was my first song. I knew what other guys in the Village were trying to write. They were all trying to catch up with Dylan. He wasn't a star yet but he had this incredible output already. He would leave us in the dust. But we all came to the realization that if he could turn out six great songs we could maybe do one or two."

In "Four Strong Winds" Ian managed to capture the loneliness that anyone who has been dislocated feels and the longing for that place where one's heart is home. In his case it was a yearning for the simple pastoral virtues of rural Alberta. "I just thought, 'God, it was so damn simple.' 'Think I'll go out to Alberta,' shit, that doesn't take a genius. But it had a universality about it. People could relate to it. The Americans loved the Canadian references. They thought I had huge balls to put Canadian geography in a song. When the Nashville guys started to record it they wanted to change the Canadian references and I said, 'Nope.'"

One person who was touched by the sentiments of the song was Neil Young, who, in 1963, was a Winnipeg-based rock 'n' roller with folk music inclinations. "There was this place we used to go where you could put a nickel in the jukebox and 'Four Strong Winds' was on it," Neil remembers. "So I used to play it all the time. That's where I heard it for the first time and I loved the song. I listened to it over and over. It just caught my attention. There aren't many songs that I perform that I didn't write but that's one [Neil still performs it to this day]. It was very real to me. I don't think you can get any more real than that. Ian's the real deal. He's a very authentic Canadian country folksinger. A true original. He doesn't hide things." In his 2006 concert film *Heart of Gold* Neil introduces "Four Strong Winds" with a recollection of being at Falcon Lake, a Manitoba resort town east of Winnipeg, at age sixteen and being in a restaurant there. "I think I spent all my money playing that song over and over again." He later recorded "Four Strong Winds" on his 1978 million-selling album *Comes a Time*. The resulting royalty cheque came in handy, allowing Ian to put a down payment on his current ranch.

Released as a single in the summer of 1963, "Four Strong Winds" became a hit across Canada by fall, going on to become Ian & Sylvia's signature song. It remains so to this day. According to Sylvia, "It was Ian's song but I actually contributed one line, 'But our good times are all gone and I'm bound for moving on.' He was stuck on that so I gave him that line. He's probably forgotten that by now," she laughs. "He had been working on it in New York, then we went to the first *Hootenanny* show taping in Providence, Rhode Island, and the Journeymen were on that show. Afterwards we were sitting around with the Journeymen back at the hotel and Ian played 'Four Strong Winds' for them and everybody loved it. I really liked it." Recalls Scott McKenzie, "I was there in a hotel room when Ian first played 'Four Strong Winds.' He had just finished writing it and played it for us. I think the Journeymen were one of the first to record it. Everyone wanted to record that song, it was so good. Ian really came into his own as a songwriter and taking that step to write. And he really nailed it with 'Four Strong Winds' and later 'Some Day Soon.'"

"I'm just guessing but it must have been Sylvia that I played it for first," Ian speculates. "People loved it. Our contemporaries, they loved it. Waylon [Jennings] loved it. He was the second to record it after Bobby Bare. He had a hit with it. It was a hit single in Canada. Bob McAdorey [CHUM deejay in Toronto], he plugged the hell out of it. Bobby Bare's version made a lot of money for me. I bought that farm in Newtonville, 350 acres, from that song, 'Four Strong Winds.'"

As the Journeymen's Dick Weissman observed, "Ian was very ambitious. He wanted that success and notoriety. I didn't know Sylvia that well but I did get the sense that she was not oriented that way. I remember we were doing a concert together with them in 1963 or 1964 and Ian was complaining that Ian & Sylvia weren't breaking through the way he wanted them to. He wanted more success. So I told him, 'You two have the best of it all. You're starting to write songs' – Ian had written 'Four Strong Winds' and Sylvia had just written 'You Were On My Mind' – 'and you can make money from this and do well in your concerts but you can also walk down the street in New York and nobody bothers you. Nobody knows who you are. You have your privacy.' But I really didn't get the sense that he understood that at the time. He was pissed off that they weren't getting the recognition others were getting but he didn't understand that there was more to it than what he thought." Adds Sylvia, "There were times when things got rough where Ian would say, 'Oh, the hell with this. I'm going to go back to being an artist.' He would get temporarily discouraged. When he would get that way I would say to him, 'Okay, but we're contracted to do this series of gigs,' and usually by the time we were done he'd have gotten over his frustration."

In July 1963, Ian & Sylvia made their Newport Folk Festival debut, marking their arrival as a major folk act. They performed during an afternoon show and went down well with the diehard folk crowd. "I know there had to be considerable lobbying on the part of Albert Grossman and Peter Yarrow to get us on the roster," notes Sylvia, "partly because we were relatively new on the scene and didn't have the history that most of the U.S. acts had. The other element was that we were Canadians and, being guests in the U.S., not inclined to be politically active or outspoken in an era when folk music was highly political and you were expected to stand and be counted. Our only experience with an event approaching that size was Mariposa. I mainly remember that first Newport appearance as somewhat bewildering because everyone seemed to know everyone else and I knew hardly anyone and was very shy. Ian did most of the socializing. I mainly stayed in my room and read. I recall that we were received very well." Ian doesn't recollect much of that event. Nor does he remember the CBC TV teleplay he and Sylvia appeared in that aired March 7 of that year. *The Cowboy and Mr. Anthony*, written by Hugh Kemp and directed by the one and only Norman Campbell, was a fantasy about a rodeo rider who gets thrown from a horse and as a result goes on to a successful singing career. Not too far from reality for Ian. "You can tell how memorable it was," Sylvia chuckles. "Ian doesn't even remember it."

Sessions began in the spring of 1963 for a follow-up album, recorded this time in the ballroom of the Manhattan Towers hotel. "That place was fabulous for folk music," glows Ian. "It was three stories high and had endless beautiful wood which gave it a natural reverb. But later when you had to have drums that changed everything. Everybody packed up and went to Nashville. But in the Manhattan Towers they just hung a Neumann microphone from the ceiling. That room just loved Ian & Sylvia's sound. You can still hear it today on those recordings." Prior to the New York sessions, the two had attempted to record the album in Toronto at Arc Sound, to no avail. "The studio claimed it had four tracks," chuckles Sylvia, "but it turned out to be two Ampex two-track machines joined together that weren't in sync. We tried some songs but the results were so appalling. We didn't keep the tracks." Once again drawing on their intimate knowledge of traditional folk ballads for the bulk of the material, the album would boast two contemporary compositions: the title track, Ian's "Four Strong Winds," and Bob Dylan's "Tomorrow Is a Long Time." "Bob told us he wrote it for us," states Ian. General wisdom holds that it was written as a love song to Suze Rotolo. "That was once he realized there was money to be made from songwriting," suggests Sylvia. Regardless, despite a blossoming demand for Dylan's songs, he did present the song to Ian & Sylvia to record.*

---

* Dylan first recorded the song at a demo session for Witmark in 1962 but did not release a version of the song until 1971's *Bob Dylan's Greatest Hits: Volume II*. The original demo appeared in 2010 on *The Bootleg Series: Volume 9*.

"Everybody thinks the folk scene was all namby pamby, nicey nice," notes singer/songwriter Tom Russell, who in later years worked separately with both Ian and Sylvia. "But it was still competitive and there were people behind the scenes running it as a business. These songwriters were all trying to outdo each other and you had to have a lot of courage and guts, and a strong front if you were an insecure person. They were all trying to cut each other. People were vicious to one another, yet the public image was of all socialists and peaceniks. Dylan learned to be vicious back and that killed Phil Ochs. He couldn't deal with that. The competitiveness killed some of these guys. It was hard-core people playing hard ball. Survival of the fittest and you needed a tough shell. And then there were the hard-core junkies like Fred Neil and Tim Hardin. To see Ian Tyson alive and well and still doing it today is astounding."

Ian & Sylvia's second album included a stirring a cappella arrangement of the old English ballad "The Greenwood Sidie (The Cruel Mother)" from Cecil Sharp's songbook and Sylvia's bluesy version of "Every Night When the Sun Goes Down." French Canadian musicologist Marius Barbeau was again tapped for "V'la l'Bon Vent." "Sylvia loved all those French ballads," claims Ian. "I was ambivalent." Two gospel numbers – "Jesus Met the Woman at the Well" and "Every Time I Feel the Spirit" – came from Mahalia Jackson, the queen of American gospel music, while the Alan Lomax collection of American Negro ballads provided "Poor Lazarus." Several of Ian & Sylvia's contemporaries were the source of songs on the album including Mary Jane and Winston Young ("Royal Canal"), the Clancy Brothers and Tommy Makem ("Lady of Carlisle") and the Country Gentlemen ("Katy Dear"). "We used to go just down the street when we played the Cellar Door in Washington D.C. to the Shamrock Tavern to see the Country Gentlemen between sets and they would do the same with us," Sylvia recalls. In addition, Greenwich Village contemporary Barry Kornfeld was the source for the old Texas ballad "Ella Speed," while the countrified "Long, Lonesome Road" came from a Peggy Seeger album. "By now we had albums available to us that we hadn't had before," notes Sylvia. Ian brought the old western ballad "Spanish Is a Loving Tongue" in to the session, written by cowboy poet Charles Badger Clark and adapted for song by Richard Dyer-Bennet. "He kind of homogenized it," he relates, "and made it politically correct by removing the line about 'She was Mex and I was white.'"

Accompanying the duo on the album once again was the respected guitarist from the Greenbriar Boys, John Herald, whose lead guitar work added much to the tracks. "Johnny Herald was a great guitar player but not an instinctive player," Sylvia reveals. "He had to work out every note. We had to send him every song we were going to do months in advance and he would painstakingly work out methodically note by note what he would play. People would hear his work on our albums and call him to do sessions but he couldn't do it on the spur of the moment. He was a lovely player but a very meticulous, hard-working player. That's why that stuff is so great." On bass was ex-Greenbriar Boy and member of the Tarriers, Eric Weissberg, a graduate of the Julliard School of Music and later famous as the banjo picker on "Duelin' Banjos." "There weren't too many bass players who knew the folk idiom as well and could play it on bass," notes Eric. "Russ Savakus was a jazz guy who played folk because he liked it and so was Bill Lee. With Ian & Sylvia the music was great. Ian had the arrangements pretty much in his head and taught them to us and things moved along easily. There were never any problems. They played really great country music, too. There were no downsides to working with them. But I remember Ian was the nattiest dresser. Those double-vented suits he had freaked me out."*

Released in early autumn 1963, *Four Strong Winds* was the break-through album for Ian & Sylvia. Driven by the popularity of the title song, the album sold in excess of 100,000 copies, big business for folk albums in general and for Vanguard Records in particular. Those kind of sales numbers rivalled Joan Baez's. In its year-end issue *Maclean's* magazine noted that 1963 was the year that folk music challenged rock 'n' roll. "The best of the new Canadian stars were the superb team of Ian Tyson and Sylvia Fricker," the short, uncredited article declared, "who succeeded with two LPs during the year. One song, 'Four Strong Winds,' written by Tyson, beat its way up through the raucous gibberish of most popular records to become number two in eastern Canada in November. Not all purists are in favour of Ian and Sylvia, who arrange their material to suit their own unique musicality. But no one denies they are pleasant to listen to." *Chatelaine* had already prepared a major feature on Ian & Sylvia for their January 1964 issue.

"When the second album, *Four Strong Winds*, came out we did a signing at a record store in Washington, D.C.," recalls Ian, "and there was a riot. A very non-violent riot – all well-behaved, well-dressed college kids – but it was a big crush of people. That was the first eye-opener for me that maybe something big was happening."

---

* Ian bought his suits at Lou Myles in Toronto. Lou outfitted the local jazz community and later fitted Bob Dylan in several distinctive hounds-tooth suits for his 1965 electric world tour.

4

NED AND MAUDE: THE LOVIN' SOUND

"Sylvia fell in love with New York when Joe Taylor took us there," states Ian. "She wanted to live there right away." Because she enjoyed dual citizenship, Sylvia was able to take up residence in New York and work from a base there. Her older sister Sonia was already living on the Lower East Side. It was Sylvia who, initially, was the more determined of the two and affixed her sights firmly on a career in New York. "My mother was an American citizen at the time I was born so I was able to claim dual citizenship," she confirms. "They changed the ruling after that. If I had thought that I was going to lose my Canadian citizenship I wouldn't have claimed my American citizenship. But I knew the Canadians weren't going to write you off if you did do that. I never had a passport until about ten years ago because you didn't need one to travel back then. I had my birth certificate and an American immigration card." Ian was granted resident alien status which allowed him to work in the U.S., although for the first few years he continued to return to Toronto when the duo had rare time off. Being a resident alien also put Ian on the compulsory military service list. "They grabbed me," he reveals. "I had a draft card. But my knees were shot from the rodeo. I'd have ended up in Viet Nam. Shit, I wasn't even an American. They said, 'You report,' and I did. I thought it would be a lark but it wasn't.

"I didn't exactly have a permanent place," Ian continues. "I was kind of floating from place to place with friends." For a time, he and Edgar Cowan shared a house on Roxborough Street in central Toronto near the posh community of Rosedale. According to Edgar, "The house was owned by a notorious Mafia figure but there were never any problems. Bobby Dylan came up a little later and stayed at that house with us. He wrote some songs in our backyard on my old Remington typewriter." Edgar contends that Bob wrote "Mr. Tambourine Man" on that particular Toronto visit.

When in New York, Ian resided at the Earle Hotel (now the Washington Square Hotel) located at Waverly Place and MacDougal Street near Washington Square, a popular hangout for artists, writers, and musicians. Sylvia stayed at the Earle, too, until moving to a fifth-floor walkup on Stanton Street in the old Jewish neighbourhood of Manhattan two blocks from Delancey. The apartment previously belonged to folksingers Len and Nancy Chandler. "It certainly was a walkup, alright," smirks Ian. "I had to walk up those stairs with my guitars. It was a funky little place complete with cockroaches. The cast-iron bathtub was in the kitchen and it had a kind of counter over top. There was no place to park near the apartment or anywhere in Manhattan without spending a lot of money. Eric Weissberg always had his motorcycle. Most people in the Village didn't have cars."

By her own admission, Sylvia paid little attention to her appearance in the earliest days of the duo. "I just wore what I wore and did what I did," she states. "We were very natural. We weren't glitzy or glamorous. Canadians weren't generally like that back then." However, with her shimmering long straight hair, luminous skin, and captivating eyes she was a natural beauty, and as the duo's profile rose, much of their appeal was drawn from Sylvia's entrancing presence. After the duo's move to New York, "she kept getting better looking," notes Edgar Cowan. "She filled out, and being on the road and playing colleges and clubs, her sophistication grew. And that, I think, started to appeal to Ian as well." It also appealed to their contemporaries. "She was utterly gorgeous back then and she still is," offers Tom Paxton. "I wouldn't call her painfully shy but she was certainly content to let others carry the ball conversationally. But so what? She was so damn good looking and I loved being around her. I liked being around Ian, too. He had a very strong personality but Sylvia sang with such confidence that it was clear she had an investment in it. She was truly a musical partner and an equal; there was no doubt about that. It wasn't 'Ian with Sylvia' it was 'Ian & Sylvia.'"

Michelle Phillips, later of the Mamas & the Papas, remembers, "When I was a teenager in southern California all the girls wanted to look like Sylvia Tyson. She was so beautiful." California-born singer/songwriter Tom Russell first saw Ian & Sylvia in the early '60s in southern California folk clubs like the Ash Grove and the Golden Bear. "Every young folkie was in love with Sylvia," claims Tom. "She was as real as you can be and so beautiful. She looked like what a beautiful folksinging lady should look like. I became aware with each of their records I bought that she was a big, big part of who they were. It was very much an equal thing with them despite the public image. A lot of the groundwork, the homework, and finding the songs was Sylvia. I read the liner notes and realized she was the one doing the research. But she didn't get the credit because it was a very chauvinistic world back then. It was very hard when you have a guy like Ian with such a huge presence. And Ian was a bit of a rounder back then and she wasn't of that kind of life."

But while others took note of Sylvia's burgeoning allure and key role in the duo, few were emboldened enough to approach her for fear of riling Ian. The relationship between the two Canadians remained somewhat ambiguous. "I just assumed they were a couple back then," insists close friend Suze Rotolo. "I never questioned it." Dick Weissman recalls, "There was a mystery about the two of them. Musicians would always be having these conversations among themselves about whether they were really a couple or not. Nobody knew what their relationship was. Were they just working together or were they, in fact, sleeping together? Seems kind of funny now. There were a couple of male folksingers who were quite interested in Sylvia but afraid to approach her for fear of what Ian might do. They weren't sure if it was a cool thing to do or not. And I think Ian was quite happy to have it implied rather than stated."

"There may have been guys who wanted to date me but they were terrified of Ian," laughs Sylvia. "Even though we didn't have a relationship right away, Ian was quite proprietary. I don't think he wanted to lose his singing partner." Confirms Ian, "There was no romantic attraction between us. It was completely platonic for the first two years." Nonetheless, travelling, recording, and performing together constantly drew the two closer. They even came up with pet names for each other. Sylvia was Maude, based on American television comedian Jonathan Winters's character Maude Frickert (Ian was a big Winters fan), while Ian became Ned for Harry Secombe's character Neddie Seagoon from the British comedy *The Goon Show*.

"I didn't date a lot," reveals Sylvia. "I had a couple of boy-
friends but nothing lasting or serious. Once we started working
we were on the road most of the time so there wasn't really an
opportunity to have a relationship outside the duo." Ian, on the
other hand, continued to woo the womenfolk. "He was not overt
about it," offers Edgar, "but he certainly had lots of women before
he and Sylvia became a couple." As Jutta Maue Kay, working at
the time as a waitress in Yorkville, remembers it, "All the guys
wanted to date Sylvia while all the girls wanted to bed Ian." The
distinction is noteworthy. Ian was sexually attractive, all masculine bravado and confidence, and regarded as a desirable conquest.
And he never lacked for female company. "Ian was a real lady's
man," Scott McKenzie smiles. "It was just in his nature. It's like
he couldn't help it. Ian loved the women and they loved him, too."
At one point Ian was the subject of a paternity suit in the Village
but it was ultimately exposed as merely a shakedown. Sylvia, con-
versely, was the dark, mysterious, ethereal girl whom men wanted
to get to know rather than have a quick roll in the hay with.
"Other guys were having a look-see at Sylvia," avers Edgar, "and
Ian didn't like that much. And there were guys looking hard. They
had been working together for quite awhile and were also enjoying great success. They were sharing everything. They were singing together, writing together, travelling together, living together.
They were doing quite well."

Among those few who dared to approach Sylvia was Tom
Paxton. "I think I went out with Tom Paxton a couple of times
when Ian had gone back to Toronto. Then he came back to New
York and said, 'Okay, that's enough of that.'" The personal relationship between Ian and Sylvia had been growing closer since they
left Toronto for New York. The steady work week in, week out
on the road increasingly drew them together. It was inevitable that

a relationship would emerge. "We worked together, living day to day," notes Ian. "We were very fond of each other. It wasn't something that was planned or even anticipated. We didn't know any more about our relationship than those other guys knew. We weren't into analyzing our love affair like all those people in New York." As Carolyn Hester states, "I think everyone was hoping a personal relationship would develop between them because we all fell in love with them as a couple."

"It wasn't romantic in the least," confirms Sylvia. "We worked together for a considerable time before we became a couple. He loved me and I loved him but it was not romantic. It had more to do with it being a very compatible partnership borne from working together and sharing common interests, and a lot of respect for each other. It just wasn't very romantic. Friends have told me it was fascinating watching us onstage for the implied relationship rather than for a real one. They found it very interesting that we put out the impression of there being a relationship without looking in each other's eyes or touching each other. It was not overt in any way, especially onstage." Edgar Cowan agrees. "Did they ever show any of the playfulness of two young lovers? No. It was business as usual. I never saw arguments, negativity, or bitterness but I also never saw any passion. They both are a little cold anyway. All the television guys wanted them to look at each other and show that passion but they would never do that. They wouldn't cooperate."

According to Tom Russell, "No, there weren't any of those loving glances exchanged between them onstage. If they looked at each other it was likely because one thought the other had made a mistake. Ian told me that once he put his foot on her foot in the middle of a song because he thought she sang the wrong harmony. It was tense looking and very professional looking but it wasn't all lovey dovey like Peter, Paul & Mary. A lot of that was Ian, who was a very macho kind of guy with testosterone flowing."

Rather than the fabled great Canadian love story, Ian terms their relationship "a deep and abiding affection. It wasn't this great, classic passionate love affair. It was a very affectionate relationship that was ultimately hard to maintain with my philandering. We liked each other a lot." As Ruth Jones McVeigh recalls, "I thought they were a team and had a friendship more than a passion. I saw them as very close musicians and very good friends with a lot in common." Regardless, by the end of 1962, Ian & Sylvia were a couple in more than a musical sense. Ian, however, still had a roving eye, although as some suggest, it may not have been anything more. "It certainly wouldn't have been easy in the early years because they were together all the time," Edgar points out. "How do you fit in other relationships? I think it was a 'look but don't touch' situation. Ian may have been doing the looking [or looking back] but it didn't mean it went much further than that."

All the while Ian & Sylvia were basking in folk music success and earning both respect and acclaim far and wide from critics and peers, Ian never abandoned his partiality for rural life nor his dream of one day being a cowboy. Meeting Ramblin' Jack Elliott only served to reinforce that dream. Born Elliott Adnopoz in Brooklyn, New York, in 1931, the son of upper-middle-class parents, Jack grew up nurturing that same dream. At the age of nine he attended his first rodeo at Madison Square Garden and he returned for many years thereafter. "I've always been interested in that life," Jack admits. "I was twelve when I got a book by Will James, who was a Canadian cowboy born in Quebec province. He started cowboying out in the Calgary area. I read his book *Lone Cowboy: My Life Story*, which was his autobiography, and then I proceeded to read every Will James book I could get

my hands on. Then I found out that Ian was also a big fan of Will
James and still is."

Ian, too, had been smitten as a youngster by Will James's books.
Born Joseph Ernest Dufault in Saint-Nazaire-d'Acton in 1892,
Dufault assumed the name Will James after heading out west.
Initially it was his artwork, drawings of cowboy life, that caught
people's attention, but when he turned his talent to writing and
illustrating a series of books for children set in the west, he found
fame. Beginning with *Smoky the Cow Horse* in 1926, James wrote
twenty-three books in all before his death in 1942. Ian later wrote
a tribute to his early hero, "Will James," on his 1983 album *Old
Corrals and Sagebrush & Other Cowboy Culture Classics*. Jack recorded
the song for *The Gift*, Stony Plain Records' 2007 tribute to Ian. "I
left one of the verses out," he chuckles. "I couldn't remember it
and was playing it from memory and Ian sure let me have it. He
called me up and said, 'God damn it, you left one of the verses
out! You had my phone number. You could've called me!' So I apol-
ogized profusely."

By the mid '50s Jack fell under the sway of Woody Guthrie and
adopted a pseudonym. Dressing the cowboy part, Ramblin' Jack
(his name derived from his penchant for telling long rambling stories rather than for a transient lifestyle) found success performing
and recording in the U.K. and Europe. Returning to New York in
late 1961 Jack was surprised to discover he was already somewhat
of a legendary figure in Greenwich Village. He became a mentor
to Bob Dylan as the two developed a close friendship. Bob adopted
Jack's guitar style and stage personality. And Jack also met up with
Ian Tyson. "I think we met down at the Gaslight," recalls Jack.
"I am very fond of Ian and I had some marvellous good times with
him. He's one of my favourite people. I was staying at the Earle
Hotel at the time. I saw Ian & Sylvia playing a couple of times. I

loved the way they sang together. Their voices blended so beautifully. Sylvia had a great singing voice even without Ian but together
there was a wonderful sound that came out. I loved hearing them
sing 'Four Strong Winds.'"

For a wannabe cowboy like Jack, Ian Tyson was the real deal.
"I liked the fact that they were from Canada, especially the fact
that Ian was from Western Canada," he points out. The two connected over their mutual love for the cowboy lifestyle. "Whenever
Ian and I would happen to meet up out on the road in some distant town or city we'd usually end up looking for some western
store together and look at saddles or maybe pick up a *Western
Horseman* magazine," says Jack . "One time it was around Christmas
and Ian & Sylvia were heading west to a gig in L.A. It must have
been 1964. I was heading for California and I was in Santa Fe, New
Mexico, to play a gig. They discovered I was playing in Santa Fe.
My wife and I had just arrived in town and we were having a cup
of coffee in the main square in town and Ian & Sylvia walked in.
My coffee hadn't even cooled enough yet to drink. I looked up at
them and said, 'Well, howdy! Welcome to New Mexico!' So Ian
and I had to find a western store to go to and we did. Ian bought
me a fine cowboy hat for Christmas, a fine chocolate brown hat.
And I bought him a nylon lariat rope. He said he never roped much
so I figured it was time he had his own lariat. But that was kind
of a dude's store, not a real western store, so the next day I looked
up in the phone book to find a more authentic, real cowboy store
and found a saddlers called Slim's. Ian and I went up to Slim's and
spent several hours watching him build a saddle. I bought myself
a rope while I was there. I figured now that Ian had a lariat I needed
one, too."

Jack encouraged Ian to let loose his inner cowboy. "When Ian
was in New York I didn't see him wearing jeans much, never on

stage. He dressed in nicely tailored clothes, expensive shirts and trousers, and looked almost like a photographer's model. Ian was one of the greatest looking guys I ever saw. Everyone admired his good looks on stage. But he didn't even wear cowboy boots. I guess that's the way he thought he had to dress to please the crowds in his chosen profession in a folksinging duo. So I said to him one day, 'Why don't you just wear your cowboy clothes?' I always wore my cowboy clothes. Of course, I was just an amateur cowboy and he was the real thing. It was part of my whole make-up, wearing cowboy boots and a cowboy hat. So I told Ian to do the same and I think he took my suggestion and started wearing boots and a hat on stage. The first time I played up in Toronto Ian drove me up there in my truck and I didn't know that truck could go that fast. He was a helluva driver. Ian had an apartment in Toronto and he had his saddle there and sheepskin pads on the chairs and stuff like that, a very western decor. I went shopping with Ian to look for a ranch up north of Toronto. I got back and my second wife, Patty, who was from Toronto, greeted us at the door in tears and told us that President John F. Kennedy was shot. It was a terrible day. Ian didn't buy that particular farm."

The hectic touring pace continued for Ian & Sylvia through early 1964. They played a two-week residency at Washington's Cellar Door beginning January 20 and followed that with a return to Canada for an Atlantic Canada college tour, ending with a major concert at Toronto's Massey Hall on February 21 for which they earned $3,400. Back in the U.S. they continued playing college shows, mostly down south, through to late May. By the end of May they were in Los Angeles for rehearsals and a live appearance on *The Steve Allen Show* (produced by Canadian Daryl Duke) before performing at the annual Monterey Folk Festival on May 30. They followed that with a two-week stint at the Golden Bear folk club on the Pacific Coast Highway in Huntington Beach. Much like the Cellar Door, the Golden Bear was another Ian & Sylvia stronghold and they appeared at the folk club frequently in the early to mid '60s. Among those to catch Ian & Sylvia there were singer/songwriters Jackson Browne, Steve Gillette, and Tom Russell, as well as Chris Hillman, then a bluegrass mandolin player, later to become a founding member of the Byrds and the Flying Burrito Brothers. As Steve Gillette describes it, "The Golden Bear was pretty typical, one large open room. The club was right on the Pacific Coast Highway. The stage was at the far right corner, angled across. At the left of the stage was a divider, which hid the door to the kitchen and the dressing rooms. It had seating for about 200 people." He also remembers another unique feature. "Down in the basement, a cook and dishwasher named Patrick (an artist who went on to work for Bill Graham, designing posters) had decorated it and made it into a special dressing room. Around the dressing table and mirror he had painted a shrine to Sylvia. I think she was a little embarrassed about that.

"Ian & Sylvia were captivating to watch onstage," Steve continues. "Sylvia had long straight hair down to her waist and was absolutely beautiful with a voice that was entrancing with that vibrato of hers. She was so enchanting and had a real star look about her. Ian was very masculine and had that gunfighter bravado thing about him. We all looked up to him as a kind of hero to us. He would call everybody 'Hoss,' No one ever knew if he remembered your name because he'd just say, 'Hey, Hoss!' But the chemistry between them was so amazing. They seemed to us like a mysterious and wonderful couple."

The axis of the L.A. folk music scene swung between three clubs. Doug Weston's Troubadour on Santa Monica Boulevard was central to the Hollywood music scene and the spot where the music industry types hung out. The Ash Grove on Melrose Avenue, run by Ed Pearl, catered more to the folk purists ("the folk Nazis," as some called them) with more traditional or authentic folk artists. The Golden Bear, operated by Delbert Kauffman, took a more open and eclectic approach to its folk fare and offered a more laidback atmosphere that suited the vibe of the beach scene. While the latter was more of a home base for Ian & Sylvia they also appeared at the other two clubs.

Tom Russell was tuned in to folk and country music while still in high school in the early '60s. "You'd hear that stuff together on the radio and I didn't even think of it as being different," he notes. "It was all just music, great music. I became aware of Ian & Sylvia by about their second album, *Four Strong Winds*. You would hear that song on these weird folk shows. We had a little record store in Inglewood and I went in and bought the first two Ian & Sylvia albums and was immediately blown away. At that time I was steeping myself in anything that was folk music – the Kingston Trio, the Limeliters, Bud & Travis – but Ian & Sylvia were different, more authentic. I saw them live several times but I think the first time was at the Ash Grove and later at the Golden Bear. You could get very close to them at the Golden Bear. I remember Ian being very funny. He would make fun of the local beer. He had a great sense of humour, very sarcastic, but it wasn't that rehearsed shtick that a lot of folk acts did; the same jokes and the same patter every night. All the folk acts did shtick. Ian's humour was very off the wall and I identified with that. He certainly never kissed the audience's ass."

Of the folk boom in general, Tom observed, "From Joan Baez to the Kingston Trio, it was all very nice and wholesome and appealed to a college audience. You got the feeling like we're all very nice and we're all a part of this folk community. That was the schtick. Peter, Paul & Mary tried to promote that community thing; that we're all in this together. Ian never tried to promote that kind of trip or sang protest songs. They weren't political and didn't kiss a lot of butts and that probably hurt them. They didn't go along with the political line and I thought that was great. Being a singer/songwriter is a very isolated experience and Ian & Sylvia were very much like that. I didn't see them as being a part of any community. They were just damn good. That made them unique to me, a kid who had good ears.

"When they hit the stage back then it was very strong musically," recalls Tom. "The first song would always knock you over. And they always had really good guitar players with them.* It was always about the music with them, as opposed to an act. That was the transformation for me; when Ian & Sylvia and Dylan got in on the act, I realized this wasn't just showbiz, these were creative people. It was the start of the singer/songwriter thing, which was very cool. The other guy who was also very much that same way was Ramblin' Jack Elliott who kind of linked all those traditions. I must have seen Ian & Sylvia two or three times but I was terrified to go up and talk to them even though you could because they would be standing around after their sets. Ian would be out there having a beer. I remember him talking to a bunch of us about early Buck Owens records which he was really into and we were just overwhelmed. 'Wow, this guy's hip to Bakersfield music,' which we were really into as well. 'He's not just a folkie.' And my first and lasting impression of Sylvia is that if she wasn't onstage she was reading a mystery novel. As I learned later, she would read one a day. Both of them were very literate and well-read. I've done songwriting workshops with Ian and he always stresses, 'Read,

---

* By this point Eric Hord had left, replaced by Monte Dunn, a well-respected guitarist in the folk community.

read, read!' I had been educated and I kind of gravitated towards where they were coming from. To me they seemed like a very European act because it wasn't so much a commercial American show biz thing with them. They were much more sophisticated than that."

Ian recalls a particularly memorable character who would come to their shows at the Golden Bear. "Gilbert Roland, the great Spanish actor, used to come and see us. He would come almost every night and come in the back door. He took us to Mexico to the bullfights in Tijuana. I remember it very well. We went down there in a big white Lincoln. I've got pictures of it."

Life on the road for travelling folk music performers was hardly glamorous and for the one and a half to two hours spent on stage, they often spent more than that on planes, cars, or in hotel rooms. "There was a lot of wasted time when you weren't singing," Sylvia points out, "especially if you were in a town that you didn't know very well. I read a lot and Ian would go out, read, or practise his guitar. We'd go fool around with the sound system at the venue, maybe rehearse a bit. You might make a friend or two while you are there. You'd always get sucked into going to dinner at some-body's place, especially if you got so lonely you just couldn't stand it anymore. You'd accept a dinner invitation from some well-meaning couple and it would be a disaster. You had nothing in common. They didn't have anything to say to you. They wanted you to come and sing. No idea that you weren't like some animal in a zoo. Not their fault but that's just the way it was. You can spot a situation like that a mile away. When we were down south they would invite us to the fraternities. Whoever put on the concert would invite you to the frat house, which would consist of guys who didn't have dates getting drunk on beer as fast as they could, or guys who did have dates sitting with one arm jealously around their date. Whereas you were the occasion for the party, they didn't really want you there. I don't know how girl singers on their own on the road could do it."

Sessions for a third album, *Northern Journey*, were held in early March of 1964, again at New York's Manhattan Towers Ballroom. Both Ian and Sylvia regard *Northern Journey* as the full realization of the Ian & Sylvia sound and approach to folk music they were trying for. "I think it's the best one of our Vanguard albums, actually," Ian points out. Joining the usual backing crew of John Herald and Eric Weissberg was guitarist and mandolin player Monte Dunn. Guitar connoisseurs often point to this album as the finest example of John Herald's nimble playing. Released later that summer, the album offered a balance of traditional folk, country, and bluegrass-flavoured songs, and original material (two songs from Ian, one from Sylvia). There was even a nod to their Canadian roots with "Brave Wolfe" and "Nova Scotia Farewell." According to Sylvia, titling the album *Northern Journey* reflected the origins of much of the material drawn from Canadian sources.

Sylvia's lone compositional contribution proved to be an enduring one. "You Were On My Mind" was the first original song she had attempted back in 1962. Inspired by Ian's inaugural effort, "Four Strong Winds," Sylvia retreated to the bathtub of her suite at the Earle Hotel to get away from the cockroaches ("Those buggers were big enough to throw a saddle on," Ian smirks) and with her autoharp in hand wrote the song within a matter of minutes. Long-time friend Larry LeBlanc claims, "Sylvia is a very unusual songwriter. She doesn't write anything down until she's conceived the entire song in her head. Then she writes it down. They are all formed, top to bottom, by the time she writes them down." As Sylvia explains, "It was loosely based on something I had heard Odetta sing. Not the same, but it started a train of thought in my mind and it developed from that. It was the first song I ever wrote. The first one's easy! But it wasn't about anyone in particular. It's pretty amazing that Ian's first song was 'Four Strong Winds' and mine was 'You Were On My Mind.'" As Ian suggests, "It never occurred to us before to write." With its twelve-string guitar intro, the arrangement draws from the Rooftop Singers' hit "Walk Right In." Picked as the lead track, the song set the pace for the rest of the album. Surprisingly, Vanguard did not release "You Were On My Mind" as a single. That distinction would belong to a West Coast rock group the following year.

Ian's two original numbers reflected his country/bluegrass leanings. "Four Rode By," with its lightning fast picking from John Herald and Ian ("that certainly turned some guitar pickers' heads around," boasts Sylvia), was based on real-life Canadian outlaws, the three McLean Brothers and accomplice Alex Hare, whose crime spree in 1870s British Columbia ended when they were hanged at Westminster. Ian & Sylvia later assisted in the production of a documentary film on the McLean gang. Ian's other composition would, like "Four Strong Winds," take on a life of its own and, according to Ian, go on to become his biggest money-maker. "Some Day Soon" has become a country music classic, recorded dozens and dozens of times, and become as identified with its writer as his first song.

"I just wrote it in Sylvia's apartment down on the Lower East Side," says Ian. "I don't know where I got the idea for doing a song from a girl's perspective. I stole the first line of that song from an old Stanley Brothers tune, an old bluegrass song. I filched that and I don't think I've ever admitted that. But I don't know where I got that plotline. It was pretty clever and I didn't steal that, I know that. I was hanging out with Jack [Elliott] a lot then and Jack was also hanging out with Peter LaFarge. Peter was one of those wannabe cowboys. Jack and I were trying to be cowboys in Greenwich Village and that's why I was trying to write that. I was kind of homesick in Greenwich Village and 'Four Strong Winds' has that in it, too. I didn't like the East. You couldn't be a cowboy anywhere east of Winnipeg. And cowboys weren't hip then. But the folkies kind of liked cowboys, they thought they were sort of exotic." Judy Collins and later Suzy Bogguss both enjoyed success with "Some Day Soon." Ian named the indoor cutting horse training building on his ranch "the Suzy Boggus Arena" after a substantial royalty cheque came his way from her recording.

"That was a big, big song for me for years," he admits. "But it had just been lying there until Stephen Stills was living with Judy Collins and told her, 'You've got to record this song.' She didn't want to record it but he pushed her to and that recording was magical. It was huge. And it was because of Stephen Stills, God please him. Its next huge resurrection came after another old guitar player of mine, Tommy Spurlock, was on a session for Suzy Bogguss and he told her, 'Y'all should do that Tyson song about "Some Day Soon.' She had never heard it but Bam! What a monster hit."

Of the other songs on the album, "Moonshine Can" came from an old Newfoundland song by Pat Troy of Goose Cove, while "Nova Scotia Farewell" was a song Ian & Sylvia had heard Maritime singer Catherine McKinnon sing at a party. "We didn't know her but we liked the song," says Sylvia. "Brave Wolfe" was gleaned from a Peggy Seeger album. As for "Little Beggarman," Sylvia explains, "We just needed one more song for the album. We had been working at Martha's Vineyard with the Clancy Brothers and Tommy Makem and this was one of Tommy's songs. I was a great Tommy Makem fan so I said, 'Why don't we do it?' And that was it." The a cappella version of "Texas Rangers" was based on a

Mike Seeger arrangement from a New Lost City Ramblers album; however, the verses were derived from the Cecil Sharp book of traditional ballads. "We hated 'Captain Woodstock's Courtship,'" Sylvia insists. "It was one of those songs that was requested but it was just like doing 'Bill Bailey.' You hate the song but you always get asked for it." Helen Creighton's music book of Maritime folk songs yielded "The Jealous Lover," while "Green Valley" was another traditional song from the Maritimes. "The Ghost Lover" was derived from the Child ballad number 248, "The Grey Cock," which was gleaned from Toronto folksinger Karen James. "Swing Down, Chariot" was pulled from *Precious Memories*, an album of gospel music from R&B singer LaVern Baker.

By their third album a dichotomy was beginning to emerge between Sylvia's traditional folk leanings and Ian's cowboy/country inclinations. "Truthfully," Sylvia explains, "throughout our whole career together our musical influences were quite different. In many ways that was what was interesting about our sound and created the musical tension between us."

Released in September 1964, *Northern Journey* was a critical and a sales success. "Another superb album from this pair of Canadian folksingers who are, as a team, without peer," declared *High Fidelity*. "Again, we have the glinting interplay of counterpoint and harmony that is the Ian & Sylvia hallmark." "We were about the third-biggest sellers in folk," acknowledges Ian. "We sold out Carnegie Hall twice and Town Hall. We did Symphony Hall in Chicago. We sold out Place d'Arts in Montreal and they didn't understand a goddamn word we sang. But they loved us. That's the point where I believed it was going to go on forever. The demand for tickets in that little window of time was phenomenal. We were hot then. We'd sell around, I don't know, about 150,000, which was a lot of albums in those days."

The duo was also hot property in other markets. "One of the things about Vanguard," reveals Sylvia, "was that they didn't really want us to know the kinds of numbers we were selling. We sold a lot of albums in Japan and could have gone over there if we had known. We had no idea we had a following there because Vanguard never reported that to us. Who knows how big we might have become had we toured outside North America."

"Ian & Sylvia made great records," says Tom Russell. "They're all great records but Vanguard didn't have the promotional budget that other labels and artists like Dylan or Lightfoot had. But they sold records because they were just too damn good not to sell records. I think those albums are filled with strong songs. Those songs are by and large still strong today. Every album had three or four or five gems on them. When I tell people that the first songs both Ian and Sylvia separately ever wrote were 'Four Strong Winds' and 'You Were On My Mind' they can't believe it. It's unfathomable to consider that, and all written within a couple of days of each other. When you add in Dylan and his output including 'Blowin' in the Wind' that's incredible; that amount of great songs happening around the same time. People were writing songs that have lasted. It wouldn't happen like that today. Today we have all the technology and know-how – the books, magazines, and the Internet – but has that meant better songs and better songwriters? No. Nowadays it's not so much about songs – and this is something the Internet promotes. The young indie rock writers and the new folk songwriters today are more about sound and sonic pictures, windows and curtains of sound, than about lyrics. It's kind of a blurred sense of lyric writing. When you boil it down where is the song that you can actually sing on a guitar? Back then you had these guys who had the ability to sing hundreds of songs on an acoustic guitar and blow you away."

As their career continued its upward course, many of Ian & Sylvia's colleagues and contemporaries were surprised in early June to receive an invitation to the wedding of Sylvia Anne Fricker and Ian Dawson Tyson to be held on Friday, June 26, 1964, at St. Thomas' Anglican Church on Huron Street in central Toronto, with the Rev. Brian Freeland presiding. Certainly the two had been a couple in the fullest sense of that descriptor for the past two years but, according to several friends, the announcement of their pending nuptials came as a bit of a shocker. "I wasn't surprised when they separated years later," muses Ruth Jones McVeigh. "I was almost more surprised when they got married. It was a natural thing but that doesn't say it was passionate. It was one of those things they kind of fell into. I couldn't see a great spark between them except professionally. They were two very different personalities."

Ian had been back in Victoria visiting his family when his mother caught him off guard by inquiring when he and Sylvia intended to tie the knot and make it official. "She basically told Ian that it was about time that we were married. So Ian told her we were thinking of getting married, which was news to me," states Sylvia. "And his mother made him set a date. So he came back east and told me, 'I guess we're getting married.' That was the proposal. I didn't hesitate although it was not my big dream to be married. But I didn't have anything against the idea." Interesting to note that in Ian's calendar entry for that date are the words "Wedding day. Oy Vay!"

"It wasn't like we met a year earlier, fell in love, got married, and had a brood of kids," offers Sylvia. "It wasn't that kind of thing at all. The relationship was well-established because we had been working together for years and living together." "We got married," explains Ian, "because it just seemed like everyone thought it was the thing to do and everybody kind of expected it of us. I certainly wouldn't say we were pushed into it because neither Sylvia nor I are that kind of person. But in a way it was fulfilling a national image, completing the package." It was the romantic notion of the two good-looking Canadians who started out as singing partners only to fall in love. At some point the relationship evolved from professional to personal. "I fell for Sylvia. We were in love. I fell for her when she started growing up, that kind of thing. At first she was just so young and a country girl. I liked her a lot. But it was pretty gradual. She had her gentlemen friends and I had been just hound-dogging it around."

As befitting their status as Canadian music royalty and the fairy-tale nature of their relationship as the public perceived it, the wedding was a major event on the Toronto social calendar and received coverage in all the media. "It was a big affair," confirms Sylvia, on the formal service and extensive guest list boasting many music world luminaries. Bob Dylan was invited but was unable to attend. "My wife Nuala and I were very close with both Ian and Sylvia," notes Edgar Cowan. "We kind of officiated at their wedding and they at ours, that kind of stuff. Ian had been best man at my wedding at a Reform Jewish synagogue. As we walked up to the canopy who should be the cantor but one of the singers we knew from the CBC. We just cracked up seeing him there." Ian's best man was John Court from the Groscourt agency, while Estelle Klein served as Sylvia's matron of honour. "Ian did all the arranging himself," Edgar continues. "I don't remember him being nervous about anything. Ian came from a somewhat upper-class family with a strikingly austere yet quite divine mother, Margaret, and a father, George, who was a rather U.K.-style West Coast type. They gave the Tysons broadloom carpeting for their new place as a wedding present." Ian & Sylvia performed a song at their own wedding.

The reception was held at Fantasy Farms, a banquet and wedding facility in the Don Valley off Pottery Road just north of Bloor Street. It's still in existence. "It was a funky western-style large reception hall on the grounds of an old restored lumber mill site, Todmorden Mills, located right in the centre of the city," Edgar explains. "My wife and I remember some country music and dancing to the Twist, the first worldwide dance craze in the early '60's." "One of my favourite photos," chuckles Sylvia, "is of Jack Elliott talking with my uncle Ted who was a prison guard. I have no idea what they were talking about or what they could have found in common but they were very intently talking." As Ramblin' Jack recalls, "I flew up to Toronto from New York but I forgot the address of the church. So when I got to Toronto I phoned up the Albert Grossman Agency back in New York and got the address, jumped in a taxi, and arrived a little late. I ran up the steps of the church just as Ian and Sylvia were coming out after the service. They had just gotten married. They saw me coming and Ian said, 'Well, here's Jack! Kiss the bride, Jack.'" So I was the first to kiss the bride and I didn't even get to see the wedding. The next day we all went out to the racetrack and I got to meet Ian's father, the only time I ever met him." Ian's family came in from the West Coast for the wedding. Sylvia had met them previously. "Possibly I knew Ian's mother better than he did. I liked her. She was kind of an enigma. Ian was kind of distant from her and closer to his dad. I didn't know his dad that well."

Emblematic of their immense popularity by that point, the newlyweds were denied a honeymoon and instead were off to Washington, D.C., for a two-week engagement at the Cellar Door beginning the following Monday. The unrelenting demands of their booming career overshadowed their personal lives. Despite having wed, the two were without a permanent residence in Toronto.

Sylvia still retained her New York apartment which was beneficial to their career, based as it was out of New York, but Ian had been floating from place to place. "We didn't even have an apartment in Toronto at the time," notes Sylvia. "We were staying at a kind of apartment hotel when we were in town." Not long afterwards, the Tysons jointly bought into a triplex at the corner of Elm and Dunbar in central Toronto, not far from Rosedale, with friends Jack and Estelle Klein. Jack was a successful architect and Estelle was a major force on the local arts scene. The Kleins occupied the main floor with the Tysons on the second. The third floor was rented out. "Jack was a partner in an architectural firm, and his company did the renovation work to his specifications," offers Sylvia. This would serve as their Toronto home for the next four years.

Though they had separated their songwriting and publishing, upon marrying they had further issues regarding their joint finances. Once again, Albert Grossman's choice of advisers for Ian & Sylvia proved foresighted. As Sylvia remembers, "Our accountant in New York, Marshall Gelfand, sat us down and said to us, 'I know you're young and I know you're in love but the mortality rate of show business marriages is extremely high so I'm separating your finances.' That certainly was good for us when we split up years later. It made things very simple. I thank Marshall for that."

In late August, Ian & Sylvia embarked on a Western Canadian tour beginning in Winnipeg and carrying through with dates in Edmonton, Calgary, and Vancouver, as well as with dips across the border to Spokane, Seattle, and Portland. On the 31st they arrived in L.A. for a week at the Golden Bear, followed by a week at the Ash Grove on Melrose Avenue in Hollywood, coinciding with the release of *Northern Journey*. During their Hollywood stint they once again appeared on *The Steve Allen Show*. Returning to Canada in early

October they played Sudbury and London, Ontario, before resuming their usual college circuit in the Eastern U.S. Later that month they joined the Lady Bird Johnson campaign tour in Allentown, Pennsylvania. It was a brief jaunt through several American cities in support of Democrat Lyndon Baines Johnson. Sylvia admits their reason for supporting Johnson was less to do with his policies or personality and more to do with stopping his right-wing opponent, Republican Sen. Barry Goldwater, from winning. "So we were whistle stopping with Lady Bird Johnson down through Arkansas, Ohio, that sort of heartland Middle America. And we were on the bill with [country music star] Faron Young. Faron loved what we were doing. He was a great singer." Faron's band included Ottawa-born drummer Dewey Martin (a.k.a. Dwayne Midkiff, later of the Buffalo Springfield with fellow Canadians Neil Young and Bruce Palmer), as well as Ben Keith from Kentucky on pedal steel guitar who would later join the Tysons in the Great Speckled Bird. "Faron was a mess at the time," chuckles Ben Keith, "running around pinching Lady Bird on the ass."

Among the many recording artists to cover Ian's "Four Strong Winds," country singer Bobby Bare of "Detroit City" fame garnered the biggest hit with it in 1964. Bobby had already mined the folk catalogue and come up with a hit single of Hedy West's "500 Miles" earlier that year before he released his version of Ian & Sylvia's signature song. The single rose to number 3 on the *Billboard* country charts and earned Bobby two Grammy nominations for Best Country & Western Vocal Performance and Best Country & Western single. It also earned Ian a substantial royalty cheque. And he knew just what he intended to spend it on.

Ian's dream was to own a ranch, raise horses and cattle, and return to rodeo riding. The success of Ian & Sylvia in the United States and Canada had not dampened his desire. While the duo earned impressive concert and club fees, ranging from $1,000 to $5,000, maintaining a modest lifestyle, living on the road, and keeping two residences (Sylvia had since let her New York apartment go to the Journeymen's Scott McKenzie and moved to another apartment on 48th Street*), plus investments, did not leave enough for a down payment on his dream. Since 1963 he had been on the lookout for suitable property in rural Ontario not too far, no more than a two-hour drive at most, from Toronto, allowing him to still be able to fly out to their concert dates in the U.S. It was a singular dream nurtured only by Ian. Sylvia had no interest in a rural retreat. She was hardly about to become the dutiful country housewife raising a gaggle of young 'uns. "I grew up in the country so I'd had that experience," she stresses. "I wasn't completely out of my element there, I just preferred being where I could walk out and do things. I wasn't into the rural life the way Ian was."

After scouting out several properties, Ian finally found what he was looking for, a 350-acre spread near Newtonville, Ontario, an hour's drive north east from Toronto off Highway 401 (formerly Highway 2) past Oshawa. When the Bobby Bare cheque came through in 1965, Ian plunked it down on the property, taking possession November 19, 1965. The community boasted a population just under a thousand and was predominately agriculturally based. "My neighbour showed up to meet me in a horse-drawn buggy," says Ian. "It was fifty miles from Toronto but it was like going back one hundred years." The property included a 140-year-old stone house (pictured on the *Great Speckled Bird* album inside a gatefold cover), streams, and rolling hills. It was a working farm with cattle, and Ian's goal was to raise quarter horses. "It was a

---

★ Ian's twelve-string Gibson guitar was "stolen right out of the back of the moving van. The only guitar of mine that ever got stolen." Responds Sylvia: "Well, if you had been there to help me move it might not have been stolen!"

pretty big place," he describes. "There were times when the place cost a lot more money than it should have, but all in all it was a pretty nice place and we had some pretty good times there." Initially intended as Ian's getaway from the rigours of Ian & Sylvia's music career where he could be a weekend cowboy, increasingly the farm came to be Ian's priority, so that he spent almost all of his available time at the farm (Ian referred to it as his ranch). Sylvia spent as little time there as possible.

"It seemed quite natural at the time, him spending time out there," she muses, "and he probably didn't have much problem with me spending my time here. If I had been out there all the time I would have driven him crazy having nothing to do. Sometimes Ian would get antsy cooped up in the city. It was just a basic difference of personality and interests."

"Ian was changing," observed Edgar Cowan, "and acquiring the farm was a huge change. He always wanted a farm. He loved it and Sylvia didn't. She didn't hate it, she just didn't like being there. There were always some really good parties up there and lots of women around. He was doing some rodeoing at that point and trying to push all of us to do it, much to my chagrin. But we had a lot of fun. Ian was a tough guy with money. He knew how to spend it and knew what he wanted to do. The farm represented something important to him. He got more involved with the farm and with horses and then came the point where he really wanted to go back into his roots with the cowboy thing. And Sylvia wanted no part of that. He started spending more and more time at the farm and she didn't, especially after Clay was born. She very rarely went there. Looking back now, that was probably the beginning of the end. He kept going off in that direction and she went off in another direction." Notes Carolyn Hester, "Ian always seemed to have a whole lot on his mind and he had that whole other life with his farm. I can see why some people found Ian intimidating. He didn't intimidate me but I just accepted him the way he was."

What the acquisition of the farm also marked was the transformation of Ian Dawson Tyson from privileged, upper-class, private school–educated, well-read and well-bred, British Columbia landed gentry to rural, brown-dirt cowboy and denim-and-leather rodeo rider, a man of the common people. He had successfully reinvented himself as the man he always dreamed of being.

"I visited Ian at that farm of his in Newtonville several times and rode horses with him there," recalls Ramblin' Jack Elliott. "In fact he once told me, 'Jack, you're the only guitar picker I know that can ride a horse!' Coming from Ian, that was very complimentary. The main attraction of course was our love of cowboy stuff but I liked Sylvia plenty, too. I thought she was a wonderful singer and a gorgeous girl. I had a great deal of respect for her and I think she knew that. But most of the time I was with Ian, riding or talking about horses. Sylvia didn't enjoy being on the farm. That may have been what caused them to separate, I don't know. They just had different lifestyles." Adds Sylvia, ruefully, "With Jack, I can never get past him hitting on me. Even now."

Charlie Rothschild laughs at the recollection of his first visit to the farm. "Ian got me up on a horse and riding and I thought I was going to fall off and die. He was roping cattle and riding horses and he loved that. He wanted to be a cowboy."

Ian & Sylvia closed out 1964 with several college dates in the American northeast, another sold-out concert at Toronto's Massey Hall on December 18, and a six-night stint at Cleveland's Le Cave club beginning on the 29th, which also allowed them to appear on popular syndicated afternoon television schmooze-fest *The Mike Douglas Show* from Cleveland. The duo would appear frequently on Mike's show over the next several years. They also made an appearance on Cleveland's *The Big Five Show* (later renamed *Upbeat* and featuring pop acts miming to pre-recordings). Recording sessions for their fourth album were slated for early February, once again at New York's Manhattan Towers Hotel ballroom. The resulting album would be distinguished by less reliance on the traditional folk songbooks and more on original material, both from Ian & Sylvia individually and from a couple of talented up-and-coming singer/songwriters. In fact, the album's title track would be from one of those young artists. "We realized after we started writing our own songs that no matter how good you are as a writer there is a certain sameness that can happen to what you do," Sylvia points out. "So we were always looking for other songs from other songwriters. Having variety and other people's songs was crucial for us in keeping everything fresh and interesting." With that philosophy in mind, Ian & Sylvia caught a set by Gordon Lightfoot at Steele's Tavern on Yonge Street in the fall of 1964 and were impressed with his performance and repertoire, in particular two songs he had recently composed, "Early Morning Rain" and "For Lovin' Me."

Gordon Lightfoot has never failed to acknowledge the enormous debt he owes to Ian & Sylvia. "Ian & Sylvia are responsible for taking my career to the next level. And they did a very unselfish thing. By them recording a couple of my tunes, that became the one break that I needed. Ian is a top guy. He's kind and gentle and witty. I have nothing but respect for him." Since leaving *Country Hoedown* and folding the Tu-Tones, Gordon had been to Europe, where he hosted a television show called *Country & Western* in the U.K. and married his first wife, Brita, in Sweden. He was now back in Toronto, honing his songwriting craft and appearing regularly at Steele's. "I certainly knew that Ian & Sylvia were successful," he continues. "I was a fan and bought their records but I didn't

know them personally until the night they came into Steele's to
see me. Ian came up to me after the show and said they were doing
an album and there were a couple of songs in my set that he and
Sylvia really liked. I had a huge repertoire myself at the time and
was doing other people's songs as well as my own. I didn't believe
Ian at first but my wife, Brita, was very excited about it. She
wanted me to succeed. We did a follow-up meeting after that, a
get-together for them to learn the songs. They came over to our
apartment and we played the songs through. They later invited
the wife and I over to a party at their house after Bob Dylan's concert at Massey Hall, which I thought was pretty decent of them.
They were very, very kind to me. Ian lifted me up to a level I had
been hoping I might find that had seemed almost impossible that
it might ever happen. There is a certain amount of luck involved.
I was lucky that they came in to see me. I was doing good business at Steele's. After that I was tearing them up at the Riverboat."

What developed was a kind of mentor relationship. "Ian took me
under his wing, so to speak. We actually used to get together and
compare each other's work without borrowing from one another,"
Gordon acknowledges. "He would show me a song and I would have
a suggestion or I would play him something and he'd have a suggestion. There was never any talk about collaboration. There were
several occasions where we assisted one another working on songs,
coming up with an idea or a lick. I would come to his place or he
would come over to mine. It was like helping each other finish a
song. It was more like, 'Do you want to look this over and tell me
what you think?' And it went both ways. I remember him and me
working on 'Red Velvet' one day.* And I remember working with
him on the changes they wanted to do on 'Early Morning Rain.'"

---

* Gordon Lightfoot later recorded Ian's "Red Velvet" on his 1998 album *A
Painter Passing Through*.

Originally entitled "Early Morning Train," at his wife's suggestion Gordon dropped the "t" from train and in so doing opened
up the song's interpretive potential. "If I change one word maybe
it'll be a bit less obvious," he recalls thinking at the time. Although
composed two years apart, "Four Strong Winds" and "Early
Morning Rain" both address the postmodern plight of urban alien-
ation and the desire to get back to a simpler life. Whereas Ian's
lament is for a lost love out west, Gordon's lyrics reflect the loneliness of the working man separated from a rural environment and
his loved ones and longing to return. It's often been suggested that
"Early Morning Rain" was inspired by Northern Ontario mining
or forestry labourers who come down to the big city with their
earnings and blow it all before signing on for any stint back up
north. The changes in technology are also reflected in the two
songs: Ian writes of sending down "the fare," implying a train
ticket, and of the imagery of the railroad opening up the west a
century earlier; Gordon's character watches as the plane he should
be on takes off in the dampness of an early morning. "You can't
jump a jet plane like you can a freight train" is perhaps one of the
most evocative lines in Canadian songwriting and says much about
the changing nature of our postwar urban society and the sense
of dislocation that many often felt. It's no wonder the song struck
a chord with Ian on hearing Gordon sing it at Steele's: if Gordon
had not written it, Ian would have. Oddly enough, both songs were
composed in an urban environment: Ian's in New York and Gordon's
in Toronto. "I could never have written 'Early Morning Rain' without being tuned in to Bob Dylan," states Gordon. "Bob Dylan was
an Ian & Sylvia fan and we were all Bob Dylan fans. He changed
the way I wrote songs. Absolutely. It could be done; it's not that
difficult. Ian was already signed before Dylan came in. There was
Ian & Sylvia already making records for Vanguard and here comes

Bob Dylan. Ian introduced me to Bob and Ramblin' Jack. I consider myself honoured to have met Dylan. He, the Beatles, and Elvis Presley are the three biggest acts of the last fifty years."

In adapting the song for their repertoire, Ian & Sylvia made a slight change that altered the melancholy mood of the ballad. "Ian wanted to change the chord progression a little bit," notes Gordon, "and I said, 'Go ahead, let's talk about it.' They put a minor chord in it and it worked. That's the way Elvis did it, so obviously he got it off their record. Judy Collins did my version. So did George Hamilton IV. The chord progression they did was actually different and actually gave the song a different feel. Peter, Paul & Mary recorded it with the minor chord although they told me they learned it from my version. Sometimes other artists take a song and change the tempo or a chord here and there, but it didn't change the way I played the song. It's still my song."

The other Lightfoot composition Ian & Sylvia recorded was "For Lovin' Me," a typical male-centric view of relationships. Peter, Paul & Mary also covered the song, releasing it as a single that climbed into the *Billboard* Top 20. "After that things really started happening for me," emphasizes Gordon. "They are my angels, Ian & Sylvia and Peter, Paul & Mary. Ian & Sylvia have always been very kind to me and so were Peter, Paul & Mary who took me on the road as an opening act." Ian & Sylvia ultimately titled their fourth album *Early Morning Rain*. "It was unbelievably exciting," Gordon remembers, on seeing the album cover. "I just thought, 'They really must like that song a lot or they wouldn't have titled the album after it.' Vanguard was one of *the* folk labels at the time. Maybe they had hopes for a hit single with it. Everybody was looking for a hit single back then."

Through Ian & Sylvia's patronage, another angel came into Gordon's corner. "Because of Ian & Sylvia I get the contract offer from Albert Grossman but I don't want to sign it," Gordon reveals. "I'm scared. It's my small-town upbringing and my small conservative Canadian brain working; the insecurity of it all. I almost backed out of it. I had been under contracts before and had to get out of my contract with Harold Moon at BMI Canada. My wife stood in his office and demanded he let me out of my contract. He was a very nice guy but my wife had to yell at him first before he would let me out of my contract. Now I had an opportunity to get with Witmark, which published all Dylan's material, which is ASCAP, not BMI. After I got out of the contract with BMI I thought about the contract with Albert for another month. Things were starting to cool off a little bit. One night Ian & Sylvia took the wife and me out for dinner. During the dinner I told Ian what a rough time I was having trying to make up my mind about whether to sign the contract with Albert or not. Ian had a napkin and he got out a pen and wrote one word on the napkin and pushed it across the table to me. I picked it up and looked at it and it said 'Sign.' Shortly after that I signed with Albert. Albert got me a thousand-dollar advance from Witmark and when that came in the mail I thought to myself, 'Wow, this is real!' They got me the deal. None of those other people whose songs they recorded got the deal. With me they went a step further. But I was sitting on a lot of material. I had a lot of songs." Ian & Sylvia also provided advice in another area of the business. "Ian had learned about publishing. He made a study of it and he helped me. Barry [Harvey, Gordon's long-time manager] and Ian spent time together and Barry learned about it from Ian.

"Ian & Sylvia's legacy is their kindness to others, their caring," muses Gordon. "They are great people, very unselfish. They helped me get ahead in this business by giving me a hand up the ladder. It takes a lot of caring and a lot of energy on their part to have done that. That's a quality that a lot of us don't have. I'm not willing to go out on a limb and help somebody. I'm too insecure to do that. But Ian was secure enough to do it. There are very few who will do that. But they went to bat for me. I love those two." There's little doubt that Gordon Lightfoot would have become a major star without Ian & Sylvia's patronage. His talent was undeniable. But as Gordon's star rose he soon eclipsed his mentors, leaving Ian & Sylvia far behind. Being the man he is, Gordon felt guilty about surpassing them. "By giving me that helping hand, later that became a bit of an albatross for Ian. He was watching me move ahead of them and just take off on that great racetrack. I even had hit singles when they didn't. It bothered me that I was doing so well and they weren't doing as well. I was with a powerful record company when I got with Warner Brothers. They didn't have a powerful record company behind them. I felt guilty and wished they could have had the kind of backing that I had. Here I was pulling ahead of them after they had helped me up. But I don't feel that way now. Ian & Sylvia's legend is very powerful in this country. They're legendary figures. They opened the doors for a lot of people although they never got that number 1 record. That's the elusive butterfly, the brass ring."

During one of their engagements at the Golden Bear in Huntington Beach, Ian & Sylvia's opening act was a twenty-two-year-old singer/songwriter named Steve Gillette. "He wasn't well known at that point," Sylvia suggests, "and I think was still in school." Born in Las Vegas, Steve had grown up in southern California and met songwriting partner Tom Campbell in college. The story of the unfortunate young girl Darcy Farrow, who's thrown off her horse and dies and whose lover, Vandermeer, in his grief, takes his own life, was purely fictional, although the setting references – the Walker River, Carson Valley Plain, Yerrington, and the Truckee River – are real. "My sister's name was Darcy," reveals Steve, who drew inspiration initially from her experience of being kicked by a horse, "but as we worked with it and took it in the direction of the old cowboy songs, I was much more comfortable with it. So many of the old cowboy songs take their melodies from Scottish-Irish musical traditions. The big thing was that we were so inspired by Ian & Sylvia that the whole idea of writing something that sounded traditional really was partly due to their influence. The story that Tom and I wrote the song to fool a college professor isn't true but Ian told that story for years. That wasn't the case. We really wrote it just as a song."

Steve vividly recalls introducing the song to his heroes. "They were staying at a motel out near the beach but we gathered together at a friend's little house out by an oil field. We'd grab a bottle of cheap wine and have song circles. I played 'Darcy Farrow' for Ian & Sylvia and Ian looked at Sylvia and said, 'What do ya think, Maude?' and Sylvia replied, 'Yeah, I think we can do that song.' Tom and I were just beside ourselves. That was the first song of ours that anybody recorded so it was the greatest endorsement we could hope for." Ian & Sylvia became the first artists to record "Darcy Farrow." It would ultimately log some three hundred recorded versions, becoming a modern folk classic. Steve Gillette would go on to enjoy a long career as a respected singer/songwriter. "They were very supportive and very friendly," notes Steve. "They gave Tom and me a lot of advice about songwriting. It got to be a bit of a ritual where they'd come out to southern California over a period of about two years and I'd be the opening act. Then they invited me to come along on some other dates they had around southern California. It was a very magical time."

Like they had done for pal Gordon Lightfoot, Ian & Sylvia extended a helping hand to Steve Gillette. "They pretty much presented my tape to Maynard Solomon at Vanguard," he states. "So I credit them for getting my recording career started. They really went to bat for me. I admire them both so much."

Of the other originals, Sylvia contributed the uptempo "Travelling Drummer," the title referring to the old description of a travelling salesman, and "Maude's Blues," illustrating her facility with the blues idiom as well as Ian's lead guitar dexterity. Ian's "Marlborough Street Blues" drew its theme from his former residence in Toronto out near the train tracks and once again played on the theme of loneliness in the big city. The chorus of "I don't know one woman in this town" must have given rise to a few smiles. Ian claimed that he was inspired to write "Red Velvet" after driving through Saskatchewan. "I mainly wanted a feeling of loneliness against the vastness of that part of Canada," he wrote in the album's liner notes. Once more he was working within a country music framework and in doing so creating a whole new Western Canadian country music songbook. "If a song had a western theme, it held my interest," states Ian.

"Song for Canada" was a one-off collaboration between Ian and journalist and later CBC radio host Peter Gzowski intended as a plea to French Canadians for unity at a time when Quebec nationalism and separatism were on the rise and threatening to rend the country apart. It was a gamble for Ian & Sylvia, taking a rare and ultimately misguided political stand. "I hate that song," grouses Ian. "It's awful." As for Sylvia, "I always thought that was a bit awkward. Sorry, Peter. Lyrically it was a bit awkward. Peter was a brilliant man but not a lyricist or poet. His ideas were good but the execution was a bit suspect. It was timely, it's just the use of the language left much to be desired. You don't use 'How come' in a song. It was trying to be a bit too populist and not really our thing." Ruth Jones McVeigh remembers Ian & Sylvia performing another Canadian political song around that time. "They wrote a song when the new Canadian flag came out in 1964. They weren't fans of the new flag."

Writing more of their own material as well as drawing from contemporary singer/songwriters reduced Ian & Sylvia's dependence on traditional folk music. "It was getting to a point," explains Sylvia, "that a lot of the good traditional songs had been done to death. There were people in some cases who did it better than us. Their versions had been done. We were looking for fresh stuff people hadn't heard. Because we were writing more we were aware of what other writers were doing and we were looking around." Country singer Johnny Cash was the source for "Come In, Stranger." Johnny had been accepted into the folk community after appearing at Newport in July 1964 and celebrated by the likes of Bob Dylan. Nonetheless, three tracks on the album came from traditional folk music sources. "Awake Ye Drowsy Sleepers" was drawn from traditional folk music matriarch Jean Ritchie and boasted modal harmonies ("An experiment," claims Sylvia), while "Nancy Whiskey" was a traditional Scottish song Sylvia learned from Len Chandler, although it's more likely it came from Greenwich Village Scottish singer/songwriter Logan English, a contemporary on the coffeehouse scene. Sylvia's stirring solo a cappella rendition of "I'll Bid My Heart Be Still" is among the album's highlights. The song came from one of her songbooks about a woman mourning the death of her soldier husband, cut down in the prime of life. "I didn't think about it at the time," she muses, "but afterwards that song struck me very forcibly in terms of the Kennedy assassination."

Released in May 1965 (with a cover photo shot just outside Toronto) during extended appearances at their old stomping grounds, the Cellar Door in Washington, D.C., and the Golden Bear in Huntington Beach, *Early Morning Rain* sold well to the faithful but also marked the end of an era of sorts for Ian & Sylvia. No longer would they record at the Manhattan Towers, nor would they be working exclusively within a folk/country music context. Furthermore, their competition in the record-buying marketplace was no longer made up of folk music contemporaries. The musical and cultural landscape had altered significantly and irrevocably in 1964, leaving many acoustic folkies in the dust. It became a question of adapting to the new reality or packing it in. Ian & Sylvia were not about to be relegated to the "where are they now?" category. "The second, third, and fourth albums were really fine albums at the time," Ian acknowledges. "They were important albums for us. After those albums, things just got more repetitious, with isolated good songs on each album. That was the peak period for Ian & Sylvia, '63–'64 before the Beatles wiped us all out."

Hyperbole aside, Ian & Sylvia found themselves having to re-evaluate their position in the popular music pantheon. Testimony to the changing tide was their appearance[*] March 30 on NBC TV's prime-time pop music cavalcade *Hullabaloo* alongside the likes of Peter & Gordon ("World Without Love"), Dionne Warwick ("Some Other Time"), the Vibrations ("Shout"), and Cannibal & the Headhunters ("Land of 1,000 Dances"), with the gyrating Hullabaloo dancers and host Michael "Little Joe" Landon from *Bonanza* doing "The Freddie." The times were, indeed, a-changin'.

---

[*] Ian & Sylvia performed "Makes a Long Time Man Feel Bad" and "Moonshine Can."

SO MUCH FOR DREAMING

On Sunday evening February 9, 1964, an estimated 74 million Americans, and likely several million Canadians, tuned into CBS TV's *The Ed Sullivan Show* to witness the North American debut* of U.K. music sensations the Beatles. The group had already taken the British Isles and Western Europe by storm and were establishing the all-important North American beachhead with their Sullivan show appearance. The next day there was only one topic of conversation across the continent: the four moptops from Liverpool. Beatlemania had arrived† and what followed would be dubbed the British Invasion.‡ Few would be immune, not even the folk music community, including Ian & Sylvia. As one musicologist articulated, it was as if the whole world had

---

* The Beatles had already appeared Friday, January 3, 1964, in a BBC film clip on NBC's *The Jack Paar Show* and had also been the subject of a feature on NBC's *The Huntley & Brinkley Report* on November 18, 1963.

† The term Beatlemania had already been coined in the U.K. in 1963 to describe the Beatles phenomenon.

‡ Gerry & the Pacemakers, Herman's Hermits, the Searchers, Peter & Gordon, the Dave Clark Five, et al.

been in black and white and suddenly it was now in Technicolor.

"I don't recall seeing it [the Beatles on *Ed Sullivan*] at the time," Sylvia admits, "but subsequently saw news clips of it. It certainly was the death knell for the Great Folk Scare of the '60s." Not immediately, but in due time. Ian & Sylvia were in the midst of a tour of colleges in Atlantic Canada that weekend. They had played Dalhousie University in Halifax on Saturday, February 8, and were en route to Prince Edward Island to play Charlottetown's Prince of Wales College on the Monday. They would not have been aware of the seismic shift in popular music that began that weekend. The changeover, however, would be gradual, though all-pervasive. Their accompanist, Monte Dunn, was instantly smitten. "Young Monte was just totally immersed in the Beatles," notes Ian. "He was always talking about them, trying to get their records, and listening to them on the radio. I remember we were driving to some gig down on the Eastern Seaboard out of New York and we were listening to 'I Want to Hold Your Hand' and Monte went nuts over that." As for Ian himself, "I loved them. I'm not very progressive in that sense but I loved them. I thought they sounded a little bit country to me. We had an inkling of it starting to happen but it became even bigger than we imagined. I knew the Beatles would have an impact because it reminded me very much of the Elvis thing on radio back in the '50s. You could hear one hit after another getting bigger and bigger. I didn't like Frank Zappa and the Mothers of Invention when I was playing next to them in New York a few years later and I didn't like the Jefferson Airplane either, but I liked the Beatles. I hated the Rolling Stones and still don't care much for them today. But the Beatles were great. I guess it was 1965 before they wiped out the commercial folk thing. There's always a bit of a lag period in terms of out on the street. Then all those West Coast bands started plugging in and that put us all on the sidelines. They cleaned the slate and that's a good thing. There was a whole fresh start. In terms of large numbers of people going to coffeehouses and listening to folk music, they really wiped that out. By 1969 or '70 there weren't more than a couple of coffeehouses left in Toronto, the old strongholds." It would take folk music's fair-haired boy Bob Dylan to put the final nail in the coffin some seventeen months later at the Newport Folk Festival.

"I would agree that the Beatles coming along was pretty much the beginning of the end for folk music," states the Journeymen's Dick Weissman, "although it re-emerged a few years later in all the singer/songwriter guys of the early '70s. But there weren't any more college boy trios in button-down shirts." Notes Scott McKenzie, "I didn't make the transition after the Beatles. I wanted to sing jazz. John Phillips's transition was really due to Denny [Doherty] who convinced John to write songs like the Beatles." Leader John Phillips, never a folk purist and always with an eye toward the next trend, began writing songs in a Beatles pop vein. As Denny Doherty remembers, "I came over with a copy of the first Beatles album and made John listen to it over and over again. Then I told him, 'Write some songs like that!'" From this would ultimately emerge the Mamas & the Papas. According to Eric Weissberg, "The Tarriers kept gigging into 1965 but the writing was on the wall. It was pretty much the end of the folk thing." Adds Gordon Lightfoot, "The Beatles were on the scene and eating up all the air time on radio. There were a whole bunch of us waiting on the backburner for about six or seven years, including Ian & Sylvia. I didn't get my first hit single until 1971 and that was after five albums. Ian & Sylvia were making albums and I was making albums but we couldn't grab a hit single."

"We were well aware of the Beatles music and thought it was

great," reveals Sylvia. "I liked the Buddy Holly influence because I was a big Buddy Holly fan and could hear that influence in their music. We loved the Everly Brothers, Buddy Holly, Little Richard, Jerry Lee Lewis. But suddenly nobody was interested in listening to folksingers anymore and that was because of the Beatles and the Beach Boys. It was the end of life as we knew it," she laughs.

For their own influences, the Beatles drew from early American rock 'n' roll (e.g., Little Richard, Chuck Berry), southern rocka-billy (Carl Perkins, Buddy Holly), R&B (Larry Williams, the Isley Brothers) and Soul/Motown (the Marvelettes, Smokey Robinson) with a little Broadway thrown in ("Till There Was You," "A Taste of Honey"). George Harrison and Ringo Starr were also country music fans. The four Beatles were not appreciably enamoured with folk music, commercial or traditional, at least not until Bob Dylan's influence was felt by the time of *Help* in mid 1965.* The American folk boom of the late 1950s beginning with the Kingston Trio had failed to cross the Atlantic in anything other than a minor way. The U.K. version of folk music was "skiffle," as represented by Lonnie Donegan's "Rock Island Line" and "Jack of Diamonds," an extension of the U.K. Dixieland-inspired Trad Jazz craze of the '50s. While the Beatles may have started out as a skiffle band (the Quarrymen) they quickly abandoned that style for American rock 'n' roll. Where folk music was cerebral, rock 'n' roll was a jolt of electricity aimed a bit lower.

And yet despite few discernible folk nuances, Roger (Jim) McGuinn, who would abandon his own folk career for Beatlesque music in 1964, insists he heard something familiar in the Fab Four's chord patterns and harmonies. "I might have been one of the first people to dig what the Beatles were into musically," claims the

---

* *Rubber Soul*, released in December 1965, is generally considered the Beatles' most folk-influenced album.

former accompanist for Judy Collins, Bobby Darin, and the Chad Mitchell Trio. "In their chord changes I could see degrees of complexity that folk music had gotten to by that time and it struck me as being a groovy thing. They were doing fourth and fifth harmonies like bluegrass modal or Appalachian modal songs, mixing elements of folk and rock because they had been a skiffle band, but kind of doing it subconsciously. They were shooting for a 1950s rock style but they were blending a lot of things together, sort of under the hood. I don't think they were really aware of what they were doing. Anyway, I picked up on it and started singing their songs in coffeehouses. But I was really getting a terrible audience reaction, the total cold shoulder. The folk purists absolutely hated what I was doing. It was blasphemy. They wanted to stone me or burn me at the stake."

While some folkies determined to ride it out in the hope that America would soon come to its senses over the Beatles, others jumped on the bandwagon, ditching their acoustic guitars for electric models or simply attaching a pickup to their Martin or Gibson acoustic. There's a telling scene in D. A. Pennebaker's documentary *Don't Look Back* chronicling Bob Dylan's last acoustic folk tour of the U.K. in the spring of 1965 where Bob seen staring pensively into an instrument shop window at various electric guitars.

But if the Beatles' folk inclinations were muted, some of their Merseyside contemporaries', were more overt. The Searchers, onetime rivals of the Beatles on the Liverpool club circuit, wore their folk influences openly on their collective sleeves, recording electric versions of American folk music performer and social activist Malvina Reynold's "What Have They Done to the Rain" and ex-Limeliter Glenn Yarborough's "All My Sorrows" in 1964. The following year they cut an electric version of Ian's "Four Strong Winds." as did London pop/folk duo Chad & Jeremy that same year.

Ian & Sylvia were certainly not equipped to compete with the British Invasion sounds. But the sudden change in public tastes was something they could not ignore. As Ian suggests, the Beatles and the British Invasion did not shut down the folk scene automatically. Ian & Sylvia continued touring the still lucrative American college circuit and playing their folk strongholds like the Cellar Door, the Golden Bear, and San Francisco's Hungry I. Beatlemania, initially at least, was very much a teen phenomenon that isolated the high-brow college crowd and thus did not threaten the duo's income stream. Nonetheless, it did give them pause to reflect on their direction and their own future. Ian's calendars reveal that by early 1965 the college gigs were beginning to thin out slightly, with an increasing reliance on the club engagements. Beatle-besotted teenagers were beginning to enter university. As for recording, it was clear that cutting another purely folk-oriented album was not an option unless you wanted to be relegated to the "has-been" bin.

The first indications of a switch in direction came during a May 1965 stint at the Golden Bear when Albert Grossman arranged for Ian & Sylvia to try recording a pop single in L.A. under the direction of producer Jim Dickson at World Pacific studios in Hollywood. Jim was well-connected in the Dylan camp and had earlier procured an acetate demo of "Mr. Tambourine Man." As Svengali to a quintet of ex-folkies-gone-electric he convinced them to work up an electric arrangement of the trippily poetic number, then secured a recording contract for the group, now under the name the Byrds, with Columbia Records. Released in April 1965, their electrified version, complete with electric Rickenbacker twelve-string "jingle jangle" guitar (played by Jim McGuinn), Appalachian triad harmonies, and tambourine, was burning up the pop charts by May on its way to number 1 the following month. And with that achievement and that signature sound, folk rock was born. This, of course, made Jim Dickson a hot property, and Albert thought perhaps some of his fairy dust might be applied to Ian & Sylvia. The session ran over two days but in the end yielded nothing worth releasing. "The session was rushed together by Grossman," Jim reveals. "I had no time to create a connection with Ian & Sylvia. I got a few studio musicians and we all met at the session. With no planning, I remember it as a failure." Tracks cut included a new song of Ian's, "Play One More," and "Red Velvet."

"We were on the West Coast when that whole folk rock thing exploded from there and we knew a lot of those guys," Ian points out. "It was huge there then, those folk-rock songs. We wanted one of those hits, too, but we didn't have the right producer. If we had had a decent producer, who knows what might have happened? John Phillips and Scott McKenzie [formerly of the Journeymen] weren't doing anything but Lou Adler saw the potential and look what he did with them? We didn't hang out with the Topanga Canyon gang. We knew Neil [Young] slightly and Chris Hillman, of course. He always wanted to be a cowboy. We knew McGuinn back in Chicago but he was a different person in L.A. So was John Phillips. That blew me away. He had reinvented himself since the Journeymen. I didn't understand reinvention then. I was so green. I just thought people that reinvent themselves were phoneys. Nowadays reinvention is the name of the game."

But if Ian & Sylvia themselves were not yet successful in adapting their songs to the new electric folk-rock reality, others were. The previous month, an obscure folk quintet from Los Angeles known at the time as the Ridge Runners had ventured up to Kingston Trio manager Frank Werber's Trident recording studio in San Francisco to cut their debut single. The connection with Trident and the Kingston Trio came via Ridge Runner Mike

Stewart, whose brother John was a member of the Kingston Trio. Mike and his Claremont, California, high-school buddy Jerry Burgan had formed their own group a year earlier, ultimately expanding to a quintet with the addition of Pete Fullerton, Bob Jones, and nineteen-year-old singer Bev Bivens. Under Frank Werber's auspices, the group's name was changed to We Five and the song they chose to lay down at Trident studios was a cover of Sylvia's "You Were On My Mind." John Stewart was a friend of Ian's. As Jerry Burgan tells it, John turned him and Mike on to Ian & Sylvia with "Four Strong Winds." "He sat on a bed and played and sang it. I loved it. I also loved when [Journeymen singer] Scott McKenzie would sing it. He was my absolute favourite singer."

How did the We Five come to record Sylvia's song? "By the time we were in college we were already looking beyond folk music," recalls Jerry Burgan. "We were looking for good songs anywhere we could get them. Mike got the *Northern Journey* album and he picked up on 'You Were On My Mind.' He said to me, 'Sing this.' He had been working on an arrangement for it and had me sing it before I even heard the original by Ian & Sylvia. Then our guitar player Bob Jones who had been a rock 'n' roll guy, he and Mike started fooling around with the rhythm. The way we did it was like one long continuous build to a crescendo, then we'd start it again. It was like a mini symphony. We put a rock rhythm to it and put in the twelve-string inspired by the Beatles' 'Ticket to Ride.' But Bob played it on an acoustic twelve-string with a pickup on it, giving it a remarkably unique sound that everyone still thinks is a Rickenbacker. When you listen to our song you hear six guitar chords that enter early on. We had gone back down to L.A. and played it for some deejays and were told that if we had the twelve-string come in sooner we'd have a hit on our hands. So the Rickenbacker was overdubbed after. We had brought in a drummer for our first sessions and we taught him 'You Were On My Mind' in about ten or fifteen minutes. So we started recording it and it was the drummer's idea to give it the rock beat. We shortened the opening from Sylvia's version, and with a band and a drummer and a rock arrangement, magic happened in the studio."

Not before another slight alteration to Sylvia's original. "We changed some of the lyrics because of the phrasing," Jerry explains. "For the speed we were doing the song in, it was just easier for us to sing 'When I woke up this morning' than 'Got up this morning.' It got to where we were going faster. But the lines about getting drunk and getting sick, Frank Werber had a bad experience with the Kingston Trio's 'Greenback Dollar' where the word 'damn' was edited out for radio by Capitol Records. He didn't like that that was done and was determined that he wouldn't let it happen again. Also, Sylvia was older than we were. I was the oldest in the group and I was twenty. The idea of putting us on television shows and into mainstream music as cherubic kids singing about getting drunk, Werber knew that wouldn't play. We toyed with changing the words but it wasn't our song to change. So we just repeated the first verse. In doing so it made the song more esoteric and less defined, so it allowed the listener to interpret the song as they chose. That boosted the song's success."

Released in May 1965, We Five's "You Were On My Mind" reached number 3 in *Billboard* by August, selling in excess of a million copies and earning the group a gold record as well as a Grammy nomination the following year. Alongside the Byrds' "Mr. Tambourine Man," We Five's "You Were On My Mind" came to define folk rock, a style of popular music generally regarded as America's answer to the British Invasion and characterized by poetic lyrics, chiming Rickenbacker twelve-string guitars, and folk-based harmonies. Where folk music was perceived as emanating from New York's funky-chic Greenwich Village coffeehouses, folk rock was a West Coast invention originating in colourful Sunset Strip teen clubs like the Whisky a Go-Go, Ciro's, and the Trip, with nubile young bodies gyrating to a pulsating electric beat.

Sylvia always maintained she was unaware of the We Five cover version until hearing it by chance one day on a California radio station. "That was quite a surprise. It was actually a hit before I knew about it. We were on the road in California, driving down Highway 101 between Los Angeles and San Francisco, and turned on the radio and there it was, by God. If I had been driving we would have probably driven off the road. Publishers didn't notify you of anything in those days. Mike Stewart heard it on our album. The publishers hadn't even placed it for cover versions." And how did she feel about their arrangement and alterations? "I wasn't that thrilled with how they changed the lyrics. But I certainly knew the limitations of pop radio in those days and that the lyrics 'I got drunk and I got sick' probably wouldn't pass muster." Ian, who says he liked the We Five version, counters her assertion. "She knew it had been cut and maybe the first time we heard it was in the car. The We Five made a hit song out of it. The only hit they ever had."*

According to We Five's Jerry Burgan, "I had always been told that Sylvia didn't like our version. But she has admitted that our version changed her life. It went somewhere Ian & Sylvia had not gone yet. It kind of forced their hand to move in a more folk rock direction. I'd been afraid to talk to Sylvia for over forty years but

---

* We Five had minor hits with "Let's Get Together" and "You Let a Love Burn Out" before Bev Bivens left in early 1967. Jerry Burgan continues to lead a version of We Five today.

when we finally talked recently she was very nice." Whether she approves of the changes in her lyrics, Sylvia remains eternally grateful for the hit version. "It's been used a lot in Europe in recent years in ads," notes Sylvia. "It's been enormous in Italy and has been used over and over in commercials there. It's used as a theme for a restaurant chain in Australia. Back in the '60s a Spanish group called Les Barracudas recorded it and that's the big version that's known in Europe." Comments Ian, "She got a lot of money for that. I was happy for her. 'You Were On My Mind,' boy, that sucker's got legs, like 'Some Day Soon.'"

Did the success of the single bring more than just a substantial five-figure royalty cheque Sylvia's way? "Not really," she replies. "It didn't make a lot of difference to our career because that was during a period of time when the songwriter was not as important. And a lot of people still don't know I wrote that song. I run into that all the time. They're very surprised to learn I wrote songs. They don't know who wrote that song – they certainly know the song – but don't know that I wrote it."

In July 1965, *Maclean's* magazine caught up with Canada's favourite music couple during a week-long engagement at New York's Café Au Go Go. Writer Jack Batten gushed about how New York was all agog over Canada's reigning folk music couple, despite their waning U.S. record sales. Back in 1963 Peter Gzowski had written the first major feature on the duo since their move southward the year before. Now it was time for an update. Introducing "Four Strong Winds" to the packed house, Jack quotes Ian stating, "It's a combination love ballad and winter weather report." Commenting on Sylvia's vocals, he writes, "She could charm the angels out of heaven." Between sets, old friend Don Francks, in the city for a role in the off-Broadway production *Leonard Bernstein's Theatre Songs*, joined the two along with Jack Batten over drinks across

Bleecker Street at the Dugout to reminisce about the early days back in Toronto. "Don was the hippest thing around Toronto in those days," offers Ian. "Me, I didn't know what I was doing."

In the *Maclean's* piece, Ian gushes effusively about the current state of popular music. If he was experiencing any apprehension about where Ian & Sylvia fit into the new reality he did not let on. "Everything's coming together. Jazz, rock, folk, we're all meeting. We listen to each other, we use each other's material, and a lot of guys move back and forth across the different styles. Rock 'n' roll is a lot more interesting than it used to be. It's full of really difficult harmonies – Paul McCartney, John Lennon, and George Harrison had a lot to do with that."

By the Café Au Go Go stand, accompanist Monte Dunn had been replaced by Boston-based guitarist Rick Turner. "Monte was hanging out with Tim Hardin, the junkie songwriter," reveals Ian. "One of Monte's great heroes was Tim Hardin," adds Sylvia. "That's when Monte got into hard drugs. We were playing once in Huntington Beach and Monte said to us, 'My friend Tim Hardin is coming out' and asked if we would put him up. Monte didn't have a car, we had the car, so we drove Monte to the bus station to pick up Tim Hardin and this quivering jelly of a man got off the bus. He stayed in Monte's room and that was an unfortunate connection for Monte. He did get straightened out later but he never did quite come back. He ended up living in upstate New York, married, and had a child. He would get in touch once in awhile."

Monte recommended Rick as his replacement. "There was no auditioning," recalls Rick. "They just called me up and said, 'Come down and start rehearsing.' They sent me their albums and my job was to learn the tunes and come join them. There weren't that many of us who could come close to playing that stuff at that point. Flatpicking per se was in its infancy outside of the outstanding virtuosity of Doc Watson or Clarence White. My inspiration in terms of my flatpicking initially was Ramblin' Jack Elliott." Although hardly a novice to softer drugs, Rick remembers Ian's advice to him, then twenty-two years old, upon his hiring. "One of the first things he said to me on the phone when I got the call to do the gig was, 'Okay, you're going to be bringing stuff in so put it in your pants when you cross the border.'"

Travelling with two established folk music stars was a real treat for Rick. "Together they were incredible to tour with. It was really a wonderful experience. They travelled well, they ate well on the road, and it was really good. I couldn't imagine a better way to tour at that time. They were making good money and doing fine in those days. We had no roadies and carried everything ourselves. Ian is quite the comedian and we had a lot of fun. And, of course, the music was great. They had a very unique approach to what I guess at the time was like a pop folk sound. They kept a level of authenticity and a demand for virtuosity that contemporaries like Peter, Paul & Mary, the Kingston Trio, the Limeliters, and the New Christy Minstrels did not have and that made them unique. Starting right off they had hired Johnny Herald as accompanist and that set the bar pretty damn high. And their harmony singing was amazing. Their a cappella songs were spine-chilling. And a lot of that was Sylvia. No one was doing the harmonies they were doing. Sylvia was quiet but she has this sly sense of humour that was just killer. It would come out in a slightly acerbic comment or a raised eyebrow.

"It's certainly no secret that Ian was quite the skirt-chaser then," Rick continues, "but the way we were touring there was more talk than action; more looking than touching. Ian was sharing a room with Sylvia, for God's sake, so he certainly wasn't bringing anyone back to the hotel. I didn't ever really pick up on him following up beyond looking. Sylvia certainly knew what he was up to but she was putting up with it. Ian was a cowboy. That's what cowboys were like. I do remember, though, that Ian was quite jealous that Sylvia's song 'You Were On My Mind' had become a pop hit before his songs did. That sort of burned in him. She got the big songwriter's cheque." Ian's "Four Strong Winds" had been a major country hit for Bobby Bare and while that in itself was both satisfying and lucrative, Ian craved the higher profile pop hit.

On the evening of Saturday, July 24, 1965, Ian & Sylvia made their second and ultimately final appearance at the annual Newport Folk Festival on a bill alongside Oscar Brand, Theodore Bikel, Lightning Hopkins, Odetta, and the Kweskin Jug Band, among others. They also took part in various workshops over the three days they attended the festival. "The first year we played Newport we went over well," Ian acknowledges, "but the next time we played I think we bombed. I was drunk, I think." Gordon Lightfoot made his Newport debut playing a Sunday afternoon set. But history barely remembers those artists who appeared that year, overshadowed as the event was by the dramatic appearance on the Sunday evening concert closing by an electrified Bob Dylan backed by members of the Butterfield Blues Band and keyboardist Al Kooper. Volumes have been written about this epochal moment when Bob turned his back on his folk constituency for a bid at rock 'n' roll fame. By that point he was virtually a rock star in all but name anyway. It shouldn't have surprised anyone that he would don an electric guitar. He'd been motioning in that direction for the past four or five months. His most recent album, *Bringing It All Back Home*, included electric rock 'n' roll backing on a number of songs, notably the opening track "Subterranean Homesick Blues," and his current single off the soon-to-be-unleashed full-on rock album *Highway 61 Revisited*, "Like a Rolling Stone," was already riding the top of the pop charts. He had all but abandoned protest songs for more esoteric lyrics as far back as *Another Side of Bob Dylan* in 1964. The die was cast. Apparently many of his devotees failed to read the signals. The only thing left for Bob was to perform live backed by a rock band. This he did at Newport that Sunday evening.

If the Beatles appearance on *The Ed Sullivan Show* the previous year was the first salvo fired across the bows of folk music, Bob Dylan's brief Newport set marked its imminent demise. All that was left was the eulogizing and there would be plenty of that in the forthcoming months. Once again, the kid from Hibbing, Minnesota, was changing the game for everyone. But in doing so he had to suffer the rancour of those diehards who felt a profound sense of betrayal by their chosen one and assailed him with boos. Some argue the booing was for the poor sound, the mixer unaccustomed to handling a loud and loose electric band. Others contend it was for Bob himself, for either the brevity of his set or his decision to go electric. The controversy has never been settled. After three loose and under-rehearsed electric songs (Dylan having decided the day before to mount an electric set), Bob left the stage only to be coaxed back by Peter Yarrow of Peter, Paul & Mary to soothe the unruly crowd with an acoustic song. Bob's choice spoke volumes about the incident and the future of folk music: "It's All Over Now, Baby Blue," followed by "Mr. Tambourine Man," a recent hit for the Byrds.

"The crowd was against him," insists Mary Martin, who was part of the Dylan-Grossman retinue that day. "Those boos were real. I was in the audience. I think a big reason Dylan did what he did was because of the Byrds and their recording of 'Mr. Tambourine Man.' He realized it could be done."

Witnessing all this tumult that momentous weekend were Ian & Sylvia, Rick Turner, and Gordon Lightfoot. All were affected by the unfolding scene. "We were there that afternoon when Albert Grossman and Alan Lomax were rolling around in the dirt having a brawl,"* Ian recalls. "Johnny Herald was hysterical with laughter. He thought that was the most incredible thing he'd ever seen. Sylvia and I were there the night of the famous debut of Dylan's new electric approach. It was really quite frightening to see his fans who were so totally devoted to him – he was idolized perhaps as no American artist had been on that artistic level – he was their spiritual and cultural leader all rolled up in one for that generation. And to see all these kids, 18,000 or whatever, turn on him within two or three songs was really quite frightening."

"My feeling about the whole night that Bob Dylan was backed by the electric band," muses Sylvia, "was they played badly. They played so loud you couldn't hear him singing. They hadn't rehearsed but Dylan doesn't like to rehearse anything. It could have been great but it wasn't. I think it was a mixed reaction. There was certainly a visceral reaction against Dylan doing anything that wasn't acoustic. But Paul Butterfield had played at the festival, they knew his band. Dylan wasn't up there with a bunch of strangers. It just wasn't very good. It was all over the map and the sound levels were totally off. Pete Seeger's wandering around backstage with tears running down his face, as if it's some great betrayal. The people who really hated it were quite volatile about it. What happened after that was that at the end, the whole audience was in a very unsettled state. And the organizers didn't know what to do. So they turned off the stage lights. And that

---

* Noted musicologist and folk purist Alan Lomax had provided a rather condescending introduction to Albert's clients the Butterfield Blues Band and Albert took exception. Their brawl is almost as notorious as Dylan's electric set.

whole audience was sitting there, not knowing which end was up."

Gordon Lightfoot, on the other hand, is more positive about what transpired onstage. "I thought it was great and the people loved it. It was the musicologists who didn't like it. Bob might have got booed somewhere but by the time it was over people loved it and were cheering. They settled down after the first tune." For Rick Turner, Bob's appearance marked a major turning point. "I was there in the fourth row when it happened. I thought it was really sloppy and loose but still great. Frankly, there was not as much booing as is often reported. But it was certainly a game-changer and pretty exciting. After that everybody started thinking about how to make the transition from acoustic to electric instruments. Everyone was thinking, 'How do you pull it off?' Back then PAs and gear were pretty primitive and that made it tough. There were no monitors. So often the quality of the acoustics in the places we played was very important to us."

For many folk artists there was no going back. While Ian & Sylvia were not in a position to compete with the Beatles and the British Invasion, they were better positioned to adapt their approach to that of folk rock. The first move in that direction was the addition of an electric bass player to their lineup. Bronx-born Felix Pappalardi was a classically trained musician who, besides adding electric bass to Ian & Sylvia's sound, would also contribute to arranging several of their songs on their next album. He would go on to great success as producer for the Youngbloods and Cream's recordings and as a founding member of the hard rock group Mountain. "Felix was this scrappy Italian kid and a sharp dresser," notes Rick, "who was the consummate accompanist. He really understood his role. He was also pushy in a way but not obnoxiously so. He had a Danelectro bass and we'd rent an Ampeg amplifier wherever we went. Felix and I would room together on the road. We had this tradition every time we played a college or university field house. We'd go out before the gig and smoke a joint on the fifty-yard line. I remember we played *The Tonight Show* once and they didn't want to pay for Felix and me to be seen on screen so they stashed us about twenty-five feet away offstage."

Despite the declining fortunes of many folk artists, Ian & Sylvia's booking calendar remained busy and their fees healthy. In August they made a return to the Mariposa Folk Festival followed by a week at the Golden Bear* and a concert at the Hollywood Bowl on August 13 alongside Judy Collins. Another Western Canadian tour opened in Vancouver on the 17th and ended in Winnipeg four days later, for which the two earned $10,000. The remainder of the month was spent on location in rural Saskatchewan filming a CBC documentary on the South Saskatchewan River. "We did a lot of documentaries," Ian reveals. "It seemed like every summer we did one." The duo would also write and perform the soundtrack music. In September, Ian & Sylvia headlined at Toronto's annual CNE (Canadian National Exhibition) over two nights (for $4,500) before heading down south for a two-week stay at the Cellar Door ($3,000 per week). Every weekend in October through November was booked with two college dates, often not in close proximity to one another, necessitating some hasty white-knuckle flights. "We played in Lynchburg, Virginia, in the afternoon at a women's college," Rick Turner recalls, "then took a little Piper Cherokee up to Troy, New York, to play a polytechnic that night. It was almost a Buddy Holly moment, five of us, including the pilot, Felix and me, all crammed into this small plane which was overloaded with stuff. Sylvia was stuck in the single back seat

---

* Stephen Stills and Peter Tork, later of Buffalo Springfield and the Monkees, respectively, were working at that time in the basement at the Golden Bear as dishwashers waiting for their big break.

on the plane and was pregnant and miserable. The plane barely made it over the wires on takeoff. I tapped Felix on the shoulder, he was in the co-pilot seat, and told him, 'See those pedals down there? If the pilot has a heart attack you're flying this thing!'" During the week Ian and Sylvia would return either to Toronto to work on the documentary soundtrack or to New York to begin recording their next album.

Unlike their previous four albums, *Play One More* was cut in a proper recording studio, RCA studios in New York at 155 East 24th Street, and done piecemeal over several scattered recording dates. Both circumstances created some adjustments for the two, who were also grappling with augmenting their sound with additional musicians. "It was a very transitional period for us," acknowledges Sylvia. As Rick Turner recalls, "There was this search beginning to start on the *Play One More* album with stuff like bringing in a full orchestra and using drums and electric guitars and Felix's influence. Ian was a bit of a control freak and suddenly recording sessions were getting out of control with orchestras and studio musicians. It was getting a bit pop commercial and it took away some of that grit Ian & Sylvia always had. It was a case of trying to chase what's coming next but how do you chase the Beatles, the Rolling Stones, or the Byrds? The folk scene was changing by then and we were all starting to embrace electric instruments and seeing where it would go. I got the sense it was very experimental for them. There was a desire to like the results; I think they wanted to like the results more than they ultimately did."

Both Ian and Sylvia are generally dismissive of their fifth album, citing particular highlights in an overall lacklustre collection of recordings. "That was more of a poppy album," Sylvia admits. What was going on or not going on in their career at the time has coloured their perspective on the actual songs and recordings. At that moment both were wondering where they fit in on the new musical landscape. That tends to temper their feelings about the experience of recording *Play One More*. "It definitely was a grab bag of styles," admits Rick. "It does not hang together as an album and was very different from anything they had done before. It might have gone too pop for the pace of the folkies who stuck with them and yet it was too sincere or too musical to appeal to the Sonny & Cher crowd."

"RCA was our first experience in a real honest-to-God recording studio," states Sylvia. "We actually had an engineer[*] on it. There wasn't the same natural echo in the vocals which we were used to and which made the early albums so distinctive. Now we had to get used to headphones for overdubbing, which is very rough. We had to learn how to be a hell of a lot more careful about certain music. The organ thing on 'Tulsa' I thought was lousy. You really can't get a studio guy and expect that he's going to do the right thing for you. Vanguard booked him [Paul Griffin, who had previously recorded with Bob Dylan] for us." Indeed, generally the organ is over the top and distracting where used on the album. It was all a learning experience for Ian & Sylvia.

By this point, Vanguard Records was becoming hip to the notion that folk-rock 45 singles might just sell. Better late than never, in their case. Between 1965 and 1967 the label would experiment on folk rock recordings by the likes of Patrick Sky, the Vagrants (featuring future Mountain guitarist Leslie West), Bonnie Dobson's roommate Judy Roderick, Steve Gillette, Circus Maximus, and Project X, which included former Journeyman Scott McKenzie as well as ex-Rooftop Singers leader Eric Darling. As far back as October 19, three weeks before the album sessions were set to

---

[*] A recording engineer manages the recording console, operates the tapes, and balances the sound.

begin, Ian & Sylvia had attempted to record a possible single at RCA studios. What they cut would remain unreleased until 2005 when it appeared on Big Beat Records' *The Vanguard Folk Rock Album*, a compilation of unsuccessful attempts by various folk artists on the label to plug in and go for a hit. Boasting a full rock backing – drums, electric bass, and electric guitars, as well as Hammond organ – "When I Was a Cowboy" is slightly more up-tempo, rollicking, and appealing than the version that would appear months later on the *Play One More* album. It's a shame it wasn't released in late 1965 as it might have meant a whole new career for Ian & Sylvia. As it was, the recording was abandoned for the next forty years.

Play One More was, indeed, a grab bag of styles and instrumentation. There was familiar acoustic folk/country territory on "Short Grass" (one of two songs on the album composed for the soundtrack to the CBC documentary on the South Saskatchewan River); a cover of Phil Ochs's evergreen "Changes"; "Lonely Girls" (the other documentary track); and Ian's pensive "Friends of Mine;" – all given a more strident feel courtesy of Felix's electric bass. Steve Gillette and Linda Albertano's "Molly and Tenbrooks," based on a legendary nineteenth-century horse race and featuring Eric Weissberg's superb banjo picking, and "Satisfied Mind" were countrified arrangements, the latter a one-time hit for country star Porter Wagoner and recorded a month earlier by the Byrds on their *Turn! Turn! Turn!* album. Eclectic is an apt descriptor for the rest of the tracks, ranging from baroque to pop and R&B-flavoured to full-on rock, drums and all. There's even a smattering of mariachi horns à la Johnny Cash's "Ring of Fire." Clearly, Ian & Sylvia were throwing everything at the wall, hoping something would stick and offer them a commercial breakthrough.

Sylvia's musings on relationships, "Gifts Are for Giving," and

"When I Was a Cowboy" both offer a funky R&B feel (despite the annoyingly cheesy organ). "I thought 'When I Was a Cowboy' was a great song and really funny," recalls Sylvia. "I loved the humour of it. We got that one from Leadbelly." "Hey, What About Me" was a rare composition from old friend Scott McKenzie who had recently opened for Ian & Sylvia at the Golden Bear. It's an attempt at a pop folk sound.* But the biggest departure from the signature Ian & Sylvia sound came on the title track and on "Twenty-Four Hours from Tulsa," a Burt Bacharach–Hal David composition turned hit single by Gene Pitney in 1963. Both were given the full rock spin with added horns and strings. What is remarkable about these two tracks, both arranged by noted New York session man Al Gorgoni and featuring legendary studio guitarist Vinnie Bell, is how Ian is transformed into Roy Orbison. "That was my idea to do that song," states Ian, a Gene Pitney fan. "I liked it but no one else did. It wasn't a hit." Adds Sylvia, "Vanguard was trying to make the jump to more commercial pop music. We thought it was a great song. But initially when people heard us play it they were outraged. Later it became a popular requested number." And if they had managed to score a hit single with that song? "I'm sure some major label would have tried to buy out our contract with Vanguard and turned us into pop stars," avers Sylvia. Surprisingly, the thought of becoming pop stars held some appeal to both at the time. "We were searching for some direction," Sylvia admits.

But if taking a pop rock turn was out of character and less successful, their attempt at orchestrated baroque music, on the other hand, proved to be a possible direction Ian & Sylvia could very well have followed, coming on the heels of the Beatles' "Yesterday", and predating the Left Banke's baroque rock hits

---

* "Hey, What About Me" would become a hit single for Canadian singer Anne Murray in 1972.

"Walk Away Renée" and "Pretty Ballerina" by a full year. "The French Girl," one of three atypical collaborations between the two on the album, was orchestrated by bass player Felix Pappalardi and is nothing short of exquisite in its execution. With lyrics from Ian, music by Sylvia, and a score arranged and conducted by Felix, it was a winning combination. "We didn't write together very much," admits Sylvia. "We tended to write solo and there were very few collaborations, but 'The French Girl' was one we worked on together. It was our first collaboration. I wrote it as a classical piece on piano." "That's one of the best melodies I ever wrote," states Ian. "Melodically, it's a good song. Felix was a classically trained rock guy."

"I think Ian was a little taken aback when Felix wanted to do the arrangement for 'The French Girl,'" reveals Rick. "I don't think Ian knew how well-schooled a musician Felix was. Everyone around Ian & Sylvia were all folkies. No one had any classical background, whereas Felix could sit down with music paper and write down an orchestral arrangement. I think there was a little push and shove there but the results speak for themselves. Ian is very proud of those results, which were brilliant. Personally, that should have been the direction they might have been better off moving into, because it was more unique. It kept that distinctive sound they had and expanded it just the right amount."

Despite Felix's skill at crafting an orchestrated arrangement, the session was fraught with some apprehension. "One thing Vanguard did for you was find good string players," states Sylvia. "Even Felix was uptight these guys were such heavies and here was this little guy up there leading them with a baton. It was the first time he'd ever done that." David Rea later worked with Felix backing Ian & Sylvia and offers this assessment of his friend's approach to recording. "The recordings that Felix made were earmarked by the fact that he knew all the material backwards and forwards. Although he was able and willing to make allowances for the artist to make last-minute changes, it was his thorough familiarity with the material that enabled him to do so. It was his consistency and intimate knowledge of all facets of the recording process that made him such an innovative musician and producer." Unfortunately Ian & Sylvia did not have further opportunities to work with Felix nor to follow this new and potentially exciting direction. More than a year later, ex-Byrd Gene Clark would record his own baroque version of "The French Girl," arranged by legendary L.A. studio wizard Curt Boettcher, who out-baroqued Felix's arrangement with harpsichord, flutes, and heavenly chorus. L.A. rock band the Daily Flash released a folk rock version of the song, scoring a minor West Coast hit. Bob Dylan even cut his own rendition in 1967 as part of *The Basement Tapes* recorded in the basement of Big Pink in upstate New York. The song was a stretch for his limited vocal abilities and the recording includes him changing the key to something more manageable for his range.

With what is arguably the least attractive cover photo in the Ian & Sylvia canon, a pregnant Sylvia intentionally obscured by a reclining Ian over a faded orange background, *Play One More*, released in May 1966, does have its moments but is clearly a diverse collection of songs in an attempt to find a direction to follow. Not quite folk, folk rock, or pop, it was not a big seller and holds few fond memories for either its creators or their fans. Perhaps had they pushed more for the title track, "Twenty-Four Hours from Tulsa," or even "The French Girl" to be released as a single, things might have turned out differently; however, given Vanguard's track record in promoting singles, it's likely they would still have turned deaf ears to the idea.

With Sylvia pregnant with son Clay, touring dates reduced slightly through December 1965 and January 1966, although they did perform a week-long engagement at Miami's Gaslight South club in mid December. Ian found time that month to attend the National Finals Rodeo Championships in Oklahoma City, a harbinger of things to come. There was, however, a longstanding U.K. tour booked for mid February that they had to honour. Accompanying Ian & Sylvia on their one and only U.K. jaunt was Gordon Lightfoot. Neither were household names on the U.K. music scene, dominated as it was at the time by all things pop and rock. As a result the tour proved to be very low key and failed to break Ian & Sylvia in the U.K. market. "I was five months pregnant at the time," notes Sylvia, "so I don't remember a lot of that tour." Backing them onstage were Felix on bass and David Rea on guitar, both serving double duty as Gordon's accompanists. Rick Turner had left Ian & Sylvia's employ at the end of 1965.

Ohio-born David Rea was already a name on the Toronto music circuit, having worked with the Allen Ward Trio (who recorded one album on Vanguard) and most recently with Gordon Lightfoot, both in concert and on his debut album. David had met and befriended Ian & Sylvia at the Mariposa Folk Festival and was even invited to their wedding. He got the call from Ian to be their accompanist just after Christmas 1965. "I was having a wonderful time playing with Gordon," he admits. "I was still a teenager fresh out of Ohio when I started with him. But the big thing in Toronto was to be Ian & Sylvia's guitar player. Ian approached me and asked if I wanted to come to work for them. 'You think about it,' he said to me. We both agreed to keep it quiet and not talk about it in public until I made my decision. So neither of us said a word but somebody was listening and the next thing I knew Gordon came up to me and said, 'Congratulations!' Gordon and I remained good friends after that. There was no acrimony between us when I left." "I don't think Gordon ever forgave us for stealing David Rea away from him," smiles Sylvia. Accompanying the duo offered a challenge for the young guitarist. "One thing you can say about Ian & Sylvia's music," remarks David, "was that it was never boring. It was very demanding music to play."

The arrival of the Canadian contingent in London on February 15, 1966, coincided with a nation-wide rail strike that forced the oddly billed Anglo-American Folk Concert touring party – Ian, Sylvia, Gordon, David, and Felix, plus the Ian Campbell Folk Group who were, in fact, the headliners, plus Australian singer Trevor Lucas, Colin Wilkie & Shirley Hart, and the Settlers – to travel from gig to gig via a rented coach. Not the kind of luxurious land cruisers touring artists use today; no, this was simply a bus with bench seating. For Sylvia this mode of transit was decidedly distressing. "I was five months' pregnant and showing, so a lot of it I just blotted out of my memory. I was at that placid stage and largely oblivious to most of what was going on around me by then. I was not very social at the best of times and even less so on that trip. We also discovered that the English equivalent of Howard Johnson's hotels was not to be believed. Worst food I ever had."

"Sylvia is a very strong, resilient lady," notes David, "but she was uncomfortable and not happy. Nonetheless, she was a rock, no matter how badly she felt." To add to the misery it rained for much of the ten-day tour. "We were all rather disenchanted because we had been told we'd be welcomed with open arms," David recalls, "and that wasn't the case. Our expectations were very high. While some might have heard of Ian & Sylvia, they didn't know Gordon Lightfoot from a hot rock.

"After the first show [at de Montfort Hall] in Leicester we went to a pub," David continues, "but because we were North Americans we were discriminated against. There we are: Sylvia's pregnant, Ian's pissed off, Gord's confused, Felix is an Italian from Brooklyn and he doesn't know what the hell's going on, and all we wanted was some food and a drink. The barkeep put us off until closing time. 'Sorry, Yanks, but it's closing time. You'll have to leave.' Gordon got up and said, 'Oh, so it's Yankee go home, is it?' Things got a little tense so we made our retreat."

At each tour stop, Ian & Sylvia would open their portion of the show with "You Were On My Mind," only to be met with stunned silence or, worse yet, scattered booing. "At that point when we were touring the U.K.," Sylvia remembers, "a singer over there named Crispian St. Peters had had a hit with 'You Were On My Mind,' sort of copying the We Five's version. That was very peculiar for a number of reasons, one of which was that he'd put *his* name on it as if he'd written it. That got straightened out pretty quickly. It was an eye-opener for him. He didn't have a clue; he had been a plumber's mate. The other thing was that people thought we were covering *his* song. They didn't know it was my song. They had this visceral reaction to a pop song at a folk show. We were getting booed because some people thought we were doing a pop song at a folk show, and someone else's pop song at that." Confirms David Rea, "The folk music aficionados didn't like that at all. They thought it was a sell-out for Ian & Sylvia to be doing this pop song. What we heard after the song ended was the sound of one hand clapping. It was dead silence. We were on the verge of seriously bombing."

Nevertheless, there were some highlights. Gordon Lightfoot, in particular, has fond memories of the tour. "That was a wonderful experience. We had more damn fun on that trip but it was a hard trip, too, because none of us was used to getting from city to city the way we are now. We travelled all over, right up to Edinburgh and back. We didn't have huge crowds but it was respectable. We travelled around by bus and checked into all these old-fashioned hotels. It was an experience I shall never forget. Trevor Lucas* did the best damn version of 'Waltzing Matilda' that I ever heard. He rocked the place with that one every night. We also had lunch with Gene Pitney. We heard he was in the hotel and Ian wanted to meet him. Ian was very outgoing and friendly. He could interact very well with people."

Playing fiddle for the Ian Campbell Folk Group was a young Dave Swarbrick who, a few years later as a member of groundbreaking U.K. folk rock band Fairport Convention, would be the catalyst for the revival of traditional Old English folk music. "Dave Swarbrick and I became friends," acknowledges David. "I remember going up to Newcastle and into Scotland, and Felix, Dave Swarbrick, Ian Campbell, and I were sitting at the back of the bus with a few bottles of Newcastle Brown. Swarbrick would be playing all these old-time songs on the fiddle while Ian Campbell pointed out places of historical interest passing by, all this stuff about the Jacobite Rebellion and all that. It was so cool to see ruins of old castles just sitting there. It was a constant history lesson for me, sitting in the back of that bus with Ian Campbell being my personal tour guide, together with Dave Swarbrick accompanying it all on fiddle. Swarbrick had a song from every region we passed through because he knew every fiddle song ever written." A couple of years later, David would be invited by Dave Swarbrick to join Fairport Convention, which he briefly did before returning to the U.S.

Vanguard had been slow in releasing Ian & Sylvia's albums in the U.K. so the duo were surprised to discover that stores were

---

* Trevor Lucas later married Fairport Convention singer Sandy Denny and the two formed the folk rock group Fotheringay before rejoining the Fairports.

two albums behind. "The audience didn't want to hear the new stuff, even though it wasn't very new for us, because they didn't know any of it," Sylvia recalls. That would explain why "You Were On My Mind" was received with such shock. It was on their third album, *Northern Journey*, not yet released in the U.K.

The tour concluded with a show at Fairfield Hall in Croydon, a city just on the outskirts of London (they never did play in London). Long-time Ian & Sylvia fan Peter O'Brien attended the show that night. "I do remember that I went expressly to see Ian & Sylvia and couldn't understand why the Ian Campbell Folk Group should be the headliners," he recalls. In his customary fashion Ian Tyson sums up their one and only U.K. visit: "I thought it was a wreck. We had a terrible time. They didn't get us at all over there."

Ian was forced to fly home separately from the others after receiving news that his father was gravely ill back in Victoria. "I made it all the way back in eighteen hours," he states. "I had to fly to New York, then Chicago to Seattle, and from there to Victoria. He hung on and that was the last time I saw him. He was a real nice man, a great old character, and I didn't appreciate him enough as a teenager. We used to fight a lot but I missed him when he was gone." Two concerts in New Jersey and Massachusetts were cancelled as Ian remained in Victoria. George Dawson Tyson passed away March 19, 1966.

With Sylvia pregnant, touring was scaled down through the spring. Ian played Ottawa's Le Hibou club and the Riverboat in Toronto on his own, accompanied by David Rea. He suffered a broken wrist after getting bucked off a horse on the farm in early May, which sidelined him for much of that month and into June, allowing him to begin work on another documentary entitled "Bad Men of B.C." for CBC's *Telescope*, about the McLean Brothers' crime spree in the 1870s. Daryl Duke was the producer. Meanwhile,

Sylvia stayed close to home. Singer/songwriter Bonnie Dobson had moved back to Toronto from New York in 1965 and Estelle Klein found her an apartment on Dunbar Road near the triplex the Kleins shared with the Tysons. "I have a very lovely memory of Sylvia walking towards the Rosedale tube station in the spring of 1966 when she was pregnant with Clay," Bonnie recalls, "and thinking she was the most gorgeous pregnant woman I had ever seen. She looked radiant."

On the day Clay Dawson Tyson was born, June 28, 1966, Ian was out at his farm in Newtonville with Bobby Bare baling hay. "He eventually came in," mutters Sylvia. Increasingly he and Sylvia were leading separate lives although outwardly there was no sign of any division between them. For Sylvia, being in the city with a baby made sense; for Ian, the down time meant more time out at the farm.

By late July, Ian was on location out in British Columbia for the "Bad Men" documentary. Besides providing the soundtrack, Ian also narrated the project. On August 5 and 6, Sylvia returned to performing when the two appeared at the Mariposa Folk Festival, followed two days later by a taping of CBC TV's *Show of the Week*. On the 24th, recording commenced (with further sessions in October) on what was anticipated to be their final Vanguard album, or so they believed. Albert Grossman was already fishing about for a better label for his clients. *Play One More* had not fared as well as previous efforts and there was a feeling of frustration, most notably from Ian, that Ian & Sylvia needed to move in a more pop direction. "We got into a rut about the time we started the family," Ian suggests. "I guess it was heading towards a musical showdown, a crisis, and it came after the baby arrived. Sylvia had vocal troubles for about a year and musically it became very unsatisfying about that time."

"I was singing very badly," Sylvia recalls. "It was just after Clay was born and I was not very well. I went back to work too soon. I had a Caesarean for Clay and I was back rehearsing two weeks later and that's a major operation. I even fainted once at rehearsal."

Like many of their contemporaries, the duo had become disillusioned with Vanguard's inadequacies. As label mate Steve Gillette observed, "There was no promotion and, worse than that, no distribution. I remember saying to Maynard Solomon when my first album came out, 'Can we do some promotional things?' and him replying, 'Well, our experience has been that the record kind of sweeps across the country in a few weeks and everyone is aware of it.' That might have worked for Joan Baez but not for a new artist. In the final analysis Vanguard was kind of like a mom and pop organization, only it was two brothers. They had a lot of taste and were knowledgeable and worldly men who were very committed to the Weavers and that political thing but from an artist's point of view you were kind of taken in. Even the vinyl they used was not exceptionally high quality. They were nice guys but you had to look out for yourself if they weren't doing that. By the time I'd gone from Vanguard in late 1968 almost everyone who had been on the label when I signed on had left them." That would include Ian & Sylvia.

In the late summer to fall of 1966 the pop charts were dominated by the Lovin' Spoonful's "Summer in the City," the Beach Boys' grandiose "Good Vibrations," the Supremes' "You Can't Hurry Love," as well as "Cherish" from the Association and "I'm a Believer" by newcomers the Monkees. On the album charts, *Pet Sounds* from the Beach Boys, the Beatles' *Revolver*, Bob Dylan's *Blonde on Blonde*, the debut album from Cream featuring Eric Clapton, and the Byrds' third album *Fifth Dimension* were all significant releases. Was there room in this company for Ian

& Sylvia? Folk rock had already run its course, with psychedelic or acid rock still a few months away. Pop music was in a bit of a limbo period. For Ian & Sylvia that only furthered the distress of trying for a suitable path to follow.

"Ian wanted to go more and more towards a pop sound," says Sylvia. "I had no objection to it as music, I just thought we weren't very good at it." According to David Rea, "Ian listened to a lot of Burt Bacharach's arrangements. He was spending a lot of time listening to Bacharach and trying to figure out the new recording technology. At that point Ian & Sylvia were kind of searching for where they wanted to go next. I recall Sylvia inviting me over to their house on Dunbar Road and turning me on to the Bulgarian State Women's Chorus and Ian trying to come to terms with the new music of the British Invasion. By then music had changed so radically, after the Beatles came along. Everything got turned upside down. Ian & Sylvia were slowly going in that direction. It was very confusing for me. The old formulas no longer worked." David admits Ian was frustrated at the duo's decline in the wake of the British Invasion. "You don't want to be around Ian when he's angry. But he wasn't alone. A lot of people got angry at that time. For me, I thought it was a very interesting time with lots of possibilities. But all the American kids were going for the British sounds and the American music changed. But I thought Ian & Sylvia had the potential to make pop hits."

As Steve Gillette notes, "When the Mamas & the Papas and all of that was happening Ian & Sylvia didn't want to be left behind and felt they had just as much to contribute and had all the chops. It's like that song about 'McGuinn and McGuire just a gettin' higher."* They were all contemporaries of Ian & Sylvia and they

---

* "Creeque Alley," an autobiographical song by the Mamas & the Papas written by John Phillips.

made the transition. There was no reason why Ian & Sylvia wouldn't have been embraced by that new music and crowd, too. It wasn't jealousy or envy, it was their career and they didn't want to take it lying down. You want to move ahead." "I think we *were* jealous," counters Ian. "We wanted one of those hits, too, but we didn't have a producer who could do that." Whether the decision to hire or not hire an experienced pop producer with a proven track record was Ian's or Vanguard's is unknown but Ian does lay much of the blame for their commercial decline at that point on the absence of someone to take the rudder and steer the ship. Ian being headstrong and Vanguard being frugal, it may have been a combination of the two. "We desperately needed a producer but the word was that Ian & Sylvia wouldn't take direction in the studio and unfortunately they were right. We wanted to do it our way."

"Ian did want that success, that's true," confirms Sylvia. "Perhaps I was a bit less motivated at that point than he was. For me it was still always about the music and the kind of music I was interested in. I'm not a natural performer. I never have been. Anything I do onstage I've learned to do. I was never one of those little kids who had to get up and sing and dance for the folks. It was always the songs for me, initially traditional songs before I started writing. I probably wouldn't be performing today if I couldn't write. That's just a fact of life for me. The only way people are going to hear my songs is if I get up there and perform them. Performance is not instinctive for me."

David Rea reveals that there was an aborted attempt at cutting the next album in Toronto in July to allow Sylvia to be closer to home with baby Clay. "There was a whole other *So Much for Dreaming* album with Felix Pappalardi on bass and me on guitar. Ian & Sylvia wanted to make an album in Canada. We recorded at Hallmark studios. The tracks got scrapped because the sound quality wasn't good. A lot of the new technology just wasn't in Canada. That made Ian very frustrated." The session, however, was memorable for another reason. "I had some people staying at my house," explains David, "and the cops busted them and since I had the lease on the house the cops came to the recording studio to arrest me. Ian was really angry with me for getting busted but he stood by me. In those days if you were convicted it was seven and a half years in prison. There I am shaking in my boots and Ian walks up to the cops and with his gift of gab he says to them, 'Look, I've got a lot of money invested in this recording session. How about if you let young David do the session and then arrest him?' So the cops look at me and say, 'You promise you won't try to run away?' So I promised and they went away. I think Ian gave them a couple of beers. So we did the session and afterwards they carted me off to jail. But that was the way Ian could face down a couple of cops." The charges were later dropped once it was proven that David was not responsible for the stash. "It was pretty serious," Sylvia acknowledges, "because David's dad came up from Ohio. David came from a fairly well-to-do family."

As David reflects, "I grew up in a very tumultuous family situation in Ohio which was why I got out when I was seventeen. Working with Ian & Sylvia made me not only a better musician but a better person. It changed my life. Their sense of honour so impressed me. I found a family with Ian & Sylvia. And what I also got from them was a sense of purpose. If you make a mistake it's not the end of the world. Go back, review what you did, and then do your best next time. We were kind of like the Three Musketeers in a way: all for one and one for all. Some of my fondest memories are of the three of us driving a rent-a-car through the night somewhere in the southeast U.S. with the Grand Ol' Opry low on the radio, a six-pack of beer and a basket of greasy hamburgers. A lot of the conversations would just be stream of consciousness. Sylvia's a great storyteller, too. We would just lose track of time deep in conversation. Or like when I got busted, Ian was livid with me but he stood by me. My dad was furious. 'I'm coming up there and I'm hiring the best lawyer. . . . ' But we took care of it, Ian and I. They brought me over to their house after I was released on bail. 'Come on over and wash the jail stink off of you.' They took care of me like a mom and dad you carouse with. Years later I saw the cop who arrested me in a bar and he bought me a drink. He told me, 'Hey, it was just business, kid.'"

"Drugs were way down the list with Ian & Sylvia," he insists. "It was always about the music with them." "I just wasn't interested," Sylvia admits. "I took LSD on one occasion. It was the '60s and it was available. At the time that I took it I was experiencing a serious writer's block. I had always been of the opinion that anything that you were capable of in terms of creation on drugs you should be capable of in your right mind. That was always my own point of view. But I basically hit a stone wall with my writing. I hadn't written anything in about a year and a half so I thought I would try it. It certainly wasn't something I would repeat." There was a growing assumption within the artistic community that taking drugs, particularly hallucinogenic drugs like LSD or mescaline, would unlock the creativity within your psyche. That wasn't always the case, however. "The reaction I witnessed from people who were taking it was paranoia not creativity. That seemed to be the overall effect. Even if someone said they were having a good trip it wouldn't take much to turn that around. I wasn't interested in putting myself in that vulnerable a situation. Ian was more of an experimenter in that kind of thing than I was but he also had some caution, too. I could never imagine Ian shooting up hard drugs. The idea that he could become dependent on something was pretty abhorrent to him. Alcohol, on the other hand, was almost a cultural thing."

As David recalls, "Ian invited me over to the house one time. This was when they'd moved to Rosedale. It was a crisp clear January night. The whole house was all lit by a mass of candles everywhere. And he said to me, 'I just dropped LSD and I wanted somebody with me I can trust.' Sylvia was home but she was upstairs asleep. When things like that took place she would go up to bed."

By 1966 Vanguard had come to realize that the Manhattan Towers Ballroom was inadequate for electric instrumentation and drums and had built their own recording studio in a converted church in Manhattan. "They were sort of trying it out on us," Sylvia asserts. "It wasn't ready and neither were we. Once again, like *Play One More*, it was kind of a funny period for us: good material but pretty badly done." By her own admission Sylvia believes she went back to singing too early after her pregnancy and her voice was ill prepared for the rigours of recording.

There were other factors at play as well during this period that affected the recording process. "I noticed the frustration coming out when we were starting to record *So Much for Dreaming*," avers David. "When we were rehearsing for those sessions somebody brought in a copy of the Beatles' *Revolver* and that just shot everything all to hell. It was one of those, 'Wait a minute, boys, we have to rethink this one' moments. Ian was overwhelmed by that album. You have to keep in mind that the Beatles never could have pulled that album off if they hadn't had George Martin as a producer. He had a classical background. But it just knocked the flats out from under us. After that the record sales went down. So Ian was frustrated."

Maynard Solomon relinquished the producer chair on *So Much for Dreaming* to Sam Charters who, while lacking pop experience, handled many of Vanguard's blues recordings. Even so, Ian still called most of the shots in the studio (by then Felix Pappalardi had left to become a full-time producer). Despite a few nods to their original folk sound, the album is skewed in a pop rock direction beginning with the opening track, Joni Mitchell's "Circle Game." At this point Joni was still largely unknown outside of the insular folk community, where she performed on the coffee-house circuit both on her own and briefly with husband Chuck Mitchell. However, she had several champions on her side, including Buffy Sainte-Marie, Tom Rush, and Ian & Sylvia. Buffy carried a tape of Joni's songs with her and played them to anyone who would listen. Tom Rush was first to record "Circle Game" but Ian & Sylvia's orchestrated version followed soon after and received wider attention. Had Vanguard possessed the means or initiative, this could easily have been a hit single for Ian & Sylvia. "I don't remember where we saw Joni Mitchell," states Sylvia, "but we were impressed with her songs. Songwriting was always important to us." Nevertheless, Sylvia is quick to add, "That was a good song that we sang very badly." That's the general consensus both Ian and Sylvia hold for the album's tracks.

"'So Much for Dreaming' was a good song totally out of our capabilities and would have been better done by an Andy Williams type singer," she surmises. Ian's first attempt at what would go on to be regarded as another of his enduring classics, the semi-autobiographical "Summer Wages," was re-recorded four years later because he felt the vocal on the 1966 version was poor. Quebecois singer/songwriter Gilles Vignault, best known for the emotionally charged Quebec nationalist anthem "Mon Pays," had begun singing outside his home turf in the latter half of the '60s and appeared both at the Mariposa Folk Festival and at Massey Hall. Ian & Sylvia chose to cover his "Si Les Bateux" in a lushly orchestrated arrangement slightly reminiscent of "The French Girl," though the a cappella verses were not intended as such. Orchestrator Trade Martin "didn't put in any accompaniment and copped out," notes Sylvia. "There were supposed to be full chords." Of the twelve tracks on the album, ten boast drums and additional instrumentation, including, in some cases, electric guitar. Contemporaries Jim & Jean were also moving away from a strictly acoustic folk approach to integrating electric instrumentation, and comparisons can be drawn between *So Much for Dreaming* and Jim & Jean's *Changes*, also recorded in 1966.

"The transition was not planned," Sylvia admits. "It was just a progression. We felt a certain sort of growing up. Part of the progression is when we started writing. The first album had no self-written material. The second had one song, 'Four Strong Winds.' The third had three. It was like more and more written material all the time. I remember this guy came up to me and said, 'Gee, you guys sure have changed. You just totally changed your style.' I replied by asking him when was the last album of ours he bought. He said four years ago. So I said to him, 'Do you expect us to stay in the same place for four years? You don't stay in the same place for four years.' It was a really dumb thing for him to say."

"Cutty Wren" harkens back to Ian & Sylvia's earliest albums of traditional folk music and was a song they had heard the Ian Campbell Group perform on the U.K. tour. "Catfish Blues," sung superbly by Sylvia, was a B. B. King number, while "Grey Morning" was a blues number by Sylvia. Ian's country leanings remained on "Come All Ye Fair and Tender Ladies" and "Summer Wages." Perhaps reflective of the fact that Sylvia had her hands full with a new baby, she contributes only two new songs to Ian's five. Sylvia reveals there was a bit of a friendly competition between the two. "If I got a song or two ahead of Ian he'd feel he had to get off his stick and do some more and vice versa. But we would both get blocks, periods of time where we couldn't write anything. So you'd have to get yourself motivated. 'I've got to write a song because I haven't written one in six months.' But that's good for you because you start to understand how you really work."

While sessions were still underway for *So Much for Dreaming* in October, Ian & Sylvia had already begun recording what would be their first single for their new label, MGM, in New York at Bell Sound Recording Studios at 237 West 54th Street ("That was an awful place," Sylvia recalls). Albert Grossman had made a two-album deal for Ian & Sylvia for a whopping $85,000 advance. Implicit in the contract was that Ian & Sylvia would produce hits. "At the time, MGM was a squeaky clean label," notes David Rea. "Mike Curb was trying to clean it all up. They dropped Eric Burdon [of the Animals] because he admitted to taking LSD. They were trying to make Ian & Sylvia into something they weren't." Why sign with MGM? "Front money," states Ian. "Albert could use his Dylan leverage to get us front money."

Released in April 1967, *So Much for Dreaming* boasted a stunning cover photograph by renowned celebrity portrait photographer Philippe Halsman. It was, however, out of step with the burgeoning flower power summer-of-love psychedelic music scene emanating from California. Like its predecessor, the album represented Ian & Sylvia's experiments in seeking a suitable direction and comfort zone in an ever-changing popular music milieu. "We were a hot ticket in California for about a year and a half," muses Ian "but then I remember standing in the Troubadour and the announcer was publicizing upcoming acts, and when he mentioned Ian & Sylvia some of the people booed. We had gone from the hippest people around to being booed. I knew there was something wrong with that audience. I was not amused. When we went out

Walt Kelly image of Great Speckled
Bird circa 1969 (courtesy of John
Einarson)

Ian & Sylvia performing with the Great Speckled Bird circa 1971
(© Marci Blattenberger)

Great Speckled Bird 1971 left to right: ND Smart, Buddy Cage, Ian Tyson, Sylvia Tyson, David Wilcox, Jim Colegrove (courtesy of Sylvia Tyson)

The Ian Tyson Show circa 1971; left to right: David Wilcox, Ben Keith, Ian Tyson, Jim Colegrove, ND Smart. (courtesy of Jim Colegrove)

The Ian Tyson Show, 1970s (© Larry LeBlanc)

Ian at his Newtonville ranch circa
mid 1970s (© Larry LeBlanc)

Sylvia Tyson, solo artist, 1976
(courtesy of Larry LeBlanc)

Sylvia Tyson, Murray McLauchlan, Liona Boyd, Gordon Lightfoot announcing the Olympic benefit concert, 1976 (Photograph by Bruce Cole Plum Communications Inc. ©)

Gordon Lightfoot, Sylvia and Ian at reunion show at Kingswood Music Theatre,
August 1986 (courtesy of Sylvia Tyson)

Holger Petersen of Stony Plain Records presenting Ian with a platinum record award for *Cowboyography*, 1989 (courtesy of Holger Petersen)

Ian at home on the T-Bar-Y ranch, Longview, Alberta, 2004 (courtesy of Ian Tyson)

Following Sylvia's set, Ian and Sylvia discuss performing "Four Strong Winds" together at Mariposa Festival's 50 anniversary, August 2010 (© Robin LeBlanc)

Ian and Sylvia reunite onstage at Mariposa, August 2010 (courtesy of John Einarson)

Sylvia, author John Einarson, and Ian, September 2009 (courtesy of John Einarson)

of fashion, we were really out of fashion. A lot of folk acts were in the same boat. But at the time I just thought, 'How come we were good enough for these sons of bitches last year but not this year? How come we're chopped liver now?' I was pretty naive. Sylvia took it much more philosophically than I did. I was pissed off. I took it very personally. I took it badly." For Ian, the transition to the new pop reality was a hard one. "It was sort of quiet desperation. We didn't know how to play with electric instruments. We didn't know how to use drums. All of us folkies were just standing there with egg on our faces. The only one who had the guts to challenge the rock 'n' roll guys on their own terms was Dylan. He just jumped right in."

Despite the mounting frustration in the studio, Ian & Sylvia continued to be a concert draw. On October 28 they played New York's prestigious Philharmonic Hall for a $5,000 guarantee, followed the next night by a concert at Washington's Constitution Hall for $2,000. Not a bad weekend. Meantime, the CBC had once again come calling, with an offer to appear regularly on a weekly public affairs program entitled *Sunday* produced by the Tysons' friend Daryl Duke. As a replacement for the controversial and recently cancelled *This Hour Has Seven Days*, *Sunday* mixed informative current affairs stories with lighter fare and ran from 10 p.m. to 11 p.m. Hosted mainly by a trio of journalists – Robert Hoyt, Peter Reilly, and satirist Larry Zolf – and taped before a live audience, the show also boasted musical numbers from Ian Tyson and up-and-comer at the time, Leonard Cohen. Ian and Sylvia together composed and recorded the theme song, inspired by the recent hits of the Mamas & the Papas and Spanky & Our Gang, later included on their next album, *Lovin' Sound*. For the two, making it back to Toronto each Sunday from gigs in far-flung parts of the United States was often challenging. "We had to be at the TV studio at something like eleven o'clock in the morning," recalls David Rea, "so we'd have to be flying back to Toronto Saturday nights after playing a gig somewhere." The show attempted to be topical and controversial without straying too far for the CBC brass. "On one episode of the show we had gonzo journalist Hunter S. Thompson, Hell's Angel head honcho Sonny Barger, and Joan Baez. Hunter had just written his book on the Hell's Angels and Sonny Barger drove his hog right onto the damn stage. [Sylvia remembers Hunter turning white as a sheet because he hadn't seen Sonny since his controversial book came out.] That was quite a show!" *Sunday* debuted on November 6, 1966 but never garnered the ratings of its better-remembered predecessor and lasted only the one season.

A weekly television show offered several benefits for Ian & Sylvia, not the least of which was a decent paycheque and the chance to showcase Ian as a viable, appealing, and potentially marketable television personality in his role as resident performer and sometime co-host. It further gave the two the opportunity to be around their home base more. For Sylvia that meant being home with baby Clay (live-in nanny Hazel Wilson looked after Clay when his parents were on the road), while for Ian it meant more time out on the farm. The week after the television show's debut, *Toronto Life* magazine did a feature on Ian at his farm. He had just purchased eight regular cows for the ranch. In late December the *Sunday* show was pre-taped at the Newtonville farm. The duo were performing that week at New York's Café Au Go Go and were flying back each day of the two-day taping.

The year 1967 began with a hectic round of work. The first week of January was still the Café Au Go Go, while the last week of the month was at the Cellar Door. In between the duo rehearsed in preparation for a full two-day recording session in late January (followed by final sessions in late February) at Bell Sound in New York for their debut MGM album. On January 5, CBC television broadcast "Bad Men of B.C." Meanwhile, Ian continued his weekly appearance on *Sunday*.

David Rea remembers the rehearsal regimen at the Rosedale house. "We would start around ten in the morning. We'd review the previous day's work, then we had a schedule of what we'd work on that day and they'd review the whole thing at the end of the day with a lunch and beer break in between. Sylvia would cook a nice dinner and Ian and I would go upstairs and have a Scotch. Sylvia was never the dutiful domesticated little housewife [notwithstanding the cooking for and likely cleaning up after the menfolk]. She had her own mind and she had a really strong sense of what she was going to do. I was working with Joni Mitchell and Judy Collins and you wouldn't believe the shit they had to put up with. It was a male-dominated scene with ass slapping and all of that."

MGM was keen to have an Ian & Sylvia album out on the market to justify their generous advance, thus, even before *So Much for Dreaming* had been released, they were readying *Lovin' Sound*. A mere two months after the Vanguard album was released, coinciding with their first sold-out Carnegie Hall concert on April 30, MGM put out their debut Ian & Sylvia album, along with the title song as a single. If the two previous albums had found Ian & Sylvia trying out a variety of hats to see which fit best, their third in this transitional trilogy was far more satisfying and successful. Despite the two being once again disappointed with aspects of sound and execution there is no denying the strength of the songs and the comfort they were now demonstrating within a pop rock context. And their single was perfectly cast for the summer-of-love ethos, demonstrating that Ian was more than capable of writing for the contemporary pop market. The difference was, in Ian's terms, the presence of John Court as producer. John had previously worked with Gordon Lightfoot and Richie Havens, among others. "We needed a producer," bemoans Ian. "The closest we got was on 'Lovin' Sound' with John Court who wasn't really a producer, but he got pretty close to it on that record. He worked very hard on that record and it did chart."

The single "Lovin' Sound" made the Top 20 or better across Canada and was a regional hit in parts of the United States, notably in California. "It just kept building and building region by region over several months moving eastward but it never broke through nationally in the U.S.," avers Ian. "We thought it was going to. It was a smash in California. They played the hell out of it, every hour on the hour kind of thing. Everybody thought it was going to be a monster. It was a good record, too, a good country/folk record cut in New York. But it became one of those regional hits that never went national. It never got across the Mississippi, which is kind of a shame. The damn thing was bubbling under for eight months. That was the closest we ever got." The single succeeded in re-establishing Ian & Sylvia in the record-buying marketplace and gave them the biggest hit single of their career. While both tend to disparage the single today, it remains a classic artefact of that particular year when flower power and "all you need is love" were genuine sentiments for youth worldwide. "I think Ian was trying to write a pop song," states Sylvia. "I was never sold on that song myself. It wasn't that it was not a good song, I just wasn't interested in going in that direction. The pop thing didn't interest me at all. It was a bit lightweight. If it had been more R&B, I would have been more interested."

In May, prior to the album's release, Ian & Sylvia embarked on a three-week tour of Atlantic Canada, fifteen dates at $1,000 per show guaranteed. They followed this with an eight-date Northern

Canada tour, beginning in Yellowknife on June 1 and ending in Tuktoyaktuk, N.W.T., a week later. They then finished the month at the Cellar Door in Washington, D.C., three weeks for a $10,000 guarantee. During that time MGM released *Lovin' Sound*.

"The understanding with MGM was that mainly it would be stuff we wrote but that it would be more accessible to pop radio," confirms Sylvia. Opening with a funky bass line and Ian's jazzy vocal, "Windy Weather" was like nothing the two had attempted before and continued the air of experimentation of the previous recordings. "'Windy Weather' was based on a time signature thing I had," reveals Sylvia. "A 6–4 time, 4 + 2 over 4 beats. An interesting time thing we wanted to mess around with." Tim Hardin's "Hang on to a Dream" features delicate electric guitar work from David Rea. "Whatever else was true about Tim's personal habits," Sylvia admits, "he was a great writer." Indeed, they also covered Tim's well-travelled "Reason to Believe" in a bit of an over-the-top arrangement with orchestration. "I Don't Believe You" came from Bob Dylan's catalogue. "He was kind of pleased we had done that one," offers Sylvia, "because he always thought it was a good song and nobody paid any attention to it. I don't think we did it particularly well, though." Sylvia admits that she was still suffering problems with her voice during the recording sessions. "I was just very tired," she admits, "and I didn't have the energy or strength, really. I just got into a very negative, down kind of thing and it affected my singing. I was overweight, I weighed 145 pounds. When you're used to being very thin and suddenly you're fat you don't feel well. You're carrying around all that extra weight and you can't figure out why you're tired all the time and why you feel lousy."

With "Where Did All the Love Go?" Sylvia entered country music territory, allowing Ian to take the lead vocal. Was it drawn from real life? "Oh, possibly," she smiles, adding, "The point with my songs is not intently my own personal experience, although some female songwriters get away with that, Joni Mitchell being the best example. I look more for the universal in that ideal so it will connect with other people." "Mr. Spoons" was Ian's nickname for Clay and the song was written to him as an infant. It was re-recorded on their next MGM album because Ian felt he had done a poor job with the vocals this first time out. Interesting to note that none other than jazz great Mel Tormé recorded a version of the song. Perhaps the most out-of-character track on the album was Ian's campy "National Hotel," recorded in a New Vaudeville Band–inspired 1920s "Winchester Cathedral" dancehall arrangement. "We just did it for the hell of it," laughs Sylvia. "I play piano on it. Surprisingly, we would receive requests for that song for years after that."

"Sunday" was the television show theme song, complete with Sylvia mimicking a horn section in the middle eight. David Rea contributed "Pilgrimage to Paradise." "The one thing about Ian & Sylvia is that they included me in the creative process," states David. "I wasn't just a sideman. That was quite gratifying. I also had some input into the arrangements, too." The song was among David's first compositions. "I was in love with this girl and I saw her walking off in the night with another guy," he told liner notes writer Richie Unterberger on the reissue of the album on CD years later. "I was depressed. It just all spilled out. I played it for Eric Andersen and he said, 'My God, man, that's like admitting you've got acne!'" Nonetheless, Ian & Sylvia liked the song enough to record it. A dedicated Johnny Cash fan, Ian took a shot at Johnny's "Big River" and proved his country music credentials. As Steve Gillette muses, "I think Ian had an ambition to be a country star like Bobby Bare or Johnny Cash." "Trilogy" represented the most ambitious composition to date from Sylvia. "It's a weird classical type song," she admits. "It's really about the New York scene we were on at the time. There were a lot of, as Albert used to say, people you would run into in the business who felt that much taller than you if they could stand on someone else's stomach. It's about people like that told in three stories. It was just observations at the time. One of the verses was about a psychologist we knew who was always messing around with people's heads."

Lovin' Sound was proof that Ian & Sylvia could transition to a commercially appealing pop sound. However, the pop charts by mid 1967 were dominated by the likes of the Doors' LSD-tinged "Light My Fire," the Beatles' "All You Need Is Love," old friend Scott McKenzie's hippy trippy "San Francisco (Be Sure to Wear Flowers In Your Hair)," "Respect" from Aretha Franklin, Procol Harum's classically inspired "A Whiter Shade of Pale," and the Strawberry Alarm Clock's bubblegum psychedelic "Incense and Peppermints." The game was again changing. The album peaked at number 148 on the *Billboard* album charts, not what MGM had in mind for their high-priced signing. "It was the best we could do at that time," offers Sylvia. "We had obligations to meet because we'd signed with MGM and they wanted a record from us. I think it was the best album that we could have put out at that point. I don't have any particular apology for the material. It's quite strong. The performance is another matter."

"I don't remember it being a big disappointment," muses Ian. "I think at that time I was becoming disenchanted with what I thought were the limitations of our sound as a duo. The very uniqueness of our sound would create these limitations for the future. It was either go back to that pure, pure thing, which I don't think either of us wanted to do, or try adapting that duo Ian & Sylvia vocal sound to a commercial hit. We would have the standard arrangement arguments that everybody that sings together have, but I don't think Sylvia was ready to sit down and say our vocal sound isn't going to adapt itself to a major AM pop charts hit. I was getting very much more and more heavily into the country music of the time, which was pretty good. Sylvia wasn't that interested in it, she was going in her direction. Buck Owens and his Buckaroos and George Jones and his band were making real good records and I was really interested in that stuff."

FULL CIRCLE

There was something in the warm southern California air by mid 1967 and it wasn't just the sweet fragrance of marijuana. A handful of musicians, weary of the rootless meanderings and overblown excesses of psychedelic music, were turning their gaze back to a purer, simpler, more authentic Americana roots music: country music and bluegrass. Many had come from the folk music stream, made the transition to folk rock, only to be washed overboard by soulless psychedelic acid rock. Incense, peppermints, and vapid twenty-five-minute ragas offered little in the way of intrinsic musical or lyrical value. It was time to bring rock music back to its true roots.

Beginning in small enclaves such as the Palomino, Ice House, Troubadour, Ash Grove, and Golden Bear, these like-minded young musicians either played straight country music in a rock band configuration or integrated country and bluegrass textures and instrumentation into their rock. Among the ranks of these pioneers were the Buffalo Springfield, Byrds, Hearts & Flowers, Dillards, Stone

Poneys, International Submarine Band (led by one Ingram Cecil "Gram" Parsons), Nitty Gritty Dirt Band, Rick Nelson (yes, the former teen idol), and the Monkees' Mike Nesmith ("What Am I Doing Hangin' 'Round," for example). From the seeds they planted would sprout Poco, Dillard & Clark, the Flying Burrito Brothers, the First National Band, Longbranch Pennywhistle, Rick Nelson & the Stone Canyon Band, Steve Young, and Linda Ronstadt the following year. It was an invigorating time. And from this hybrid cross-pollination of styles and sounds would ultimately emerge the radio-friendly country rock of the Eagles and all their denim-clad "cocaine cowboy" cohorts (Ronstadt, Jackson Browne, J. D. Souther, Firefall, Dan Fogelberg, Fools Gold, Gram Parsons and Emmylou Harris, New Riders of the Purple Sage, et al.). Besides an abiding affection for the music of Buck, Merle, and George (even San Francisco's leading acid band the Grateful Dead began playing Merle Haggard's "Mama Tried"), all these countrified rockers had grown up listening to Ian & Sylvia.

Ironically, the musicians involved in forging this southern California hybrid were almost exclusively non-Angelinos. Although associated with southern California, country rock drew its roots from much farther afield. "Guys like Gene Clark and the Dillards coming from Missouri, Mike Nesmith from Texas, Gram Parsons from Georgia, and the guys in the Eagles coming from all over," avers latter Byrds' bass player John York, "they all had a certain amount of baggage. They all grew up on country music. When they came to L.A. they were still carrying that with them and entering into an existing music scene. I think that's one of the forces that created that particular style of music, different pieces of that puzzle were brought here. So if you have a bunch of guys playing rock 'n' roll that grew up on country music, it's going to alter the shape of the music." Once the domain of the "establishment," the Bible belt, southern hicks, segregationists, rednecks, and pro–Vietnam War hawks (Merle Haggard's "Okie from Muskogee" pretty much summed it up), country music was now slowly becoming hip with the hippie crowd. There was, indeed, something in the air and a movement afoot.

Ian & Sylvia's attempts to make the leap to a pop folk rock sound on their last three albums had met with mixed reviews and limited commercial success. Had "Lovin' Sound" managed to become the nationwide hit single it should have been, that might have changed the game for them. But as it was, they had lost some of the folk music faithful while failing to discover a whole new audience. More than that, their pop music turn had left both Ian and Sylvia feeling a bit shallow and adrift. "I don't recall feeling depressed," muses Sylvia. "I might have been a bit frustrated because I thought we had done some good work. I don't think we've ever recorded anything I'm ashamed of with the exception of 'Creators of Rain' [more on that in the next chapter]. You can sit around feeling sorry for yourself but that ain't gonna bring home the bacon. Ian was frustrated during that period and drank a bit. That's how he dealt with it. In hindsight, the way we dealt with it is that we didn't deal with it. We were working and bringing in money. And, of course, with me there was Clay. That was my preoccupation. I tend to kind of just roll with the punches. You have to get up and start punching again. I didn't get all that discouraged. I knew what we did and I knew what we did best. Our attempts to accommodate changes in the music scene had not been terribly successful. We weren't following our instincts. That wasn't the path for us."

Ian & Sylvia needed to get back to something they felt both a connection and a commitment to. That would come, strangely enough, via Vanguard Records. "They had a very ambiguous contract," Sylvia points out, "and everybody on Vanguard's roster suffered as a result. Either you had given them one album too many, or you owed them one, depending on how they interpreted it. We didn't recognize that at the time we signed. So they basically released us to do an album for another label, MGM. What they were hoping for was that we'd have a huge hit album on this other label and have to come back and do another album for them, which of course didn't happen." Nonetheless, Vanguard came a-knockin' for their contractually obligated final album. This time, Ian & Sylvia were determined to do it their way with no pressure to produce something other than the music they wanted to write and record. "The deal we did work out with them was that if we did another album for them we could go to Nashville and record there with various players because we were exploring that music at the time. That was the deal and so that's what happened."

While "Lovin' Sound" was doing its slow climb on the regional pop charts, Ian & Sylvia were relatively inactive. They played only a handful of dates in July, one being an appearance in New York's Central Park, but mostly they stayed close to home. In August they purchased a home in the toney neighbourhood of Rosedale (they had previously shared a triplex on the edge of Rosedale) on Chestnut Park Road. Built in 1914, the stately two-and-a-half-story red brick-and-stone house boasted an ornate stained-glass window in the upstairs landing (pictured on the CD cover of *Ian & Sylvia's Greatest Hits*) and a third-floor attic suite with separate entrance. Sylvia continues to live in the house today. "There weren't many other musicians in Rosedale back then," she recalls, "so we were regarded with a degree of suspicion by the neighbours. It's certainly changed a lot since then. There is a lot more variety now. It used to be the WASP bastion. I used to say the neighbourhood was so WASP even the dogs were blond." Gordon

Lightfoot would move into the neighbourhood a few years later.

With Clay still an infant it was difficult bringing him on the road but it was also difficult for Sylvia to leave him. "I had a child at home so I didn't want to be working as much. It just seemed like a really good idea to be sticking closer to home for a while. Initially we took Clay along with us as a baby, and then we had the difficulty of Hazel getting across the border. Then, too, it was becoming obvious, more to me than to Ian, that by taking him along with us, because I felt guilty leaving him, I was taking him away from where he wanted to be. He was happier being at home." Hazel was Clay's nanny from the time he was an infant until he moved out on his own as a young adult. She also served as the Tysons' housekeeper. "She was pretty tough on him and didn't take any nonsense from him," notes Sylvia. As parents, Ian and Sylvia were fairly liberal. "I often feel sorry for the children of the artists of our generation," she chuckles, "because what are they going to rebel against?"

On Christmas Day 1967 Hazel was denied entry into the U.S. en route to a three-week stand at the Golden Bear. According to U.S. law she was doing a job an American could do and thus she was turned away at Customs. "I remember we had to hire a babysitter for that gig," says Sylvia. "I was working all night and babysitting all day and I finally lost it. I screamed at Ian and he shot out of bed and I didn't see him or [eighteen-month-old] Clay the rest of the day. Clay really remembers that clearly, walking along Huntington Beach picking up stones and making whips out of the kelp. I think because it was such a unique thing for him to be spending that amount of time with his dad that it's stuck with him."

In between the house purchase and moving in, Ian went on a four-day trail ride in southern Alberta. The farm was continuing to occupy more of his time away from the road and recording studio and his dream of being a cowboy was still very much alive. "I went herding cattle with Ian one day," remembers Jack Elliott. "I had played at the Riverboat the night before and didn't get much sleep but Ian came by real early in the morning to pick me up to go to the ranch. His little boy Clay was in the backseat all wrapped up with a tangled-up lariat rope. We went into the corral and started breaking in a few colts. The little boy was practising with the lariat rope, trying to rope one of Ian's favourite old horses, Barney. Barney was standing there patiently letting the kid throw the rope at him and he wasn't doing very well. Every once in a while Ian would look over at Clay and say, 'Catch anything yet? Well, just keep trying.' Then Ian and I saddled up some horses and went to get the cows to drive them back to the ranch. We were crossing a creek and I fell asleep midstream. Soon as I did, about six cows at the back of the herd noticed and spun around in midstream and headed back to where they'd come from. Ian saw that and turned around and yelled at me, 'This ain't no gawdamn western movie!' So I woke up, spun around with my horse, and went after those cows, got them back in line and turned around. I stood up in my stirrups and saluted Ian like a cavalry soldier. 'Won't happen again, sir!' He didn't say a word. Ian had to go meet the vet so he told me to take twenty-five head of cattle and make them stand quietly at one end of the arena and the other twenty-five at the opposite end. 'Good luck,' he said, and that was my first lesson in cutting. There was nobody there to tell me what to do. I just had the horse to teach me. He knew what to do; he was a three-year-old cutting horse. Took me about an hour to do it but it was a glorious time. I felt very proud to report to Ian that I got the job done. The horse does all the work and you just hang onto the saddle." Muses Jack, wistfully, "I'd give anything to go riding with Ian again or to just sit around spinning yarns and singing a few of those old songs."

Ian's passion had become raising cutting horses. These horses are trained for ranching, to go into the herd and select the cow you want. The horse then separates that cow out from the herd. Cows don't like to be alone so they want to be with the herd and don't want to leave. A good cutting horse has to dodge and weave with her to get her away from the herd. "I got into cutting horses when I stopped riding broncs and all that rough stuff," Ian explains. "I was looking around for some rodeo thing. Roping calves is hard on your hands if you play guitar. So I got interested in raising cutting horses. It takes a lot of time, planning, and effort. Cowboys being what they are, and competitive, they turned cutting horses into an event, and it became this highly developed competitive sport." By the '70s Ian would begin competing in cutting horse competitions across the continent. "I was a pretty good trainer but I wasn't a good shower of horses. I wasn't in that top 5 percent and I never would have been."

In mid December recording sessions held at Vanguard's New York studio proved unsatisfactory. Ian & Sylvia were determined to record in Nashville. "We felt comfortable recording in Nashville," Sylvia confirms. "We had nothing to lose recording a country album even if it sank like a stone because this was a contractual obligation and we weren't feeling particularly friendly towards them at that point. So we pretty much did what we damn well pleased and damn the torpedoes, full speed ahead. This was certainly more comfortable for us, especially when you consider some of our earlier material coming from bluegrass. It was a logical progression, more so than trying to go more pop on *Lovin' Sound*. Nashville was where the greatest concentration of the best players were. There were really wonderful players there. After that, everybody started going to Nashville. They were starting to realize that country music didn't have to be old-style country. It could be a country jazz or a country rock. It was liberating on both sides, for them and for us."

"I would say that deep down, Ian & Sylvia's big influence was country music," asserts David Rea. "If you stripped away everything from Sylvia's rowboat you find Patsy Cline. And Ian grew up on country music."

Bob Dylan was the first of the folkies to trek southward to the country music capital to record his 1966 magnum opus *Blonde on Blonde*, returning in October 1967 to record the sparse *John Wesley Harding*. Buffy Sainte-Marie would follow soon after and record *I'm Gonna Be a Country Girl Again*. Ian & Sylvia set up shop in Music City, U.S.A., in February 1968, a month before the much-celebrated Byrds' *Sweetheart of the Rodeo* Nashville sessions. "What we were all doing," Ian maintains, "was expressing our love and respect for the real vital country music of the times, represented by artists like Buck Owens and Merle Haggard."

With David Rea in tow (touring bass player Ken Kalmusky from Stratford, Ontario, would join the sessions later on) and Ian serving as producer (with musical arrangements credited to Ian & Sylvia), the duo recruited the A-list of studio stalwarts, including guitarists Fred Carter, Harold Bradley, and Jerry Reed; Pete Drake on pedal steel guitar; bass player Norbert Putnam (recently wed to Buffy Sainte-Marie); drummer Kenny Buttrey; and renowned fiddle players extraordinaire Buddy Spicher and Tommy Jackson. "Those arrangements were just off the floor with those guys," notes Ian. "We got pretty close to something that was unique and special." Adds David Rea, "Ian knew I loved Jerry Reed's playing so he went out and hired Jerry Reed to play on the *Nashville* sessions. He was a real picker. That was pretty nice of Ian to do that, knowing that it meant so much to me." The sessions were held at Columbia studios where Elvis had recorded. All songs were by Ian or Sylvia or both, with the exception of "90° X 90°" from David Rea and two Bob Dylan numbers from his legendary *Basement Tapes* ("The Mighty Quinn" and "Wheels on Fire") cut as demos with the Band in 1967. "Grossman was pushing Dylan's songs," Sylvia later told writer Nicholas Jennings. "He owned a piece of the publishing so we were always getting early demos of that stuff, including *The Basement Tapes*."

Ian & Sylvia's version of "The Mighty Quinn," bolstered by fiddles and pedal steel, beat out the Manfred Mann pop version and is truer to Bob Dylan's original version; however, the latter enjoyed a huge hit single with it. "Wheels on Fire"* receives the same countrified arrangement that all the tracks on the album boast. According to Sylvia, Ian's "Farewell to the North" was written at a time when he was considering moving to the United States. "He was thinking of it more than I was. I've never worried about where I lived [Sylvia had retained her New York apartment] really. It's just that California just didn't seem like the answer to me. Fortunately we didn't do it. I think the thing that stopped him was he didn't want Clay to be brought up in the States." "Southern Comfort" was, as Sylvia suggests, an experimental piece that ran through several sections and was reminiscent of their early a cappella Elizabethan folk arrangements, only with country instrumentation and innovative pedal steel from Pete Drake. "Ballad of the Ugly Man," Sylvia explains, is about the perception that someone can be unattractive on the outside but still be "very groovy" on the inside. However, in this case, "the song is about someone who is just as ugly on the inside as he is on the outside."

---

* A.k.a. "This Wheel's on Fire," recorded one month earlier in New York by the Band, credited to Bob Dylan and the Band's Rick Danko, and released on their seminal Americana debut album, *Music from Big Pink*, in July 1968.

David Rea's inspiration for "90° X 90°" was drawn from the duo's Centennial year northern Canadian tour. "It had a profound effect on him," notes Sylvia. "We were right up to the Arctic Circle and Mackenzie Delta." "London Life" is a recollection of their time in the U.K. "Fairly self-explanatory," Sylvia admits, "if you take it as a series of images rather than try to take it as a whole." Jerry Reed's hot picking drives the track along at a brisk pace. "The Renegade" offers Ian's personal take on attempts to Canadianize First Nations people and deny their traditions. "House of Cards" is perhaps the odd man out on the album; less country and more suited to their previous couple of albums, it offers a political statement of sorts from Ian. "It was one of only a few attempts at a protest song," Sylvia explains. "We really stopped doing it after it was recorded."

While releasing a country (as opposed to country-rock) album may have appeared brazen at the time, a bold gamble with their very career at stake, Ian & Sylvia were, in point of fact, on the cusp of the movement to a "back to the roots" musical ethos that, while producing some great music, never cracked through the commercial barriers, at least not until 1972 with the Eagles' homogenized version of country rock.* The duo already leading the country rock pack given their previous body of work and their well-known country music leanings, and adjudging themselves eminently qualified to pursue the country path, their album *Nashville* was a very satisfying and cohesive musical statement that showcased their high level of comfort in the country genre. "The *Nashville* album experience gave us a very good handle on that scene," Sylvia avers. "It took us out of the New York scene, where

---

* The Byrds' seminal *Sweetheart of the Rodeo* was their worst-selling album, while the Flying Burrito Brothers' *The Gilded Palace of Sin* sold a mere 40,000 copies. Poco waited eleven years before enjoying a hit single.

we had always recorded, and put us into a whole field of players that we didn't know and who didn't know us. I think it's one hell of a good album."

It's worth noting that the Byrds' *Sweetheart of the Rodeo*, often cited as ground zero for the entire country-rock and later alternative country movements, offered little in the way of original material, with the exception of two songs by country-rock avatar and short-time Byrd Gram Parsons. Bookended by two *Basement Tapes* covers, the remainder of the album offers up cover versions of traditional country music as if to tamper with it in any way would somehow be sacrilege. Ian & Sylvia, much like Gram Parsons (and Gene Clark, Richie Furay, Mike Nesmith, and a handful of others) were taking the country music idiom and writing new original songs within that structure.

Prior to the release of *Nashville*, Vanguard hedged their bet by releasing *The Best of Ian & Sylvia* in April 1968, the first of several compilations they would trot out every couple of years. Usually a move like that is a clear indication that your label has little hope for your future endeavours and seeks to cash in on their vaults filled with your previously released tracks. Vanguard, or the Welk Record Group, continue to flood the market with Ian & Sylvia product.* *Nashville* was then released with little fanfare in September featuring a cover painting of the two on horseback, a purely fictional rendering since Sylvia was not fond of riding horses.

The weekend college circuit was still hanging on and the duo kept busy back on the road through the spring and summer, their schedule punctuated by extended engagements at those old familiar places: the Cellar Door, Golden Bear, and Café Au Go Go. A

---

* Unfortunately, royalty rates are lower for "best of" and "greatest hits" packages, so it's hardly a windfall for Ian or Sylvia. However, from the perspective of the record-buying public, the compilations succeed in keeping the duo's music available to fans both old and new.

couple of new venues appeared, such as Montreal's New Penelope club and the Embassy Club in Toronto. In April, they were booked to appear at the Liberal Party of Canada's leadership convention in Ottawa where Pierre Elliott Trudeau was anointed leader. In fact, the Tysons became friends with the charismatic prime minister and played a dinner for him and guests in November (one later band member insists Trudeau shared a joint with them backstage one time). They also made another appearance on CBC TV's *Tonight in Person* from Toronto in March.

With two Vanguard albums on the market, MGM was keen to get Ian & Sylvia back in the recording studio. Thus in June, following another extended stay at the Golden Bear, Ian & Sylvia decamped to the legendary Bradley's Barn recording facility in Mount Juliet outside Nashville. Operated by producer Owen Bradley, the man responsible for "the Nashville Sound" (often referred to derisively as "Countrypolitan" for its formulaic easy listening approach), the studio had been responsible for a long list of country music hits from the likes of Jim Reeves, Patsy Cline, Loretta Lynn, Brenda Lee, and Conway Twitty. Many of the same players from the *Nashville* sessions were retained (Putnam, Buttrey, Carter) and augmented where needed. There was no turning back from their country direction. Production duties were in the hands of Elliot Mazer, later famous for producing Neil Young's *Harvest* album. Elliot was fresh from sessions with Gordon Lightfoot (*Back Here on Earth*) and Toronto rockers and Albert Grossman clients the Paupers (*Ellis Island*). The following year he would go on to produce Linda Ronstadt's *Silk Purse* and Big Brother & the Holding Company's *Cheap Thrills*, the album that broke out Janis Joplin. Ian admits to having a brief fling with Elliot's wife during the recording sessions. Engineering the Ian & Sylvia sessions was Charlie Tallent. "Charlie had as much to do with that album as Elliot did," avers Sylvia. "He sort of mixed as he went along. Nashville engineers are really producers in a way. They're so used to coming up with a finished product in a hurry. They tend to record at the levels right for the instruments and balance as they go along."

The resulting album was given the title *Full Circle* because "we were coming back to some of our roots," Sylvia confirms. According to David Rea, who also played on the sessions, "*Full Circle* in many ways is my favourite Ian & Sylvia album. Fred Carter Jr. was supposed to be doing the lead guitar on the sessions like he had done on the *Nashville* album. But for some reason he pulled out early on, so I was given the bulk of the lead parts, acoustic and some electric." In many respects, *Full Circle* was the realization of what they'd begun on *Nashville*, strong original songwriting over country music arrangements. "*Nashville* and *Full Circle* were where we found our direction," Ian enthuses. "The good experimental records we did in Nashville I still like the best." Sylvia agrees. "We had really started getting it together with some of the guys in Nashville by this point," she says. "We found out what we needed to know from the *Nashville* album. We were surer of what we wanted. There's more consistency to *Full Circle*. I think it's a hell of an album, too." *Full Circle*'s sound was also less straight-ahead country, as *Nashville* had more or less been. While the country tones are still very much present, they are in several cases more muted, offering a broader appeal to fans.

Among the high points on the album are three extended concept pieces or suites, one each from Ian, Sylvia, and David Rea. "Stories He'd Tell" is Ian's tribute in several musical passages to his late father George. "That was about the '50s," states Ian. "The part I really liked was about the horses and Armistice Day. When you get older certain isolated memories remain vivid but there are big gaps. That song was like a testimonial to my father." The orchestration serves to heighten the sentiment of the song. Sylvia's "Woman's World," another song cycle, explores the changing roles of women. "It was about being a little girl and seeing what the lives of the women you knew were like and coming to some decision that that was not what you wanted," Sylvia explains. "It was a coming of age song. I had started writing an autobiography but as I found out when I tried doing it again in 1972 the ideas ended up being used in songs. That was a more comfortable medium for me." As David Rea recalls, "'Woman's World' came out of a book Sylvia was writing about growing up in Chatham, Ontario. She allowed me to read parts of it at the time. It was a very moving account. She later told me it all went into songs."

Was she expressing a feminist point of view in this particular song? Sylvia demurs, revealing only that she was not consciously expressing a feminist perspective, just writing about what she felt and knew. "Influencing women wasn't my intent. I certainly had it pointed out to me when I wasn't expressing that sentiment. I tended to write about women as they are rather than as they should be. It may not have been politically correct but that's the way it is. You can't change history." Although the song is piano-driven, the tasteful use of orchestration again enhances the thoughtful mood. There was no denying the maturity and sophistication that both songwriters had achieved by this time. Encouraged to develop his songwriting further by Ian, David Rea was also influenced by longer musical pieces and composed "The Minstrel" in two distinct suites, from bluegrass to rock to delicately subtle, before reprising the hoedown feel. "The fiddle section on that song was to die for," boasts David. "Buddy Spicher, Tommy Jackson, and Vasser Clements. They're the best."

Toronto singer/songwriter Keith McKie from promising rock band Kensington Market (whose two albums were produced by

Felix Pappalardi) was another in a long line of young songwriters picked to contribute a song to an Ian & Sylvia album. He did so on the recommendation of David Rea. His "Please Think" is exquisitely handled by the duo and boasts some interesting pedal steel guitar playing from Weldon Myrick. Sylvia's funky "Shinbone Alley" was inspired by an actual street name she saw in New York. "I got very intrigued by the name and thought I could write a song about it." The two also dipped back into *The Basement Tapes* for "Tears of Rage," originally a collaboration between Bob Dylan and the Band's Richard Manuel.

Released in September 1968, *Full Circle* pleased both Ian and Sylvia. The album cover, front and back, is a study in contrasts. On the front is a rather urbane portrait photo by Daniel Kramer of the two around an elegant old wooden dining-room table with matching credenza, Sylvia in a stylish velvet gown and seated, Ian standing behind her, decked out in well-worn denim jeans and jean jacket; the artsy urban lady and the cowboy. On the back the two are presented on the farm with Sylvia and Clay astride Barney, Ian's favourite horse, with Ian, dressed in cowboy hat and denims, steadying the two. No doubt it was some art director's idea to place Sylvia on horseback, a position she rarely assumed. The only one of the three looking halfway comfortable is Clay.

The album marked another turning point for the two. "We had put out a couple of pretty bad albums before that," notes Sylvia, referring to *Play One More* and *So Much for Dreaming*, "and we had a long way to come back at that point. But we were happy with *Nashville* and *Full Circle*. There wasn't a single on *Full Circle*. We just probably have never been commercial-minded enough. The closest we ever came was 'Lovin' Sound' where we actually set out to do a single and produce it as such. Other than that we always had this sort of cock-eyed attitude that maybe there'll be something on the album which they think they can turn into a single. But there were none on *Full Circle*. At that point we had very little contact with the record company. They were going through their changes and there was no one there to give us any direction. It's just one of those horror stories you hope you never hear about in the music business. Three different label presidents while we were with them. Not only that, the staff changed weekly. You just never had any consistent contact with anyone. You'd talk to someone, then go in the next week and he'd be gone, and no one knew anything about what you'd talked about."

Having fulfilled their contractual obligations to both Vanguard and MGM, Ian & Sylvia found themselves by the end of 1968 without a recording contract. The two used the time to rest, Sylvia at home in Rosedale with Clay and Ian on his farm in Newtonville. "I commuted back and forth to the farm," says Ian. "I didn't stay out there. I had a housekeeper and her mother in the house and good old Dick, my farm manager, and they were all living in the house. I was always intending to build a really nice cedar log place of my own by the pond but I never did. My neighbour to the west of me made a whole lot of money by starting a landfill dump. I couldn't do anything about it and it brought the land value down.* That was the beginning of the end. In Newtonville they were just old hillbillies who didn't give a shit about environmental regulations. They do out there now, but back then they'd just dig a hole and dump trash in it. The guy who had the dump bought my farm later. He had the cash."

They played no dates from the beginning of July through to November 1. "We were fairly frugal," states Sylvia, "so we were doing okay during that period. We didn't blow our money on big

---

* Ian tried fighting the issue in the court but ultimately lost.

cars or big houses. But our cash flow dropped because there wasn't any money coming in." It was a time to reassess and regroup. As David Rea remembers, "Ian and I were in the car and he brought it up very gingerly, saying, 'We're going to stop working for awhile. Is that alright with you?' And it was fine with me because I was looking to go out solo anyway. So it was a very clean break. Very amicable. A mutual parting of the way. Shortly after that I hooked up with Felix Pappalardi and moved to New York City."

While there was no turning back from their country music recording direction, what did that mean for live performances? "It really got to the point where we realized that it wasn't enough to be doing it on records," offers Sylvia. "We had to be doing it onstage. And that meant a band. Having recorded the *Nashville* and *Full Circle* albums it wasn't satisfying enough to go out just with a guitarist backing us. It was the same old, same old. We had never toured with a band, and knowing what we could be doing with a band behind us it, was appealing to us. We sat down in the living room here in the house, Ian and I, and looked at each other and agreed that we didn't want to do it unless we did it this way. That was the decision to put a band together. We didn't have a lot to lose at that point. It was kind of the law of diminishing returns with what we had been doing previously. The whole management thing had changed and the gigs were not coming in as much." Ian concurs. "It became apparent that if we didn't carry this through, if we went back to touring in the folk circle in the same physical make-up instrumentally, then we'd be back where we started. And we wouldn't be getting off musically. At that point, if we didn't get off musically on the road, we weren't going on the road."

In the intervening months, country rock was beginning to take root out in southern California. The Byrds' *Sweetheart of the Rodeo* had been released in July,* as had Buffalo Springfield's *Last Time Around*, both featuring country instrumentation and arrangements. The Byrds had recruited renowned flatpicker Clarence White, whose innovative pullstring or B-bender device allowed him to recreate pedal steel guitar glissandos on a standard Fender Telecaster. Ex-Byrd Gene Clark had teamed up with ex-Dillards banjo ace Douglas Dillard to form seminal folk/country/bluegrass outfit the Fantastic Expedition of Dillard & Clark (including future Burrito Brother and founding Eagle Bernie Leadon). Richie Furay and Jimmy Messina from the final Buffalo Springfield lineup had teamed up with Randy Meisner (later another founding Eagle) and two players from Colorado† to form Poco, arguably one of the first bands to fully integrate country music with rock. That fall another former Byrd, Chris Hillman, teamed up with Gram Parsons in the Flying Burrito Brothers, another groundbreaking country-rock (more country than rock) aggregation. The climate seemed right for forming a country band. "I was open to experimenting with something different," states Ian. "It certainly wasn't any good staying where we were."

Amos Garrett had already established a reputation on the Yorkville music scene as a gifted acoustic guitar player with the Dirty Shames, a much admired folk outfit featuring singers Carol Robinson and Chick Roberts. He had recently switched back to electric guitar when Ian contacted him, suggesting he put a band together to back Ian & Sylvia. "Ian told me about his idea to do a country band with a heavier-sounding rhythm section," Amos recalls. "People weren't even using the phrase 'country rock' at the time. He asked me to be the guitar player and to help him find

---

* Initially panned by critics, the album's legendary status has been achieved only in hindsight.
† Including pedal steel guitarist extraordinaire Rusty Young.

musicians to fill out the band." As early as October, Amos was onboard, and shortly after brought in pedal steel guitarist Bill Keith. Better known for his banjo playing behind Bill Monroe as well as in the Kweskin Jug Band, Bill had recently taken up the pedal steel. "The Kweskin Jug Band had broken up, "states Bill, "and I'd done some recordings with them using steel guitar. Then I got a call from Ian Tyson asking if I'd like to be a part of this new band that would involve a lot of pedal steel playing. I was still learning as far as the steel guitar goes and welcomed the gig as an opportunity to learn more; kind of a trial by fire circumstance." Ken Kalmusky was retained on bass and jazz drummer Ricky Marcus joined.

The band began rehearsing in the basement of the Rosedale home as Ian & Sylvia continued to perform on their own. From the get-go it was Ian's vision that defined the sound and approach of the band. He called the shots. "But Sylvia was also writing songs and playing autoharp and piano," Amos points out. Even so, it was still a steep learning curve for Ian. "I was a very poor band leader," he admits. "I'd never done that, and never learned to do it. I could lead that band now. But it was one of those democratic '60s bands and that never works. It was a high-energy group but we really didn't know what we were doing. Don't let Amos tell you any different. He didn't know any more than the rest of us. He didn't know how to put his instrument out there in front of electric instruments. We weren't like those West Texas boys or Tennessee boys who'd been using amplifiers for the previous ten years. It was all new and I didn't have a clue." Ian's leadership style rubbed Bill Keith the wrong way. "In recalling the whole experience," he avers, "Ian's sharp edges and his authoritarian style were the salient characteristics of that gig for me. With Ian & Sylvia I was constantly made aware that I was an employee who worked for them and not at their level. There was very little camaraderie between the bosses and the sidemen. I was also learning about band dynamics and how to be a sideman in an electric band. With the Kweskin Jug Band things were very democratic, and it took some adjusting to work with the Ian Tyson mode of leadership. During rehearsals, however, things were a little more democratic. I was able to suggest things for arrangements and Ian would accept them."

Dubbed the Great Speckled Bird after an old Roy Acuff recording dating back to the 1930s (Johnny Cash, Kitty Wells, and Hank Locklin had all recorded the song more recently), it was also the name for a popular amphetamine (speed) pill used by long-haul truckers in the South and by Nashville studio players. As Sylvia explains, "The speed of choice for the Nashville musicians were these pink diet pills with red speckles and they called them great speckled birds."

By December the band began backing Ian & Sylvia out on the road. Long-time fan Wayne Reichardt caught up to them at the Cellar Door in Washington. "Even when they had the country-rock band the Great Speckled Bird they did not alienate the D.C. fans who still came out to see them," he recalls. "The diehards accepted them. They were stars there and they always got great press coverage in the Washington papers." Following that two-week stint the band played the Miami Pop Festival on December 30, where the response was less welcoming. "It was the end of Ian & Sylvia," Ian insists. "It put the nail in the coffin and probably all for the good. They were insulted, outraged – whatever. I remember the pop festival we played in Florida and we just absolutely died. It was horrible. Some strange women came up to us afterward telling us they liked it but that was two out of 20,000. Shortly thereafter our manager Albert Grossman handed us over to his partner

John Court and washed his hands of us." But not before negoti-
ating a recording contract for the new-look Ian & Sylvia and
band with his own Bearsville label distributed by Ampex, a company better known for its recording technology than for selling
records. Bert Block from the Grossman office became their manager soon after.

Ian & Sylvia soldiered on, working the kinks out of their new
band, sound, and presentation. Despite their experience at the
Cellar Door, not everyone was receptive to the new Ian & Sylvia.
"Some of our dedicated folk music fans were horrified at the sight
of a pedal steel guitar," claims Sylvia. "It was tough on Ian &
Sylvia audiences and tough on us, too, as a result. It was not what
Ian & Sylvia fans expected from us. At one of our very first gigs
at Western University in London with Bill Keith on steel guitar,
people got up and walked out when they saw that steel guitar
being set up." It is especially disheartening when your audience
doesn't even want to hear what you have to offer. "We knew we
had alienated our traditional Ian & Sylvia audience." Ian's recollections are similar. "We thought it was the right idea, and it was,
but we lost control of that once the word got out and all the
morose Ian & Sylvia fans, with their long, ironed hair, sat in front
of us, denigrating what we were trying to do." Adds Amos Garrett,
"If they saw me uncasing a Telecaster or a set of drums onstage
they might walk out. But that was just the era and it happened
to others as well. We did very well in concert, though. We drew
big crowds and didn't have a lot of that antagonistic stuff like
Dylan had when he went electric. When we played for audiences
who didn't really know the band we went over big-time. It was
just part of the period. There were folk music fans who were very
resentful about any kind of change. And Ian and Sylvia were vic-
timized to a certain degree by their acoustic music audience."

They were not alone. Most of their country-rock contemporaries experienced similar responses, although in their cases, with the exception of the Byrds, they all carried no excess baggage of expectation, given that they were all newcomers. Not only were young hippie audiences not yet sure about country music, promoters were in uncharted waters and tended to simply book country-rock artists onto the rock circuit. So you would have the Flying Burrito Brothers playing Detroit's legendary rock hall the Grande Ballroom alongside hard rockers the MC5, or playing the Seattle Pop Festival with Led Zeppelin, the Guess Who, and the Doors. Ian & Sylvia and the Great Speckled Bird were booked at New York's premier rock venue, the Fillmore East, as well as at the Electric Factory in Philadelphia and the Atlanta Pop Festival. It was all so new.

With the American East Coast and southern California the tried-and-true turf for Ian & Sylvia, their bookings still followed that pattern, only this time with the country band. "We played the East Coast from New England down to as far south as Washington, D.C.," recalls Amos. "We pounded the Northeast real hard." For Bill Keith, the steady road work was not what he had bargained for. "The way it worked on a financial level," he explains, "was that Ian & Sylvia took equal shares, which meant the two of them got half the money and the four of us split the rest. But it was up to each of us to pay our travel expenses. There were several occasions where the four of us would rent a car and drive and Ian & Sylvia would fly first-class. That didn't promote a lot of harmony within the band. I remember we had a job down in New Jersey and I drove down from Cambridge, Massachusetts [where Bill resided]. After that, Ian said, there was a rehearsal in Toronto on Tuesday and then after that there'd be no work for two weeks. It meant me driving up from Cambridge for a rehearsal and having to pay my own expenses including accommodation. So I told Ian that for me to come up there for one rehearsal wasn't logistically right for me. And Ian replied, 'If you want your job you'll show up for that rehearsal.'"

On Tuesday evening, February 25, 1969, Ian was in New York between gigs in Vermont and New Hampshire and happened into Steve Paul's Scene, a hip club and popular musicians' hangout at 301 West 46th Street. That night, the Flying Burrito Brothers were making their New York debut.* Ian was aware of the band, having known Chris Hillman since before the Byrds, but had yet to see or hear them (their debut album, *The Gilded Palace of Sin*, was released a few weeks later). What he saw and heard was both a revelation and validation of his own decision to go with a country band. Recalling the moment, he says, "The volume, which was deafening, I remember. They were right up there with Cream for loudness, tremendously loud and you couldn't hear what they were doing over this huge gigantic wall of drawl and twang. But Gram [Parsons] was a real charismatic kid. I really liked what they were doing. After that I started persuading Sylvia that we should move in that direction." That direction meant adding more of a rock kick to their country music. It also meant changing personnel. Ian caught the Burritos several times that week. The five Burrito Brothers were festooned in their distinctive sequined Nudie† suit finery with enough sequins to make Little Jimmy Dickens envious. "I remember Gram's Nudie jacket. I said to him, 'That thing looks mighty hot' and he said, 'Yeah, it is, but it's my Nudie jacket and I'm wearing it anyway.'"

---

* Their debut was in fact slated for the night before but a snowstorm in New England delayed their arrival.

† Nudie Cohn (not Cohen as is often spelled) had been designing custom suits for country and western artists for decades out of Nudie's Rodeo Tailors shop on Lankershim Boulevard in L.A.

Although they were touring with the band, Ian & Sylvia made a guest appearance alone on *The Johnny Cash Show*, taped between May 27 and 29, with Charlie Pride and Mason Williams also guesting. The episode aired September 6. Long-time fan Johnny gave them a warm introduction. "I suppose I really know when I like a piece of music. I hear it and say, 'I wish I'd written that.' In the case of the two people you're about to meet I've said those words many, many times concerning their songs, believe me. From the land of the maple and the Douglas fir meet my sweet-singing friends Ian & Sylvia." The duo performed "Lovin' Sound" live before the audience at Nashville's hallowed Ryman Auditorium and followed that with what Ian announced as a brand-new song from Sylvia entitled "Give It to the World." The appealing gospel-flavoured country singalong would ultimately be recorded during sessions for their debut with Columbia Records in 1971 and released as a single the following year. It did not appear on an album until a 1996 Bear Family Records compilation out of Germany, under the rather uninspired title *Ian & Sylvia – The Beginning of the End*.

On the weekend of August 15 through 17, 1969, when over half a million young people converged on a farm near the community of Bethel in upstate New York and the world first heard of Woodstock, Ian & Sylvia and the Great Speckled Bird were in the general vicinity, playing Friday the 15th at Nassau County College in Garden City, Long Island, followed the next night by the Singer Bowl in Flushing Meadows, New York. One assumes they were aware of the events further upstate from the extensive media coverage. The next day they travelled to Washington for a week at the Cellar Door. It was at that point that Bill Keith had enough and quit. Drummer Ricky Marcus was also not cutting it and Ian, with a heavier drum sound in mind, gave him his walking papers. "He was a terrible drummer and was a hippie kind of guy," grouses Ian. "It didn't work."

According to Amos Garrett's recollections, "I don't think Ricky and Bill anticipated being on the road as much as Ian & Sylvia did. That was primarily why Bill left. Sylvia didn't want to be away from Clay for long periods at a time so we developed a touring routine of out for four days, home for three. We might do a two-week gig but mostly it was out for a few days, then home for a few days."

With the band in a state of disarray, Ian and Sylvia took the down time for separate holidays, reflective not of any marital strife but merely of diverging personal interests. The last week of August, Sylvia travelled to California, and upon her return in the first week of September, Ian then headed out to Alberta. Back in Toronto by the middle of the month, they set about lining up replacements on drums and pedal steel guitar. N. D. (Norman) Smart II came highly recommended by Felix Pappalardi. A veteran of rock bands the Remains and Mountain (with Felix), N.D. would put the rock in Ian & Sylvia's brand of country rock. "I was playing in Mountain at the time and living in New York," states N.D. "But I got tired of playing so loud, the volume was getting to me. Felix and I had an agreement that he would find another drummer, and he knew of a band up in Canada that Amos Garrett was playing with. Felix knew Ian and Sylvia and he gave them a call. Me and [pedal steel guitarist] Buddy Cage joined the band at the same time." N.D.'s rock experience brought a stronger drum sound to the band. "That's what made it country rock," he chuckles. "That's probably one of the positive influences Mountain exerted." Adds Amos, "Mountain was a hard rock, almost heavy metal, band."

"N. D. Smart was a helluva drummer," stresses Ian, "but he wasn't a country drummer. He was a rock drummer. N.D. and I never got along but he was a good drummer. He, Buddy, and Amos helped define the sound of the Great Speckled Bird." Pedal steel guitarist Buddy Cage (Gary Saul) was recruited from the local Toronto country music bar scene. "I'd heard about Buddy through the local musical grapevine," Ian recalls. "He used to play at the Matador and the Horseshoe Tavern. Waylon Jennings used to play at the Matador when he'd come through. So I knew about Buddy. We found him playing in a country bar in Oshawa. We went out to see him there and offered him the job." The intricate interplay between Buddy's pedal steel and Amos's Telecaster became a hallmark of the Great Speckled Bird's sound, an aggressive attack like no other contemporary country-rock outfit. As N.D. recalls, "Amos composed all his solos. He didn't play them off the top of his head. He wasn't an improviser. He would go out there and start a solo and have it fall apart. That's why Amos and Buddy worked so well together, because they caused each other to compose things in the music and the band would really sound polished because of that. That band with Ian & Sylvia was up for *anything*. We could have gone anywhere."

"Buddy had a huge impact on my style of guitar playing," Amos acknowledges. "I envied the fact that a pedal steel guitarist could glissando more than one note simultaneously, and I thought it would be great if I could do the same. The multi-string bending that I came up with was an attempt by me to play some figures in unison with Buddy or harmonize with him.* We worked out some interesting acoustical things, almost panning from one side of the stage where Buddy was to the other side where I was. One of us would memorize the last couple of bars of the other guy's solo and we would double each other in unison and then the

---

* Amos Garrett's calling card remains his innovative string-bending solo in Maria Muldaur's 1974 hit "Midnight at the Oasis."

next solo would immediately follow. So it was like the solo instantly panned across the stage." With Amos and Buddy driving the instrumentation, the Great Speckled Bird became an incendiary live act. Even non-fans of country-rock had to acknowledge the dynamics and excitement of their performances, and other musicians took note. "We loved the Great Speckled Bird," says Craig Fuller of Pure Prairie League, who enjoyed several country-rock hits in the wake of the Eagles, including "Amie" and "Two Lane Highway." "Amos Garrett and Buddy Cage were incredible." Another admirer was Bernie Leadon, one-time Burrito Brother and founding member of the Eagles, who cites the Bird among a handful of influential pioneering country-rock groups. "The interplay between those two was the real driving force at that time in the band," acknowledges later Great Speckled Bird bass player Jim Colegrove. "That became the sound of the band, Amos and Buddy. My memory was that it was Ian's idea to put a band together that was based on Buck Owen's Buckaroos, who had a real raw electric sound."

There was no denying that the Great Speckled Bird band rejuvenated both Ian and Sylvia and they began in earnest writing for a band sound. It was an exciting time for them. They were taking a risk musically and it stimulated their creative juices. Ian was in his element, country music, and although not steeped in that genre to the same extent as her partner, Sylvia nonetheless stepped up. "Ian & Sylvia were writing a great volume of material at that time," notes Amos, "and much of it was inspired by the people they were playing with. Ian & Sylvia were not your typical country music songwriters. Their songs were more sophisticated and adventurous. So I knew we were on some kind of new path. We didn't call it country rock. Someone else put that label on it later."

Reconstituted, the band hit the road running in October, playing dates on both coasts and appearing on *The Mike Douglas Show*
(Philadelphia), *The Della Reese Show* (Los Angeles), Joey Bishop's
late-night talk show (Los Angeles), *The Wayne & Shuster Show*
(Toronto), as well as another CBC TV special from Toronto.
Despite the higher profile, the gigs had been booked months earlier for Ian & Sylvia, folk duo, and often audiences were unpre-
pared for a hot pickin' country-rock band fronted by the two.
"We'd play these colleges," avers Ian, "and they'd say afterwards,
after everyone had walked out on us, 'That's it for these guys. Not
having them back again.' And we'd never get invited back. A lot
of Ian & Sylvia fans were pretty square. As long as we were playing acoustic we were fine. That's all they wanted, acoustic music.
That shows their lack of discrimination or tolerance of something
new. If you were acoustic you were okay and if you were electric
you weren't okay. A lot of the long-time Ian & Sylvia fans just
shut it down when we went electric. So we lost our old fans but
didn't build up enough new ones."

There were further problems in their new electric direction.
"When we first started out we played too loud," Ian recalls. "It
sounded pretty bad, pretty garbled. It was tough performing live
because you often couldn't hear yourself. There were no monitors
back then. So being on pitch was a challenge sometimes because
we simply couldn't hear the blend of voices." Amos Garrett concurs. "The first incarnation of the Bird was playing way too loud.
Ian was losing his voice and had to quit smoking because he
couldn't smoke and sing. When the second lineup came about, even
with N.D., we actually played quieter than the original one. We
found the volume level and dynamic that worked best for the music
and Ian was real happy after that."

"Our reputation started to get around the country and people turned off," Ian continues. "The old fans wouldn't come. The reputation had gone ahead: 'Oh, Ian & Sylvia? They've got a loud country band and it sounds awful and they don't do their old stuff anymore. Don't go.' All of this would have been instantly rectified by a hit but we didn't get one. But, you know, I don't regret any of it. I think it got us out of a very bad musical perspective we had got into with the round of college concerts. It was like a rerun every night you worked. Having something new shook us out of a complacency thing. Performers that we knew, contemporaries on the folk scene, got lulled into this myth that people don't want you to change. People always request the old songs because that's what they know. I was open to experimenting with something different. It certainly wasn't any good staying where we were." Rejection by their fan base had nothing to do with any image shift on the part of Ian or Sylvia. Neither were decked out in rhinestone-encrusted Nudie suits and Stetsons onstage. For all intents and purposes they looked the same as in their folky duo days, only Ian's hair and sideburns were longer. No, the rejection was based solely on the music. Country music had yet to find wide acceptance among both the younger hippie audiences and the diehard folk community. Ian & Sylvia were a couple of years off the mark.

"There were some fans who really liked it and were ready to go with it," affirms Ian. "They figured any change we wanted to make was okay with them. They're the kind of fans you'd like to have but there weren't enough of them. The worst date we ever played was with Tom Paxton in Central Park in New York. There was so little musical communication with that crowd and I was so mad that when we left the stage I made an obscene gesture to the crowd. It was a dreadful night. We boogied hard that night and they hated us. It was awful. But somebody had to pave the way. There were triumphs; it wasn't all that bad. I remember playing in Philadelphia and the hundred or so kids that were there loved it. We played the Atlanta Pop Festival and everything gelled and they liked us. We blew a lot of chances but I don't regret it. We were still creating and making valid, honest music."

Sessions for an album began on early November 1969 at Jack Clements's Belmont studios in Nashville. Charlie Tallent was once again engineering the sessions but Albert Grossman parachuted eccentric rocker Todd Rundgren, late of the Anglophile band the Nazz and a recent Bearsville signing as a recording artist in his own right, to produce the album. It was a bizarre matchup. Todd had as much of an association with country rock as Ian & Sylvia had with psychedelic acid rock. In the event, much of the direction of the album came from Ian and Charlie, despite the production credit going to Todd. "Todd Rundgren freaked me out," Ian insists. "I couldn't stand him. That was Albert's decision, not mine, and I didn't agree with that at all. I respected Albert because he was a very smart man but I didn't think Todd was the right guy. He was supposed to be producer but he didn't know what he was doing. Charlie Tallent was the engineer and producer, sort of."

"Talk about your basic culture clash," laughs Sylvia. "There was Todd looking like the fourteen-year-old-girl who never got invited to the prom. He was skinny with his long stringy hair. And he had with him Miss Christine from the GTOs [Girls Together Outrageously, Frank Zappa's protégés]. They were sort of twin-like, with long hair. She'd be sitting there in the studio every day knitting him a sweater. Nashville did not take to Todd or her. I don't think they had ever seen anything like it. They took one look at them and said, 'Unh unh.' But the musicians didn't seem to have a problem with Todd, it was the police and the establishment who did."

The sessions had their fair share of shenanigans. As Ian explains, "Back then record companies were throwing money around. In the studio we were doping and had black hookers in and out – not when Sylvia was around, of course. It was ridiculous. We were completely irresponsible. If you did that today the budget would be just astronomical. I wouldn't put up with that kind of shit now but we were young and stupid. A lot of the guys would get high every day. I didn't get high every day. But we screwed around in the studio. Once we were playing baseball with tennis balls in the studio. It was just crazy. But in spite of that there was some great music made. It was done off the floor and the vocals were done live. Everything was done live although Amos would *still* be over-dubbing if we'd have let him."

This was Amos Garrett's first time in a Nashville recording studio and he has fond memories of the experience. "I remember Harold Bradley who was hired to play rhythm guitar on the album. He was a really neat guy and a great player. He liked my playing. He had an immense guitar collection, everything and anything you could imagine. At the end of every session he'd ask, 'Do you want me to bring any special guitars tomorrow?' I asked him if he had any Telecasters and he replied, 'Well, I've got about twenty-five of 'em.' He'd be bringing in these amazing archtop guitars, too. His collection must have been worth millions. I also remember Waylon Jennings and Willie Nelson wandering into the studio once when we were recording. Waylon still had a greasy DA haircut and Willie had a brush cut. And they were so drunk Willie could barely play. I knew who Waylon was because he was one of my favourite Telecaster players and I'd met him up in Canada when he played the Horseshoe Tavern. But I had no idea who Willie Nelson was. So I pulled Waylon aside and asked him, 'Who's the guy in the crewcut?' and he said, 'That's Willie Nelson!' I replied,

'Who's he?' and Waylon looked at me and said, 'He wrote "Crazy,"' and sang a bit of it. I went, 'Oh, *that guy!*' They were just wall-eyed drunk and just as nice as can be."

Studio misbehaviour aside, the Great Speckled Bird managed to lay down twelve tracks, eleven of which were originals from Ian or Sylvia or both, the lone cover being "Crazy Arms." Although Nashville was initially wary of the long-haired band, the band members were ultimately welcomed. "Getting the acceptance of the Nashville crowd was tough," notes N.D., "but we earned that. They couldn't get used to the longhairs but they got to like us. They were taking us out to dinner. They were surprised that we could play. 'These long-haired assholes can really play!'" With N.D.'s pounding drumming setting the pace (Ian tried session player Kenny Buttrey on one track but he didn't have the same punch) and the twin leads of Amos and Buddy, Ian & Sylvia's songs took on a whole new attitude and swagger as the album took shape quickly. The experience of working with a band over the last few months had recharged their writing and the group had a wealth of material. "What made the Great Speckled Bird different from the other country-rock groups like the Burritos," asserts bass player Jim Colegrove, who joined the group following the record-ing sessions, "was that Ian and Sylvia were singing the songs. To me it was a tremendous difference in style. Most of the material was theirs, too. They came at a lot of it from a different angle. Sylvia certainly had her say on how her songs were going to go, but I just always felt like the band represented Ian's vision. He thought he was forming a band akin to the Buckaroos and it worked, arrangement-wise, like the Buckaroos." As Sylvia reveals, "I was writing during a very optimistic period so I was writing very optimistic songs. We had gained confidence. Part of it was having a band that we worked with all the time." That optimism is best exemplified in "We Sail," whose lyrics reflect the hope for a new beginning, not only for humankind but for Ian & Sylvia's new venture. "That song became popular for high school graduations," smiles Sylvia.

Bass player Ken Kalmusky had been dropped from the lineup prior to the recordings ("He wasn't a good enough player," states Ian) and Nashville session player Norbert Putnam took on the bass duties, with David Briggs contributing piano, on the album. "They all figured that you had to have the hit done before lunch or there was something wrong with you," recalls N.D. on the Nashville recording routine. "But we weren't in there for two or three hours watching the clock. We were in the studio for eighteen hours at a stretch. And David Briggs and Norbert Putnam were loving this because they were getting paid triple scale."

Released in April 1970, the album, simply titled *Great Speckled Bird*, opened with a thundering drum intro, thumping bass, and screaming guitars that left little doubt where the direction of the music was going, with the band in full flight right out of the nest. Ian's "Love What You're Doing Child" is a funky rocker, with Ian singing with bold confidence. From that auspicious start the album covers plenty of country-rock territory, from ballads like "Calgary," "Flies in the Bottle" ("A hell of a song," boasts Sylvia), and "This Dream," to the honky-tonk swing of Sylvia's "Trucker's Cafe" (later covered by Kitty Wells), "Smiling Wine," and "Crazy Arms" sung *en français* (with Ian on a rare harmony part), based on an arrangement by the popular French Canadian chanteuse Lucille Starr.* "Rio Grande" was a collaboration between Amos and Ian and has a Marty Robbins feel and contemporary twist with the

---

* Winnipeg-born Lucille Starr's "The French Song" became an international hit in 1964. She once held the top 5 positions on the South Africa charts and was number 1 in the Netherlands for nineteen weeks running. Sylvia still regards Lucille as the finest country singer Canada ever produced.

line, "There was cocaine falling like snow on the mountains." One of the standout tracks is Ian's "Long Long Time to Get Old," propelled by Smart's thundering tom-toms and cowbell. "'Long Long Time' is one of the best songs I ever wrote and the band played it great," says Ian. "That became N. D. Smart's signature, the cowbell and the groove. It all came together on that song." Boasts N.D., "I was playing that beat in his basement, he liked it, and he wrote that song around it." The song would go on to become the theme song for Ian's television series *Nashville North*.

Beyond the superb songwriting and incomparable musicianship, what was further astonishing about the album was the complete absence of Ian & Sylvia's name on the cover. The album was simply titled *Great Speckled Bird*. "The thinking behind that," Sylvia explains, "was that it was to be a band and that we were a part of that band. We tried to make the band into an entity and submerge our identity into it. We were naive. We didn't think at that point we had anything to lose, so why not submerge our names within the band?" Ian concurs. "That was all planned. We thought we needed to get away from the Ian & Sylvia label because we were doing something different." The decision only succeeded in confusing record buyers. Bearsville later added a sticker to the front cover stating "Ian & Sylvia" to alert fans that this was indeed an Ian & Sylvia album. But by then it was likely too late. To Ian and Sylvia's misfortune, Bearsville Records' distributor Ampex put little energy into promoting or distributing the album, which came and went without much fanfare. "I think that album had an impact among musicians," claims Ian, who remains very proud of the *Great Speckled Bird* disc. "It was like a little rocket that went off, left some carbon sparks, and then died. I had to check out the remastering for the CD re-release a few years back and I was blown away. Stuff like 'Flies in the Bottle' stand up well. There's some good stuff there." If the record-buying public failed to notice, musicians did not. "*Great Speckled Bird* is considered a landmark," says Sylvia. "I've talked to people over the years in Nashville who recall that album as a signpost that things were changing both in country and in folk. It had an influence." Notes singer/songwriter Tom Russell, "That album is a cornerstone of the country-rock movement that emerged in the 1970s."

In the New Year, Jim Colegrove joined the band on bass, rec-ommended by his friend N. D. Smart. He attended a rehearsal in the basement of the Rosedale home and "after about an hour or so Ian was satisfied and told me I was in the band. Ian was the guy calling the shots and the one we listened to. If he wanted something done he got it. Ian was a tough guy, no question about it. But I think I got along with him better than anyone else in his band. That's why I lasted the longest. Sylvia brought her material to the band and had a say in how she wanted it arranged but we still saw it as Ian's band." Gigs continued through the spring of 1970, concentrating more on week-long club dates than on one-nighters. Jim recalls an incident at Mr. Kelley's club in Chicago. "One night someone in the audience was talking too loudly and Ian was P.O.'d because it was interrupting his show. He didn't like that. If someone was messing with him he'd mess with them right back. During that period Ian would play an electric Fender Telecaster near the end of the set. I can't remember exactly what number it was but at the end of the song Ian walked off the stage toward this guy with the Telecaster in his hand. I thought, 'Oh shit! He's going to cleave that guy's head open with his Tele.' But as it turned out the guy was very apologetic to Ian, which was a good thing because Ian would fight at the drop of a hat and usu-ally kick their ass."

In June, the Great Speckled Bird made its Troubadour debut to a packed house, many in the audience country-rock players themselves who had heard the album and the buzz surrounding the group. "Everybody associated with country rock in southern California was there to see us," boasts Jim Colegrove. "We got a great review in *Cashbox*." Sylvia recalls a humorous incident during their Troubadour stand. "We were playing three sets a night and it was full every night. Amos kept getting louder and louder with each set. We couldn't figure it out. It was deafening; people in the first few rows had their fingers in their ears. Finally we said to him, 'Why are you playing so loud?' And he said, 'Well, my friend Fritz Richmond says he can't hear me.' So we said, 'Where is Fritz?' It turned out he was sitting in the bar at the front, not in the club itself where we were playing."

That same month the Speckled Bird flew to Osaka, Japan, for a two-week engagement beginning May 24, playing the Canadian Pavilion at Japan's Expo 70 world's fair. "The Japanese *love* country music," enthuses N. D. Smart. "It was encores and standing room only every night." Sylvia describes the striking pavilion, designed by renowned Canadian architect Arthur Erickson. "It was like a pyramid with the top chopped off and it had entrances in each of the corners. It was covered in mirrors so it would change every hour as the sun moved. The stage was set up over the water that flowed through the pavilion. It was quite spectacular." The band members were housed in an apartment building in Osaka. "We were there for two weeks and stayed in these new-rise apartments that were built to house people coming to the World's Fair," recalls Jim Colegrove. "We were paid in advance and we only worked twice a day, an afternoon and an evening set. It was over by 8:00 p.m. The rest of the time was ours. So the whole thing was wonderful. The five of us – the band and road manager Michael

Friedman – rented a car and toured around for a couple of days.
Ian and Sylvia might have done that too, but not with us. In general they didn't hang out much with us." Amos continues. "The
five of us went into downtown Osaka, which was like the Chicago
of Japan: very industrial, not very pretty, but the second-largest
city in Japan. The dollar went quite far in those days. We just
rented a taxi cab for a whole day and it cost us about fifty dollars
in total. We went up as far as Kyoto one day and Nara the next.
Those were the temple cities with the most magnificent Buddhist
temples."

"They loved us in Japan," Ian attests. "It was a lot of fun. But
we saw the American soldiers coming back from Vietnam for some
rest and relaxation and they were like ghosts. You could spot them,
these haunted-looking guys with hollow eyes. There was no mis-
taking them, nineteen-year-old kids who looked seventy-nine. I
could have ended up like them."

Returning to Canada, the band joined the infamous Festival
Express tour, a kind of rolling thunder revue of the hottest acts
in popular music at the time, travelling across Canada on a spe-
cially equipped (including several bar cars) Canadian National
Railway chartered train. The brains behind the tour were promoter Ken Walker and backer Thor Eaton of the Eaton's department store dynasty. In the end the tour lost over half a million
dollars but it remains a legendary event in music history. With a
lineup boasting the Band, Janis Joplin (and her Full Tilt Boogie
Band), the Grateful Dead, Mountain, Delaney & Bonnie & Friends,
and Eric Andersen, Ian & Sylvia were among friends. "Everyone
on that train was at their peak," Sylvia avers. "If you look at the
Band, that was them at their best; and Janis, too. She was just
coming into her own as the singer she really was just before she
died." Initially intended as a cross-Canada tour beginning in

Montreal and ending in Vancouver, these two cities backed out of hosting the concerts, so instead the tour began in Toronto at CNE Stadium the weekend of June 27 and 28. Ian & Sylvia and the Great Speckled Bird played the Saturday date, but instead of boarding the train they headed to North Tonawanda, New York, just across the border from Ontario between Niagara Falls and Buffalo, for a concert Sunday night. They then flew out to join the tour and train in Winnipeg on July 1.

On the train the partying never paused. "One lounge car was for blues and rock, and the other was country and folk," recalls Sylvia. "We all got along fine. There were jam sessions non-stop." The unending reverie had its memorable moments. "The Grateful Dead ran out of other substances around Winnipeg and started drinking and it was not a pretty sight," laughs Sylvia. "I didn't really drink at that point, but I think Janis Joplin outdrank Amos, and *that* was quite an accomplishment." Recalls Ian with a smile, "I was drunk the whole time. I recall getting into a drinking contest with Janis Joplin and I was seriously overmatched. She drank me under the table. I remember me and somebody else [the Grateful Dead's Jerry Garcia] crawling onto the roof of one of these train cars and howling like coyotes." The train had to make an emergency stop in Saskatoon to refill their depleted liquor stock.

"Jerry Garcia was a great person," maintains Ian. "He was perfect for that situation and just loved to play, a real California hippie the way they were supposed to be. A lot of seeds were sown on that trip. Everyone acquitted themselves quite honourably." Adds N.D., "We were the darlings of that tour. We were the one everybody stood on the sidelines and watched. And they'd come out and jam with us." Indeed, Jerry Garcia had recently gotten into playing pedal steel guitar and was taken by Buddy Cage's virtuosity. He would stand onstage at Buddy's side to watch him at each of the concerts, unfettered by the audience seeing him. "Jerry was fascinated by Buddy's playing," Sylvia remembers. One of the more unforgettable moments on the train was when Jerry and Buddy jammed. "The New Riders of the Purple Sage were a new group then," states Jim Colegrove, "and Jerry Garcia was playing pedal steel guitar for them. So the two were playing and finally Jerry just stopped and said to Buddy, 'Sorry, I can't keep up with you.'" A year later, when Jerry left the New Riders, he recommended Buddy as his replacement. "Jerry was just starting to fool around with the steel at that time," says Amos, "but Buddy had been playing since he was a child, so he was very advanced."

Sylvia insists she did not partake in the partying, preferring to retreat to her sleeping compartment. "I remember talking to Jackie Burroughs who was married to Zal Yanovsky and working in Albert Grossman's office," chuckles Sylvia, "and her telling me later that her memory of me on the train through all the partying was my sitting in a corner reading a book." The subsequent film of the event, compiled by Gavin Poolman and Bob Smeaton and released in 2003, includes much footage from the endless boozy jam sessions, including Sylvia and Jerry Garcia, a former bluegrass banjo player himself, harmonizing on an old bluegrass song.

Despite the non-stop reverie and exciting performances, the tour was plagued by protests at every stop, which cut into attendance numbers. Requiring a total tour attendance figure of roughly 150,000 people to break even, the tour barely attracted 70,000. Tickets were priced at between $10 (Winnipeg) and $14 (Toronto and Calgary) for the multi-act concert, but a protest group calling itself the May 4th Movement picketed each venue, insisting the ticket price was a rip-off and demanding the concert be declared free to everyone. "It was ridiculous because it was a cheap ticket price for the top acts in music at that point," states Sylvia.

"We were going through the parking lot with Janis who was going to her car and a couple of little teenyboppers from the protest group yelled out, 'Janis Joplin is a rip-off.' She started in on them, telling them how much it cost for her band to travel, to put on a show, how much it cost for her clothes, concluding with, 'And furthermore, if I looked like you I'd sell my ass.' That was Janis. When we were in Calgary, which was a very strange scene there, someone had stolen Janis's fur coat that the Southern Comfort company had given to her. So she was ready to chew nails and spit rust. She was not happy."

Protests in Toronto were fuelled by a claim that the local police on horseback were beating young people. "The police weren't busting heads," Sylvia insists. "The road manager for the Dead was agitating the situation by claiming all this so the Grateful Dead could appear to be the band of the people and go play for free in a park. The police in Toronto were so good. Yes, they were mounted but they were acting cool about the whole thing. Under the circumstances the police were remarkably cool." A hastily organized alternate concert was staged at a nearby public park to placate the protesters. "The presenters in each city were terrified there was going to be some kind of riot from this May 4th Movement. That had such an adverse affect on the whole thing. The mayor of Calgary got in on the act, declaring, 'Let the children of Calgary in for free,' with Ken Walker saying 'Screw you' and punching him. Then the manager of the stadium said, 'I have a solution. We'll let them in for free but they have to pay to get out!'"

At Winnipeg Stadium (where the concert was part of the annual Red River Exhibition, temporarily renamed Manisphere), Delaney Bramlett of Delaney & Bonnie & Friends joined Ian & Sylvia onstage during their set. "In Winnipeg some drug-crazed hippie climbed up on the stage and tried to grab N.D.'s drum sticks," laughs Sylvia. "Big mistake. N.D. put down his sticks, punched him, and went back to playing without missing a beat. By the time we turned around it was all over." On the last date on the tour, Calgary's McMahon Stadium, the Speckled Bird was joined by a whole host of players and singers for a rousing version of "Will the Circle Be Unbroken." Following the concert, Ian got into an altercation as the band was driving out of the parking lot. Someone in a passing car shouted out a comment that N.D. took offence to. "N. D. Smart with his big mouth got us into this brawl," notes Ian, "a genuine street brawl. N. D. Smart started it and I had to finish it. And I ended up breaking my hand on this guy's head and had to play two days later."*

What the Festival Express tour underscored was the fact that Ian & Sylvia's country-rock excursion with the Great Speckled Bird was received far better by their peers than by their fans. "The Speckled Bird album was almost music for musicians," muses Ian, "and that can be a trap somehow. Almost without exception the people that I know who really liked that album and who played it a lot were musicians. It's very nice to have the respect of your colleagues but the recording business is not based on selling records to musicians or it would go broke. I'm very proud of the *Great Speckled Bird* album. It was a very uncompromising album, a statement of how we felt modern country-rock music should be played and interpreted. It was certainly uncompromising from a commercial perspective. A lot of artists won't admit any knowledge or motivation to the commercial end of it but one has to take that into consideration whether one admits that or not." The fact

---

* The *Festival Express* DVD released in 2004 includes footage of Ian & Sylvia and the Great Speckled Bird performing onstage, jamming on the train, plus interviews with Sylvia.

remained that the album had sold poorly despite the commitment of all the participants. Like almost all country-rock albums before 1972, its groundbreaking stature has been conferred largely in hindsight.

"I'm all for Gram Parsons," muses Tom Russell, who witnessed first-hand the birth of country rock in the late '60s, "but Gram gets all the credit for *everything* that happened in country rock pre Eagles and that simply wasn't true.* Ian & Sylvia were doing it with the Great Speckled Bird. They just never got the recognition. It was a transitional period. Then, of course, the Eagles took all that everyone was doing, filtered it, smoothed it out, and made it commercial. Ian & Sylvia just weren't able to fly it. They couldn't put that sound on the road unless they had a lot of money behind them. It had to be amplified properly and they weren't making that kind of money to do that and that's why it didn't fly."

Ian remains wistful about the Great Speckled Bird and their country-rock band experiment. "It was an offshoot of Ian & Sylvia, a fork in the road that we explored like Lewis and Clark: a tributary that we travelled up with sincerity until mutinous forces within our group and rejection by our recording company brought it to an end. It was just completely incompatible. But our karma was such that on the occasional night in the recording studio we made some music that's a little bit timeless and of that era."

---

* Parsons helped steer the Byrds in a country direction before forming country-rock pioneers the Flying Burrito Brothers. His death by drug misadventure in 1973 at age twenty-six cast him as an ill-starred country-rock Hank Williams and godfather to the genre.

NASHVILLE NORTH

If Ian & Sylvia's fortunes were ebbing south of the border by the start of the '70s, in Canada they continued to maintain a healthy cachet. They were among an elite group of Canadian popular music artists that included the likes of Gordon Lightfoot, Neil Young, Joni Mitchell, Leonard Cohen, Buffy Sainte-Marie, Paul Anka, Anne Murray, the Band, and David Clayton Thomas. For Canadians, absence only seemed to make the heart grow fonder. The longer an artist was away in the United States, the more Canadians embraced him or her back home, as if validation stateside was somehow a prerequisite for acclaim in Canada. That peculiarly Canadian phenomenon may be less pronounced in more recent years but it's still at the core of a Canadian artist's celebrity (just ask Avril Lavigne, Barenaked Ladies, Celine Dion, Shania Twain, or Justin Bieber).

As far back as early January 1970, months before the *Great Speckled Bird* album had been released or Festival Express had taken to the rails, CTV (the Canadian Television Network, a group of fifteen affiliated stations across the country) was taking a long look at Ian & Sylvia for a possible weekly television music show. In November 1969, Ian & Sylvia had hosted a CBC live music special entitled *Rock 1* and CTV was looking to capitalize on the live audience format. "*Nashville North* was a direct cop from *Rock 1*," Ian acknowledges. "But the CBC would never do anything weekly. They're little old ladies. Gerry [Rochon] saw the show and he's a pretty perceptive cat." In mid January, Ian met with Gerry (Gerard) Rochon, CTV's executive producer in charge of programming, at the Canadiana Motel in Toronto to explore possibilities. Although Ian & Sylvia's recording career was in decline by that point, the two met again a week later at CFTO's studios, the flagship station for the CTV network. In late February a pilot was shot at CFTO with producer/director Michael Steele in charge, just to see how Ian worked as host and if the concept – all music, limited host-guest banter – looked. Guests were Anne Murray (there had been brief discussions about having Anne co-host), Bobby Bare, and Sylvia. In an effort to appeal to potential U.S. syndicated stations for possible licensing, the show was given the name *Nashville North*.

Gerry Rochon expressed the sentiments of the young network. "I had been producing two other music shows on CTV and was also executive producer on the long-running *Pig & Whistle*. One of the shows was *Let's Sing Out* where we had taken it across Canada to various university gymnasiums. Ian & Sylvia had been on that show. So what we were looking for was a show like that hosted by a Canadian, rather than have Oscar Brand come in from New York all the time.* Ian & Sylvia at that point were very well liked by the Canadian public. 'Four Strong Winds' probably put

---

* Although a Canadian born in Winnipeg, Brand lived and worked in New York.

them on the map. So it was a case of doing something that would showcase Canada. We were trying to do a country music show that wasn't a country music show exclusively. Ian & Sylvia were the first performers who came to mind and CTV was all for it. So we went with them. Ian was full of charisma. He had a certain attitude that people liked. He and Sylvia were a great duo that was very popular with people. Plus he was a songwriter, so he had a lot going for him. And he hadn't been over-exposed yet. He wasn't one of those CBC graduates. That's why the show was successful because they hadn't been on television a lot up here. So they had a strong audience even before the show came on the air. Ian had a kind of audience-drawing ability, an audience that's looking for honesty in music, and they got it with him." Following further meetings through the spring, the pilot aired on May 3 as a CTV special presentation and was received well enough to warrant the network pencilling in a weekly fall half-hour time slot on Mondays at 8:00 p.m. opposite the long-running *Green Acres* sitcom, *Medical Center*, and the highly rated *Rowan and Martin's Laugh-In*.

Doing the weekly show from Toronto offered Ian and Sylvia the opportunity to reduce the road grind and be around home (Rosedale and Newtonville) more, plus pull in a decent steady paycheque. As Sylvia recalls, "I had a child at home so I didn't want to be working as much. Clay was in nursery school at the time. Ian wanted to be working and doing stuff on his own and I had no problem with that. It was fine with me. Ian had started working on his own after Clay was born. That was one of the reasons why he wanted to do the television show. It just seemed a really good idea all around to be sticking closer to home for a while." It was no secret that Ian was the draw to serve as host, of some kind of music showcase with guests. The assumption was that Sylvia came with the package. "She was asked to do every show right from the beginning," Ian insists. "Don't let her tell you otherwise 'cause she's bullshitting you. I didn't want her to do every show and that's the truth 'cause it was not going to be Martin and Lewis all the way down the line. It wasn't going to be Edy [Gormé] and Steve [Lawrence]. If I was going to do it *I* had to do it. One of the reasons, one we did agree on, was that the demands of Ian & Sylvia's musical arrangements each week were impossible because that meant nine new Ian & Sylvia charts every month." Ian admits that before the offer of the television show came along he was thinking of quitting music. "I was ready to pack it up. Sylvia wasn't, and she was right. What else could we do? We were committed to that music and weren't going back to folk. We weren't going back to do the old shows."

As Sylvia explains, "They wanted Ian & Sylvia so it was a compromise that I did half the shows. They just assumed that whatever they paid Ian they got me as well. So I went to CTV's offices with our manager at the time, Bert Block, and we sat down and they quickly realized they were going to have to pay me. They asked Bert what the figure was, he named the figure, and they went into shock. Bert then said to them, 'That appears to be a very reasonable sum for an artist of Sylvia's calibre.' And they literally admitted that they had never paid that kind of money to a female Canadian artist. That was the double whammy for me. I looked at Bert and he at me and I said to them, 'Okay, then find another Sylvia Tyson.'" Eventually the network met Sylvia's fee. "Back then if it was all male performers on the show that was okay but if it was two female performers then that was considered unbalanced. So if I was a guest that week there would not be another female that week on the show. That was the times."

There are those who infer that the television show and Sylvia's guest role was evidence of the widening gulf within the Tysons' marriage but that was not the case, at least not initially. "It wasn't that at all," Sylvia counters. Both were content with their separate roles within the relationship and the show ran for five seasons with Ian hosting (the show's name was changed after the first season to *The Ian Tyson Show*) and Sylvia guesting. However, not all was well musically in the Tyson camp. "Our musical interests started to diverge even more than they had before," notes Sylvia. "All those years it had worked for us, the differences we each brought, but now it was starting to work against us. We really didn't gel quite the same way in terms of musical directions. We were both exploring other musical ideas and not necessarily together." The weekly show became a highly rated Canadian production and made Ian into not only a music star but a television celebrity. He had star power and even managed to pick up endorsement contracts from Molson's breweries and others. It did not do so for Sylvia. She was "*and Sylvia*," occasional guest and adjunct to Ian's star; a caboose to Ian's engine.

The first episodes were taped immediately following the Festival Express tour in early July for broadcast in September. Jim Colegrove describes the routine involved in producing the weekly shows. "We recorded the TV show on Thursdays and Fridays before a live audience. We would come up from Woodstock [where he and N. D. Smart were living] on Sunday and rehearsals would start on Monday. We would rehearse what Ian and Sylvia would be doing on the show. The production team would come in on Tuesday and block out everything for the camera shots. If any of the guests were in town and needed backing they would then come down and rehearse with us. We would go into CFTO studios in the morning like we were going to work like everybody else. We would work on set on the camera shots, doing a dry run. Then we would do a full dress rehearsal and then the audience would be brought in.

There would be a solo artist who would come out with his guitar and warm up the audience before the taping started. In the first season, they taped all the shows in sequence as you would see them on TV. In other words, the first number, the second number, and so forth right to the last number. After that first season, the production team would tape things in blocks and edit them all together. We just had to learn to be on when they said, 'Roll 'em.' We had to come out of the chute running. When you know it costs a lot of money to stop tape and redo the shot you don't want to screw it up. You want it to be right. That's what we were mainly concerned with, doing it right. There weren't many times that I recall where we had to stop and reshoot. It might have happened with guests."

As N. D. Smart points out, "Doing TV is boring. Hours of boredom punctuated by a few minutes of sheer terror. When you do a song on TV it's like making movies. You film it, then it's, like, three hours before you do another one. It's just as boring as it could be. The band was always on for the filming but during the down time we used to smoke grass a lot. We had our own dressing rooms but I guess the smell got to people. So they finally bought us this big travel trailer to use as our dressing room. So the producers sent us this letter. They didn't refer to the grass but they instead asked if there was some product we could use to cover up the smell of the grass. They didn't want us to leave the show but were politely asking us if we could please hide the aroma." Prone to shenanigans, N.D. often came close to being shown the door. "Ian almost fired me one night," laughs the outspoken drummer. "The movie *Little Big Man* was out and I had the make-up people do me up like I was ninety-five years old. Ian went ballistic. They had to stop taping the show so I could get the make-up off." Comments Ian, "N. D. Smart was a troublemaker, a real redneck jerk. He played drums fine but I wouldn't put up with that kind of nonsense now. No way."

Doing the weekly show meant less road work and a steady paycheque for the band as well. For some this was appealing; for others it signalled time to move on. Amos Garrett lasted four episodes before leaving for an offer to play with ex-Kweskin Jug Band members Geoff and Maria Muldaur that ultimately morphed into Paul Butterfield's Better Days band. "I discovered that the style I had been developing really suited the sound of this new band and could be used in blues or other genres, not just country," Amos reveals. "I just thought at the time it was the best thing I could do to keep my style evolving. So I went down to Ian and Sylvia's house and told them I was leaving. I gave them a couple of months' notice and played it out." Ian accepted his resignation without argument. "I think that we would have been more relevant or perhaps more popular with another guitarist," mused Ian recently. "That sounds strange because Amos is a brilliant musician but we needed a balls-to-the-wall percussive guitar player. I think the music would have been just a little more accessible."

With a weekly show to tape, a guitarist was required pronto. Replacing the inimitable Amos Garrett was daunting but youngster David Wilcox had sufficient talent and chutzpah to rise to the challenge. "I just thought I had to take a crack at it," he recalls, "as unrealistic as it seems because I wasn't even in the musicians' union. I had done some small-time work, coffeehouses and road work. I got Ian's number from a guy named Eric Nagler who was part owner of the Toronto Folklore Centre. After bugging him for awhile he finally gave me the number and I called Ian up cold and asked for an audition. Ian was reluctant at first but I think I told him, 'Well, what have you got to lose?' I had no credits to speak of on their level. So he gave me an audition in his basement with himself and Buddy Cage on steel. I was really a novice on the electric guitar. I had played a fair amount of acoustic guitar but electric was still very new for me. I just happened to have picked one up. So Ian auditioned me and I got the job. Actually, it was more chutzpah on Ian's part than mine. Here I was, an unknown guitar player replacing a master like Amos Garrett. How do you fill those shoes? You can't. I was just a different stylist than he was. It was a bigger gamble for Ian than for me with the lack of experience I had. But I really owe it to Ian & Sylvia for keeping me in the band while I learned. The electric guitar is certainly a different instrument than the acoustic guitar and I found that out the hard way. There were certainly some challenges for me. They had to get me an amp because I didn't have one."

David would go on to enjoy an illustrious solo career as a revered guitar slinger and recording artist ("Layin' Pipe," "Bad Apple," "Hot Hot Papa") on his own or fronting the Teddy Bears but acknowledges his debt to Ian & Sylvia for his first break. "Joining the Great Speckled Bird gave me a life direction. I wasn't sure I was going to be a musician full-time but it happening so close after my twenty-first birthday and gave me that direction. I used to fantasize about playing guitar for them long before I ever did. Theirs was the big guitar gig in Toronto on the folk scene that I was on. It was always, 'Who's playing for Ian & Sylvia?' That was a big thing. To get that gig was almost surreal for me – a kid from the suburbs all of a sudden getting hired by Ian & Sylvia was a magical thing. I learned so much from them on every level, musically certainly, but just being a professional musician on the road. It was a whole other sphere of professionalism. They were mentors to me. Ian & Sylvia were very professional and for me my overwhelming recollection is the thrill of playing with them because I went from a lower level in the entertainment business to being on TV every week and touring the continent. Just being on TV and recognized every week was unbelievable. If I wanted a date with the woman at the bank it was no problem because she recognized me from the TV show. And the money for me was astronomical. My first paycheque was for $700. I'd never made money like that before. I had been working at Sam The Record Man prior to this. It remains something that I'm very, very proud of."

Within the first few weeks on air the show had found its audience and it nurtured it steadily over the season. Ian proved to be a charming and likeable television host with an obvious ease before the cameras. Each episode opened with N. D. Smart's distinctive cowbell/tom-tom beat as Ian eased the band into "Long Long Time to Get Old" and closed with "Some Kind of Fool," a song written by Ian during their time in Japan ("In one of those dinky little bathtubs they have there"). In between was a tightly produced music show with special guests. Ian closed every show with an ecology message before the closing number. "One thing I've really always respected enormously about Ian is that on his television show he would say something about saving the environment each week," acknowledges David. "Back then it was akin to saying something about the planet Saturn because at the time people weren't aware of environmental issues. So it took a lot of guts and integrity for him to do that. He would be specific about particular environmental concerns long before the public picked up on all that. I really don't think he's been given the credit that he deserves for being one of the early environmentalists." Ian & Sylvia also put their name and drawing power behind their convictions by playing a Pollution Probe benefit concert at St. Lawrence Hall in Toronto, as well as at a benefit for Roy Ivor, the Birdman of Mississauga, after fire destroyed his bird sanctuary, and at a concert in support of First Nations people of Northern Quebec threatened with displacement by the massive James Bay hydro-electric project.

In its first season the show was syndicated in a few U.S. markets but was not picked up in later years. Ian even went on a U.S. promotional tour in mid November, beginning in Los Angeles. "I thought *Nashville North* was a clever title," Ian admits. "There was nothing dumb about it, it just didn't work. People were starting to think of Toronto as the Nashville of the north, which it wasn't. It was misleading, but they were approaching an American audience with it. It certainly had always been a country market in Canada and I guess a lot of those rural people would get touched by the TV show. Gerry [Rochon] thought country rock was going to be big in Canada and could be popular on TV. I thought he was crazy but he was right. He knew that on TV if there was a lot of care taken, country rock could be heard as it's supposed to be heard, that you could hear all the influences – the pedal steel, the folk, and the country-rock influence – blending together nicely. We worked on that eight-track sound and people thought, 'This country rock ain't so bad.'"

He does, however, feel the producers missed out on an opportunity. "They wouldn't let me do any regionalism, any Canadiana," he laments. "That hurt the show, in my opinion. That's my strong suit, I know Canada. I've travelled from one end to the other."

The show boasted an A-list of guests, mostly from the country music charts. Ian had a big hand in suggesting the guests, reflected in the names who appeared alongside him over the run of the series. As Jim Colegrove remembers, "We featured virtually all the great country acts from Nashville at the time, such as Ray Price, Porter Wagoner, Dolly Parton, Jeannie Pruitt, Johnny Rodriguez, Carl Perkins, Loretta Lynn, Jim Ed Brown, Jeanne C. Riley, Merle Travis, Chet Atkins, Jerry Reed, Tanya Tucker, Conway Twitty,

Willie Nelson, Waylon Jennings, Kris Kristofferson, Johnny Paycheck, Don Gibson, and Faron Young. Other stars such as Gordon Lightfoot, the Stampeders, Mashmakan, Ramblin' Jack Elliott, Buffy Sainte-Marie, John Prine, Lucille Starr, the Country Gentlemen, Mason Williams, Kenny Rogers, Seals & Crofts did the show, and so did Rompin' Ronnie Hawkins. Linda Ronstadt appeared with a band that would soon become known worldwide as the Eagles. One of my personal highlights was when I got to play 'Classical Gas' with Mason Williams."

"The reason that so many stars came up to do Ian's show," claims N.D., "was that they knew there was a good backup band. They wouldn't have to spend the money transporting their band, got paid a good taste, and sounded good. Word got around back in Nashville that we were playing on the show." After Buddy Cage quit halfway through the first season,* Ian became concerned that he was going to continue losing his best players. "He got real insecure about us," claims N.D. "Great musicians would come on as guests and rave about the band so he figured we were gonna split on him. He made us all sign a contract making a commitment to stay with him. He'd send me this legal document every three or four months and it had to be returned on time or else. Basically it was a loyalty document. A lot of people were wanting me to play with them. I never had eyes to leave that situation but he must have thought I did. So I would get these letters, 'Please send me your intentions for the next three months. . . . ' I used to send it just under the wire just to mess with him but if I had missed one of those deadlines I had no doubt he would have replaced me just like that. He was stubborn that way."

---

* Buddy Cage had brief stints with Hog Heaven (made up of the Shondells minus Tommy James) and Anne Murray before joining Grateful Dead offshoots the New Riders of the Purple Sage in San Francisco.

Ian had other insecurities as well, according to N.D. "Ian would get paranoid that we didn't think he was a good singer. One day he sat us all down and said, 'Listen, goddamn it. I don't care what you guys think of me. I'm paying you a shitload of money so you better act like I'm the greatest singer in the world.' He was insecure about things like that. But I thought he was a damn good singer. Ian was headstrong. He's insecure so if anybody has a different idea, he takes it personally. I always got along with him because whatever he asked of me I would do it to the best of my ability. I wouldn't make an issue with him. It just wasn't worth it to fight with Ian. If there was going to be a fight there was going to be blood drawn. But there wasn't a lot of laughing and joking around either. The relationship with the band was that you were around as long as you got your job done. If you couldn't cut it you were gone. He and I had a good rapport but there was something in me that just pissed him off. Amos really bothered him, too, because he wasn't an improviser."

Buddy Cage's replacement was Nashville musician Ben Keith (Bennett Keith Schaeufele) from Alvaton, Kentucky. He had first met Ian & Sylvia back in the fall of 1964 on the Lady Bird Johnson campaign tour when he was accompanying Faron Young. Ben had come up with Johnny Darrell to appear on *Nashville North* and was offered the steel guitar position in the Great Speckled Bird. Ben's introduction to recording came in 1961 on Patsy Cline's classic "I Fall to Pieces." "That kind of got me started," he states in his pleasant slow southern drawl. "I just thought, 'Shit, this is pretty easy.'" As Jim Colegrove tells it, "I remember the guys who became the Eagles were backing Linda Ronstadt up when she did the show. Linda sang Patsy Cline's 'I Fall to Pieces.' When they found out that Ben Keith, the guy playing with us, was the guy who played steel on the original recording, they just about shit."

Ben later played behind Cowboy Copas and Webb Pierce before hooking up with Neil Young, fostering a close friendship and musical partnership for some forty years until Ben's death in July 2010. In between playing on Neil's multi-platinum *Harvest*[*] album in Nashville (that's Ben on "Heart of Gold," "Old Man," and "Harvest") and joining his controversial *Time Fades Away* arena tour, Ben played with the Great Speckled Bird. "Ian was really good to work with," offers Ben. "He was really into the music and just wanted to get it right. He never did bother me. It was a lot of fun doing that TV show. We'd come up to Toronto and rehearse for three or four days then tape four shows; two one day and two the next. After we finished taping we'd go back to Woodstock and party."

In October, following a western Canadian university tour, Ian & Sylvia, along with the Great Speckled Bird, made a return appearance on *The Johnny Cash Show* in Nashville, airing November 11. In his introduction Johnny name checked *Nashville North* and welcomed the duo plus band to Nashville South. They then performed their bilingual "Crazy Arms," followed by an edited version of "Long Long Time to Get Old." Both Ian and Sylvia looked very hip country, Sylvia with her waist-long straight hair and her black jumpsuit and Ian sporting longer hair and sideburns. Ian & Sylvia, accompanied only by David Wilcox on acoustic guitar, closed out 1970 with another sold-out Carnegie Hall concert on December 30. David remembers the event well. "Ian was kind enough to introduce me twice. Both times the audience response was really warm and appreciative."

On the strength of Albert Grossman's still formidable clout in

---

[*] Ben had no idea who Neil Young was when he got the studio call in 1971. "They were already in the process of recording so I set up real quiet and ended up doing four or five songs before I even met Neil. I just thought, 'Who the hell is this guitar player? He's pretty damn good.'"

the music business,* Columbia Records (CBS) signed Ian & Sylvia to a three-album recording contract at the end of 1970 and sessions began at Toronto's Thunder Sound on Davenport Road across the street from the Masonic Temple, on January 7, 1971, under the direction of producer John Hill. These sessions would be marked by a return to a simpler sound eschewing the Great Speckled Bird and only recruiting David Wilcox on acoustic guitar and mandolin. Further sessions would take place in February through April at Columbia studios in New York and Nashville. In an extensive interview with the CBC's Holger Petersen (later the founder of Stony Plains Records) in Edmonton in July of that year, Ian outlined the reasoning behind the return to a less electric approach on the new album. "In the last year, even just in the last few months, there has been such a revival of interest in acoustic playing. I started thinking about that one day and realized, 'Wait a minute.' We were among the originators of that style – we didn't invent it, we got it from the country and mountain folk people who had been doing it for years – but we were in that first generation who urbanized it and brought it to the city. And people now want to hear that music and I've been playing it all these years. It really would be kind of silly not to play that kind of music for people when they want to hear it because we knew that music and grew up with it. So I started practising again, the more complicated stuff, on my acoustic guitar. And David Wilcox, his first love is acoustic music, as is mine, and he has always been a fine acoustic player. So we started to rehearse and practise extensively and the three of us went on a long tour in California, coffeehouses, and the sound really came together and we realized this is what we do best. I'm enjoying it very much because I get to play runs

---

* Although Albert was no longer directly involved in the day-to-day management of Ian & Sylvia, the duo was still a Groscourt client.

and licks and figures much more than I get to do with the band because my role in the band is a member of the rhythm section. So this new album is aimed at a broader audience. It's not pure country music for the country-rock fan. There are a variety of ballads, some pure country, and also some pop tunes with pretty arrangements and orchestration.

"I think Sylvia and I," Ian continues, "have come to the conclusion after the Great Speckled Bird experiment, if you want to call it that, which covered the last three years and a lot of effort on everybody's part, that we would attempt to perhaps broaden the base of our music somewhat for the people who come to our concerts. And if we became dissatisfied emotionally with it we would cease to do it. But if we could find that reaffirmation that one finds in music that one loves so much, and it was satisfying and we were getting off artistically on it, we would explore it more. So this new album is a departure from the Speckled Bird album but not an about-face. There are all sorts of overlapping connections."

There was one hiccup in Columbia's signing Ian & Sylvia to a contract, however. While Albert Grossman was once again able to leverage a substantial advance using his Bob Dylan calling card (Bob was still a Columbia recording artist), CBS president Clive Davis had an ulterior motive in taking on what by most accounts would be regarded as a has-been act in the U.S. Back in 1967, an obscure duo from Cincinnati, Ohio, named Smokey & His Sister (Larry and Vicki Mims) had migrated to Greenwich Village and signed with Columbia Records. They released one obscure self-titled album and a single, both of which sank without trace, as did Larry and Vicki. But the single, a Larry Mims composition entitled "Creators of Rain," was a personal favourite of Clive's and he believed that a version of the song by Ian & Sylvia might do the trick in turning it from obscurity to hit. The only problem with his plan was that Ian & Sylvia hated the song. The original recording with its schmaltzy lyrics, overwrought orchestration, and Smokey's nasally monotone singing was abhorrent to the Canadian duo. Nonetheless, Clive prevailed and, contract in hand, Ian & Sylvia agreed to tackle the song.

"Clive had a big thing for 'Creators of Rain' and really believed that Ian & Sylvia could have a hit with that song," Sylvia recalls. "And that's why he signed us. Ian later ran into the guy who wrote that song, Larry Mims, and he told Ian he was thrilled Ian & Sylvia had done one of his songs but why that one? That song did not fit our album. It's probably the only time we were put in the position of having to do a song we really did not want to do. But it was a chance for us to record for CBS. I don't think we've ever recorded anything I'm ashamed of with the exception of 'Creators of Rain.'* Clive Davis has built up such a tremendous reputation as a musical guy but he's not. He doesn't know music. He only knows what his people on the street tell him." Adds Ian ruefully, "Clive Davis had no taste in music at all."

Released in October 1971, the self-titled album, credited on the back cover to "Ian & Sylvia with David Wilcox," is an anomaly in the Ian & Sylvia canon. Neither one has much to say about the songs or the recording sessions, with the exception of "Creators of Rain." And yet there is much to recommend it. Diehard fans remain divided over the album. Much of *Ian & Sylvia* is strong if inconsistent, veering from heavily orchestrated pop ("Creators of Rain" and the rather prophetic "Everybody Has to Say Goodbye") and straight country (a much improved remake of Ian's "Summer

---

* During sessions for their debut CBS album, Ian & Sylvia recorded an ill-advised cover version of Mickey & Sylvia's 1957 hit "Love Is Strange" that remained unreleased until many years later. It rivals "Creators of Rain" for worst Ian & Sylvia recording.

Wages," John "Marmaduke" Dawson of the New Riders' "Last
Lonely Eagle") to simple, stark, unadorned folk (Sylvia's version
of Bert Jansch's "Needle of Death," "Lincoln Freed Me") and
blues ("Midnight," a smoky blues song from Sylvia). "We really
wanted to get back to that simple stuff," states Sylvia, "almost to
see if we could still do it. Just two guitars, two voices, and maybe
a bass. With the Great Speckled Bird the volume was up so loud
you kind of forgot how to sing sometimes. The band covers up a
lot and you can get lazy. We found we lost a lot of subtlety with
the band." Canadian singer/songwriter David Wiffen's* "More
Often Than Not," a lament to the itinerant life of a travelling
musician, is ably handled by Ian & Sylvia in a lushly orchestrated
country rendition and is a fitting album opener. The weekly television show closer, "Some Kind of Fool," makes its recorded debut
and, with its singalong "la-la" chorus, remains one of Ian's better
known songs. But the strongest song on the album, and for many
the hardest song to listen to without being moved emotionally, is
"Barney," a collaboration between Ian and Sylvia that tells the
true story of how Ian had to put down his favourite old horse
(pictured on the back cover of *Full Circle*) who wouldn't have made
it through another winter. "Ian had written the lyrics," recalls
Sylvia, "but couldn't face putting a melody to it so he handed it
to me." The two performed the song once, at their December 30th
Carnegie Hall concert, and would never again. It was just too pain-
ful for Ian to sing it.

"Barney was the first good horse that I owned," Ian relates.
"The first good horse I could afford to buy. And he was a pretty
good ol' horse. He just got more and more crippled in the winters.

---

* A former member of Three's a Crowd and the Children with Bruce Cockburn,
his song "Driving Wheel" has been covered by a number of artists, including
ex-Byrd Roger McGuinn and Tom Rush.

Then one winter I thought I'd better put him down. I hadn't shot a good horse before, a horse I was close to, and it shook me up pretty bad. It's all in the song, that's the way it happened. That's why you write 'em. You don't write 'em so you gotta sit around and explain 'em. Dick dragged him away with the tractor up the hill to bury him with the front-end loader. He's buried there to this day. I wrote the lyrics that same day. Sylvia had this melody she hadn't done anything with. I always thought it was beautiful and that is the melody of the song."

The Columbia album failed to meet the label's expectations and sold only moderately. The surprise for fans was that, having submerged their identity into the Great Speckled Bird moniker on their previous recording, Ian & Sylvia were here again on their own and not even backed by the band they appeared on television with each week. So there was some confusion in the marketplace. The label threw a media party to launch the album at Toronto's Variety Club headquarters on Bloor Street on September 29. Prior to the album's release, Ian & Sylvia had been performing scattered concert dates backed only by David Wilcox and bass player Bob Walker from Toronto. It was easier and cheaper than transporting the entire Great Speckled Bird band, who by now were all living in Woodstock, New York. "I think he got disillusioned with the band because of the personnel changes," suggests Jim Colegrove. "First Amos left and soon after that Buddy left and I think that really put him over the edge with the band. 'Goddamn it, I hate having to keep putting this band back together.' And he wasn't having great success with the Great Speckled Bird anyway. Nobody ever bought the fact that it was a band with Ian & Sylvia as part of the members of the band. It was always 'Ian & Sylvia with the Great Speckled Bird' or 'The Great Speckled Bird featuring Ian & Sylvia.' So I think he felt it was a failed project and he just figured he and Sylvia would go on with just a bass player and guitar player and keep the band for the TV show. Late 1970 through into 1971 there weren't many gigs. We were doing the television show. The band was even paid for every rerun during the summer months, so for us it was a pretty good job."

While the band members settled into comfortable complacency taping multiple shows before hightailing it back to Woodstock to their own projects (they cut an album entitled *Hungry Chuck* that Ian guested on), the weekly show had made Ian Tyson a bona fide Canadian television star and household name. The second season of the television show therefore changed to *The Ian Tyson Show* in recognition of his status (some American syndicated channels had been calling the show by that name during the first season) with a new day, Tuesday. But while the new title further boosted Ian's profile it also further relegated Sylvia to bit part status. Ian insists that Sylvia felt threatened by his rising stature and her diminishing role; she denies it. Nevertheless, after the taping for the second season wrapped up, Ian booked to play some concerts with the full band. According to Jim Colegrove, "After Ben Keith came into the band I told Ian that he really should be doing some gigs with us because we were a damn good band by that point. So Ian decided he would book some gigs. Bert Block was his agent and he booked some tours after that. But Ben only did one gig, at Ontario Place, then he left to rejoin Neil Young. After awhile David Wilcox left, and then Ian fired N.D. Here we were a tight band, Ian booked gigs, and the whole thing falls apart. Jeff Gutcheon had been in the band [on piano] too but he left, so everyone was gone except me! Ian just figured, 'Shit, what's the point of this?' Obviously he had to hire more musicians. We ended up with Pee Wee Charles on steel guitar, Red Shea [from Gordon Lightfoot's band] on guitar, and Billy Mundi on drums. Gordon Fleming joined on piano."

Before that there was still another album due for Columbia records. Despite the limited success of their previous release there was still some optimism that the label would recoup its investment in the duo. This time, rather than splitting sessions between Toronto, New York, and Nashville, Ian & Sylvia decided to keep it closer to home by recording the entire album at Toronto's Thunder Sound studios. Between his commitments to the television show, his ever-increasing farm and cutting horse chores, and live performances, Ian was kept busy and the recordings were booked around his schedule in April 1971 (although some over-dubbing and mixing was handled at Columbia's New York studio at the end of June). Ian dismissed John Hill and decided to produce the album himself along with pedal steel player Ben Keith (the album sleeve lists Ben's name first), who also mixed the final tracks. "I was kind of the leader of the band so I guess that's how I got the job," smiles Ben.

For this album, Ian & Sylvia made the surprise decision to share billing with the Great Speckled Bird and return to a country sound. "On that second one he wasn't thinking so much in the direction of a revolutionary country-rock concept anymore," suggests Jim Colegrove. "He was going more mainstream country." Eschewing the rapid-fire guitar and pedal steel interplay, the album, titled *You Were On My Mind*, is a more understated effort. The songwriting remains impressive, with the backing never taking the focus away from the overall arrangements and presentation. "Ian & Sylvia would allow us to develop our own parts," notes David Wilcox, recalling the recording sessions for the album, "but give us suggestions and guidance as to what they wanted. As a band leader myself I think that's a very effective approach. You get the creative best out of people but it's in a creative direction that you are comfortable with, having conceived the song. Ian was definitely the boss but Sylvia was very much a presence and a leader more than merely a participant. They generally presented a united front."

Sylvia speculates that it was probably over for Ian & Sylvia's collective career together by the time of that second Columbia album. "Nothing from that album sticks out for me," she states. It was more obvious on this album that the two were beginning to move in different musical directions. Ian's songs are more straight-forward country: "Old Cheyenne," one of his best, presages his later cowboy career, while "Salmon in the Sea" was also a strong contender. Sylvia's contributions, on the other hand, are more eclectic, reflecting her own individual musical tastes. "'Miriam' was one of those classically influenced pieces that I sometimes wrote," she offers. "And 'Joshua' was a nod to the early English music that I listened to." There may be something prophetic about a song entitled "The Beginning of the End," but the theme is not what it appears to be. A reworking of "You Were On My Mind" in a country arrangement with horns works well, while a cover of an outtake track from the Band's self-titled second album, "Get Up Jake," rocks. Ian claims the song was recorded as an intended single and might have done well if Columbia had supported the duo. In point of fact, the label had little faith in their second Ian & Sylvia effort. Although officially released in Canada in September 1972, the album kind of trickled out in the U.S. Many Ian & Sylvia fans don't even know about the album, or if they do, they haven't heard it.

Like their debut Columbia album, *You Were On My Mind* includes examples of sterling songwriting worthy of their canon from both Tysons, and their singing is always first-rate. However, both albums seem to lack cohesion and consistency. Both Ian and Sylvia were still stepping up to the plate and swinging. There was nothing "phoned in" on either album and there is commitment throughout. However, they were just not necessarily swinging at the same target anymore. Since 1966 they had been searching for the right direction and an audience. The Great Speckled Bird album had pointed the way, although its failure to connect commercially left them unsure once again. While they still retained their lofty position as Canadian music royalty, their career trajectory and commercial fortunes were pointed downward. The frustration was compounded by the feeling that the songs and recordings were good but just not catching the public's attention.

The front cover photograph, taken by Pat LeCroix, a long-time friend and former member of the Halifax Three with Denny Doherty back in the folk days, shows the two frolicking in the snow-covered fields of Ian's Newtonville farm. But it's the back cover photo that is both endearing and bittersweet: the two, arm-in-arm, walking through the snowy field, silhouetted against the setting winter sun. Whether either knew it at the time or not, this would be their last Ian & Sylvia album. The back cover photo seemed fitting.

According to their contract, Ian & Sylvia owed Columbia one more album. Neither side had much interest in returning to a recording studio. They had failed to meet Clive Davis's expectations and after two albums it wasn't going anywhere. CBS refused to pay for another album.* Sylvia was forced to go to Clive to arrange for a release from their contract. "Ian said, 'To hell with this' and went back to Toronto, so I had to negotiate to get us out of the deal. I waited about two hours in Clive Davis's office. I think he thought I would just go away. I wasn't leaving. I just

---

* The label released the rather boldly named *The Best of Ian & Sylvia* the following year, a double album that merely reprised both CBS albums intact.

figured that he would be so embarrassed he'd have to see me. Finally he met with me and agreed to let us go. It wasn't doing either of us any good. He had egg on his face anyway because 'Creators of Rain' had failed to do anything."

Nonetheless, there was still the television show, the farm, Clay, and bookings to fulfill, so Ian & Sylvia had little time to lick their wounds. February found them on familiar turf back at the Golden Bear in Huntington Beach, California, followed by a week at the Café York in Denver. The next month they appeared at the prestigious National Arts Centre in Ottawa. "It was one of the most exciting nights of our career," Ian later remarked. "It was sold out with a wonderful, energetic, attentive audience. And the best sound system for acoustic music I've ever heard. It was such a joy to play, just the two guitars and Sylvia on piano. I think we enjoyed that evening as much as any evening since we've been singing together." That same month Ian filmed a Molson's beer ad and in May embarked on a solo mini tour of Southern Ontario sponsored by the brewing company. In early June, Ian & Sylvia began recording the score to a Hollywood motion picture entitled *Payday* written by Don Carpenter and directed by their friend Daryl Duke. Co-producer on the project was noted San Francisco music critic Ralph J. Gleason. In the movie, veteran character actor Rip Torn, the only familiar name in the cast, plays an unsavoury country singer with an insatiable appetite for sex, booze, and drugs. Both Ian and Sylvia are listed separately as contributing to the soundtrack although, in the end, their work was minimized. "I don't recall having been a writer on *Payday*," notes Sylvia. "It was supposed to be the theme of the movie but Shel Silverstein was very hot at that point and our song faded into background music. It probably would have been dropped altogether if not for Daryl."

Back in late 1971, Ian had conceived of a design for a portable tipi that was quick and easy to assemble as well as conveniently transportable. The assembly required only two external poles that were easily raised once the circumference was pegged down. Naming it the Tyson Tipi, he began to explore manufacturing and distribution the following year. Canvas bags were developed to hold the poles by American Canvas of Denver, Colorado, and meetings with the Eaton's department store chain were held to consider stocking the tipi. The KOA (Kampgrounds of America and Canada) organization endorsed the tipis and by 1973 Ian was actively promoting them alongside Chief Dan George, actor (*Dances With Wolves*) and chief of British Columbia's Tsleil-Waututh Nation. "I still have my two Tyson Tipis and I still use them," boasts singer/actor Don Francks. "They're absolutely one of the most practical travelling tipis I ever had. I used to travel the country in my yellow pickup truck and I would take a Tyson Tipi along. But it was tough having these long poles hanging out. This was a real nice travelling tipi. I think I used it in a film once." Sales never quite met expectations and the Tyson Tipi soon disappeared from store shelves. "That was one of Ian's schemes," shrugs Sylvia.

Despite his diligent instructions to his sidemen on how they should transport their stash of drugs across the border and the potential consequences if caught, Ian himself was arrested for marijuana possession in April 1973. As Sylvia tells it, "We were playing a benefit in Montreal to stop the damming of the rivers going into James Bay for the James Bay hydro-electric project. Ian decided he was going to stay on in Montreal a couple more days. He and his guitar got on the plane in Montreal, he got off the plane in Toronto, and his guitar stayed on the plane and carried on to parts unknown. On its return, Canadian Customs officials opened the case and he couldn't claim he didn't know about the grass because it was in a gold cigarette case with a diamond 'T' on it. It was a little hard to disclaim it. It was only a couple of joints. When he reported to the RCMP in Toronto and told them about it they were incredulous. Busted for two joints? They told him they wouldn't have bothered. After that we had difficulty working in the U.S. They wouldn't allow Ian across the border." Apparently the guitar journeyed on to Jamaica before returning to Toronto. Suspicious of just about anything coming from that island, Canadian customs officials opened the case and discovered the small stash. The resulting conviction in June resulted in Ian relinquishing his green card, although he was allowed back into the U.S. a few years later. "I could cross with a truck and a horse trailer but not with a guitar." Nonetheless, the immediate impact was a prohibition of travel stateside.

By the third season of *The Ian Tyson Show*, Sylvia appeared even more infrequently. Ian's off time was spent almost exclusively at the farm and his involvement in training for and competing in cutting horse competitions became his primary focus. "The handwriting was on the wall at that point," Sylvia admits. "I wasn't gigging at all. Ian wanted to work on his own and that was fine." As N. D. Smart recalls, "Ian & Sylvia during this time, became two people rather than one entity. There was a feeling that something was going on between them. She stayed at the house and he was out at the farm. But they didn't let us know what was going on in their private lives." Ian had taken to carousing around Toronto in the company of Gordon Lightfoot and Rompin' Ronnie Hawkins (who would refer to Sylvia as "Bat Woman"). The three rounders cut a wide swath through the bars and clubs. Ian was a TV star and living large. The legend and the man were becoming one and the same.

"Ian and I would go out to his farm and work, haying and stuff like that," recalls David Rea. "We'd get up at five in the morning and go out and get in a couple of hundred bales of hay by eleven o'clock. Then he'd get his farm hand Dick to go into town and get three or four bottles of Bols gin and we'd make up several coolers full of gin and bitter lemon and Ronnie Hawkins would come over and we'd have a good old time." Those good times often carried over to the city. "There was this old coach house that Ian's friend A. G. MacRae owned just off Dupont in Toronto that we called the Palace of a Thousand Delights, which it was, depending on how delighted you wanted to get. I remember one time Ian and I woke up in the house and we looked outside and his Cadillac was pulled up over the curb out in front of the house with all the doors open and there's a cop standing there looking at it. And Ian says, 'Jesus Christ, there's a pound of grass in the glove compartment!' So we tucked our shirts in our trousers and went outside to try to distract the cop, an old Scottish guy. Ian says, 'Sorry about that,' and the cop says, 'Say no more, laddie. I had a few last night meself.'

"Another time," David recalls with a smile, "Ian and I had been drinking and he says to me, 'I just got a new Cadillac. Let's take it out for a drive.' So there we are driving around Rosedale at night when a police car comes up behind us. Ian makes a right; the cop makes a right. Ian turns left; the cop turns left. Ian makes another left and the cop puts on his flashing lights. 'Oh shit, there's a cop behind us.' So we pull over and the cop comes up to the car, Ian rolls down the window, the cop looks at us and says, 'Ian Tyson and David Rea. I just wanted to tell you how much I love your music!' Meanwhile, we're both trying to melt under the dash. Ian would bring people over to the house but when things started getting out of hand Sylvia would go to bed. One time, I think it was his birthday, he came back to the house with Stompin' Tom and Lucille Starr. I was staying there at the time. And he says to me, 'Go on upstairs and get Maude to wake up and come down and sing with Lucille Starr.' 'I'm not going up there, Ian.' And he says, 'Go on, go on. So I went upstairs and tapped on the door and said, 'Maude, this is not my idea. . . . ' I heard a great sigh from her and a few minutes later she had transformed herself into a lady and came down. That was quite a night."

For the 1973–74 seasons, veteran Toronto music journalist and publicist Larry LeBlanc joined *The Ian Tyson Show* as a writer along-side Bill Hartley. Larry looks back over his stint with Ian & Sylvia with great fondness. "I wouldn't be where I am today without working with Ian & Sylvia," he acknowledges. "You had to know music if you worked with Ian. He would grill you. You had to know your shit. I was brought up to speed very quickly. I was fairly knowledgeable on country music when I joined the show but I had a PhD in it by the time I left because Ian absolutely demanded it of you. But you could still have fun with him."

Each script was subject to Ian's scrutiny and the writers were required to vet every word through the boss. "We would have the scripts and we would go over to Ian's house and he would go over every line," Larry remembers. "It was Ian's vehicle and he had to approve everything. He wasn't difficult but he was very demand-ing." With each season, Ian exerted more input into the guest lists for the show. "Ian loved having people like Johnny Paycheck and Ray Price, Ian's hero, on the show because they were the real deal," Larry continues. "Ian loved the shit kickers. They were real, authentic, and he could identify with them. I remember Charlie Rich sitting at the piano in the afternoon playing jazz. He had been a jazz player originally. We got guests *The Tommy Hunter Show* people at CBC couldn't get. They paid much, much better than we could – CTV didn't have much money – but we could get better guests because they would know Ian. He was well-respected in Nashville. And if they were songwriters they worshipped the hell out of him. Jerry Jeff Walker just worshipped Ian. Tom T. Hall was a big Ian Tyson fan, too, because he was a songwriter. Tommy Hunter wasn't a songwriter and the Nashville people didn't know him. But they all knew Ian and had so much respect for him. They all knew 'Four Strong Winds.'" Each episode would include a Canadian folksinger, either established or up-and-coming. Ian measured every performer's worth by his own country music yardstick. "They were either forced upon the show or were there for Canadian content reasons and Ian hated that part of the show because it wasn't country. We used to call them the 'Bad Night in Moosonee Singers.'"

One country mega-star on the cusp of fame at the time was Dolly Parton, who appeared on Ian's show several times. Her first guest appearance was with partner Porter Wagoner. She followed that a season later, backed by her own family after breaking with Porter and launching her solo career. And on her final appearance she came up with her own band from Nashville. "I remember the time Dolly came in with her family band," notes Larry. "When we were doing the Tyson show there were other shows going on at the time and we'd run into them. Kenny Rogers's *Rolling on the River* was being taped for Glen-Warren Productions, and CTV had this circus show going on with Sherisse Laurence and Cal Dodd. I remember pulling into the CFTO studios parking lot and we had Dolly Parton and the Family Band on our show that day. There in the parking lot is an old school bus that Dolly came up in with her mom and dad and family members. Now, when Dolly talks about coming from the backwoods, she's serious. She came from the other side of the holler from Loretta Lynn, let me tell you. So as I'm pulling into the parking lot, to the right there's Dolly's mom and dad out in front of the school bus roasting a pig on a spit, and to the left are two elephants, lions, and probably a chimpanzee in there, too, going in to do the *Circus* show. It was like a Fellini movie!

"Ian was always so expressive in his delivery," Larry acknowledges. "He could take the lines someone else wrote for him and really make them meaningful. Dolly had a song called 'Coat of Many Colors' and so before Dolly sang that song Ian told the story of that coat, which is a true story of how poor Dolly was growing up in the hills. So Ian did this amazing delivery and turns to Dolly to sing it and she's crying. There wasn't a dry eye in the house. After the camera shot was done she came over to me and said, 'Hon, did you write that?' and she gave me a big hug." Dolly also had an uncanny ability to remember everyone on the production team and when she would return, made a point of going around and greeting everyone by name. "If there was a new lighting guy she'd say, 'Wait a minute. You weren't here last time. What's your name, hon?'"

On the final two seasons of the show, Ian was flexing his star power more and more. "I can remember," says Jim Colegrove, "there were a lot of production issues where [director] Michael Steele would have an idea for something and Ian would say, 'Nah, I don't like that.'" Contract negotiations, too, were becoming difficult. "We were seeing more of Ian as a star now and the network wasn't in a position to pay much more for the series," Gerry Rochon insists. "The increases from season to season were minimal. The network felt they just couldn't give him the kind of money he was demanding. It just wasn't feasible in those days. The sponsors were there but the ad rates for Canadian television shows weren't that high compared to fees on American shows. The bottom line was that we were a Canadian show, not an American show. Ian was not a happy camper towards the end. He was always professional onstage and on camera. I don't know for certain if he was trying an end run around me with the CTV top brass. But he might have. It was pretty tough to develop a personal relationship with Ian. I can't think of anybody from the show who got very close to him. You never knew where he was coming from. He could be very intimidating. I think Michael Steele found that. So we kept it on a very professional level. Ian and Michael butted heads sometimes. [According to Ian, "I was screwing his wife at the time. She was a real pistol."] Michael wasn't into country music at that time but he was probably my strongest director for music shows. He had a knack for it, the positioning of cameras and how to cut it, editing it on the fly." Larry LeBlanc agrees that Ian was becoming restless and chafing at the limitations of the weekly show. "When I came in on the television show Ian was getting bored with television. He also felt that television was hurting his record sales. He would say over and over, 'Why bother recording when people can see me live every week?'"

The weekly television show also had an impact on Ian & Sylvia's career and how they were perceived. "It kind of pitched them into the mainstream," notes Larry, "and you constantly had to remind people about who they were and what they'd done. Ian's audience for the television show was mostly an older audience. Outside Toronto the two were revered but inside Toronto, no, not necessarily. Toronto wasn't a country music city. I remember they played Massey Hall in January 1973 and it was not sold out. They did a great show and had the band with them that night but in the middle the band left the stage and they did an acoustic set of their older folk material. It was wonderful. But Ian really got bitter in later years." The professional relationship between the two was also changing. "Sylvia wasn't around all that much when I was working on the television show," states Larry. "She wasn't appearing very often. She would come in and do her spots in the show from time to time and there was no sign of discord but by the last season you could see there was some tension between them. She held herself apart from the guys, too. It was Ian's band and she didn't hang out with them or kind of joke around with them in any way. But they were still together at the time."

With an eye to establishing a solo identity, Ian signed a recording deal with A&M Records (Canada) in April 1973 for a solo album. Produced by ex-Paupers guitarist/singer Adam Mitchell, *Ol' Eon*, released that fall, was an impressive solo debut with Ian writing eleven of the twelve songs on the album. "My A&M deal came strictly out of the success of the TV show," Ian insists. "I could have told them then but they didn't know that TV does not sell records. Anyway, they signed me and they didn't know what the hell I did. They were shocked to find they had a country artist on their label," a surprising circumstance given the obvious musical direction of the television show and its guests.* "They were simply not my type of people, nor I theirs, so we didn't have any communication. Despite this, *Ol' Eon* sold pretty well. There were a bunch of hits off there. 'Great Canadian Tour' was a big hit. 'Love Can Bless the Soul of Anyone' was a big hit. So they made money on that album. But they dropped me when they found out I was country. They didn't seem to know what the hell they were doing, but they knew one thing for sure. They

---

* Larry LeBlanc helped broker the deal for Ian and counters Ian's claims. "A&M knew the were signing a country act with Ian. What else was he other than country? They were trying to widen their roster. Ian was desparate for a label after being dropped by Columbia and nobody wanted him as a solo act. It's true they weren't equipped to work a country act nor deal with an act was uncommunicative, if not hostile to them, as Ian. He loathed record company people."

knew they didn't want to be country; they damn sure knew that."
Using the nucleus of the television show band including Red Shea,
Gord Fleming, and Pee Wee Charles as backing on the album, the
tracks leave little doubt as to Ian's own musical direction. He also
toured Canada and did club dates in and around Toronto with
these same players. There was no talk of Ian & Sylvia splitting
up; Ian was simply pursuing his own path at this point.*

When taping for the fourth season wrapped up in January 1974,
Jim Colegrove left the television band and moved to Texas. "I
always had a pretty good time with Ian & Sylvia," he reflects. "The
worst times, though, were when we'd go 'Down East,' as they say,
to Newfoundland. Eew God! It was like going to another planet. A
lot of places would play the national anthem before we played but
in Newfoundland they played the Newfoundland national anthem
first. That was unusual. The Wabash gig in Labrador was in the
middle of nowhere in a hockey arena when it was twenty-five below
zero. You'd go outside and your eyelids would freeze. To me those
were the worst gigs we ever played. The best gigs were when we
went to Japan and the train tour. But by the time I left I kind of
thought they were on the outs with each other, Ian and Sylvia."

Despite efforts to launch his solo career, Ian's primary interest
lay at the farm. Besides calving, haying, raising cattle and cutting
horses, Ian was travelling more and more to compete in cutting
competitions and earning respect among the rancher constituency
for both his skill and dedication. "My thing isn't an urban cowboy
trip," he emphasized in a 1980 interview with Peter O'Brien for
Omaha Rainbow magazine, "It's a real cowboy trip, and maybe there
isn't a market for the real cowboys. Certainly the real cowboys don't
buy the records, that's for sure, because they don't live near record

---

* Ian also appeared alone on CTV's popular prime-time game show *Headline
Hunters* in October 1973.

stores. But that's what I know best and that's what I write about."

Meanwhile, Ian's partying continued. He was a star and enjoying all the spoils of fame. "We could be somewhere where no one had heard of Ian Tyson and the waitress would be flirting with him," attests Larry LeBlanc. "He was a handsome guy, a man's man." Sylvia was hardly naive but put up with Ian's antics to a point. "I'll be quite frank and say that Ian did have his dalliances," states Sylvia. "And he was becoming perhaps less careful about concealing them. I knew about his extracurricular activities. He was coming home but not necessarily to me. Fidelity was never Ian's strong suit." Did she know what she was getting when they wed? "Not really. Not when I married him. There was a fair age difference between us; he's seven years older than me. I certainly knew what his reputation was. But I was from a small town and just thought that when you got married then you were married and that's that." The prevailing attitude of most women of her generation, born and raised in the 1940s and '50s, was that you married for life. "And I did have that attitude." However, by the '70s that was no longer enough. Notes Larry, "She found Ian's carousing hurtful especially when it became public knowledge. He was no longer as discreet about it by any means."

"It was a natural drifting apart," observes singer/songwriter Tom Russell. "Ian wanted to be a cowboy out at the farm and he was a bit of a rounder anyway. Sylvia was more of a homebody. They had different lifestyles. Ian's out partying with Ronnie Hawkins and Sylvia's in her big house reading a book."

"I would always tell the various sidemen we had over the years, 'If Ian and I get into an argument about a song, don't get involved. It's not about music,'" says Sylvia. "'You don't want to get in there.' The subtext was probably the relationship but the text was the music."

By the fifth season of *The Ian Tyson Show* there was noticeable tension between them. "Ian was playing a stronger role in the show," recalls Gerry Rochon, "and we would suggest Sylvia and he'd reply, 'No, we've done that before.' He didn't really want her on the show anymore. It was his show. I think he wanted to go solo by that point." Despite Ian's decision to work alone, Sylvia was by no means inactive. She signed her own solo recording contract with Capitol/EMI Records and began recording an album in January 1975 at Toronto's Thunder Sound. Her producer of choice? Ian Tyson. Sylvia's innate insecurity and shyness meant that with Ian at the helm there was no having to prove anything or a get-acquainted period with an outsider. Besides, after all these years, who knew Sylvia's abilities better than Ian? "I was her choice," states Ian. "I don't know why because I'm the world's worst producer. I don't have the patience. That was in her Kitty Wells period." In a November 1975 *Billboard* magazine article Sylvia stated, "I don't know whether I would have trusted another producer with that album."

The same month that Sylvia began recording what would become *Woman's World*, Ian wrapped up taping on the fifth season of his television show. It had been a difficult season with protracted contract negotiations preceding the start of taping. Following the annual wrap party Ian made it known he would not be signing on for a sixth season. "They were not happy at CTV when I left," Ian reveals. "I had become this big TV star in Canada. They wanted to be able to fire me. But I walked away before they could fire me." Rather than endure a slow slide toward inevitable cancellation, Ian chose to walk away on top. He had enjoyed a good five-year run, longer perhaps than most critics expected and not long enough for many fans. It had all been a learning curve for Ian and he left the soundstage a confident television performer and a nationally recognized celebrity. "I really learned how to sing properly doing that show," he says. "But you gotta know when to hold 'em and know when to fold 'em." As Gerry Rochon recalls, "To be honest with you, I think CTV felt they'd had a good run with the show and it was time to look for something else." In a 1993 interview, director Michael Steele suggested that Ian "thought he was going on to bigger and better things" when he exited the show.

Ian continued producing Sylvia's debut solo release through to spring. By that point the duo was finished as a performing entity and their marriage was on the rocks. The studio was all business; away from the studio, though still married, they nonetheless continued to lead separate lives. "In terms of music and performance," muses Ian, "Ian & Sylvia did the right thing in breaking up. We were diverging. In fact, we should have broken up about a year earlier than we did." Certainly the signs were all there: he had the farm and she, the house; he had the TV show and she had Clay. "We sensed that at the time, that we were pulling apart. Once I had the ranch it just started drifting apart; musically, too." "Ian and I always had differences in musical tastes and in the way we wanted to live," notes Sylvia. "Those differences helped to create a musical tension between us that created our sound. But when we stopped working together, the personal relationship was affected, too, because the music was the thing that always united us." That bond had now been severed.

Timing is everything. Released in the midst of the United Nations' International Year of the Woman, Sylvia's solo debut *Woman's World* couldn't have been timed more fortuitously. Though by her own admission she was hardly a feminist, nonetheless her album's title caught the tenor of the times and carried Sylvia on a public relations wave she could never have imagined. "Every feminist in the world wanted to do a story on Sylvia," recalls Larry

LeBlanc, who was hired to serve as Sylvia's publicist. "She is not remotely a feminist but the feminists picked up on the title of the album. I had to turn down requests for interviews, there were so many. I turned down *Toronto Life* because she already had so much exposure. You would not believe the press we got. It was right off the Richter scale. Sure, the timing was perfect, but not intentionally. I remember one night at the house when they were having a party, it might have been the night the Great Speckled Bird folded, Ian turned to Sylvia and me and said, 'You two conned the press.' He saw all that publicity she was getting as a con job. Ian & Sylvia hadn't gotten much press in the latter years so he figured I somehow conjured up all this press for her. He was sceptical." Ian was somehow convinced that Sylvia and Larry were in cahoots to milk the U.N.-designated year.

It was fortunate for Sylvia that she was able, totally by coincidence, to ride that crest, because otherwise launching Sylvia Tyson as a solo entity would have been difficult. She had never been the spokesperson for the duo, rarely spoke onstage, and was seldom interviewed. It was, after all, Ian *and* Sylvia, her role in the general public's perception subordinate to his, although in reality that was not the case. She was not perceived as a Joan Baez or a Judy Collins; not even as a Mary Travers (Peter, Paul & Mary). She had an identity crisis, and five years of Ian's face and name on television only succeeded in deepening that lack of name recognition. It was not *The Ian & Sylvia Show*, nor was it ever intended to be. "It was very difficult when you have a guy with such a huge presence," muses Tom Russell. "It's generally harder for women, especially when you've been identified with a group."

"I felt sorry for Sylvia when they broke up," states Oscar Brand. "This delicate beautiful thing became a tough little lady. But she had to be. It's a tough business. And she built her own career." In a 1974 interview Sylvia offered an explanation for her new confidence. "I'm one of those people who didn't really get it together until I was about thirty. I don't think I was ready before."

Woman's World was hailed far and wide for its exceptional songwriting (all from Sylvia alone) and performances (Ian's band plus fiddler Al Cherney). Sylvia had matured into a songwriter of incredible depth, expression, sophistication, and insight. The title track was a reworking of her song from *Full Circle* seven years earlier. Despite the country music leaning of the album, *Rolling Stone* magazine declared *Woman's World* "a mature pop album whose low-keyed charm, insight and musical integrity are consistently engaging." The album reached number 54 on the Canadian album charts and a single from it, "Sleep on My Shoulder," made it to number 35 on the Canadian country charts. Unlike Ian's first solo album, *Woman's World* was released in the United States.

But as Sylvia's star was ascending, their marriage finally hit the wall with Ian's confession of a love affair. It was more than a one-night stand or a casual fling; he admitted he had fallen in love. "I was cheating on her all the time, and she knew that," claims Ian. "I had girlfriends." In the summer of 1975, Ian's indiscretions took a more serious turn. "I was having an affair with this woman from Montreal, which was really dumb. But we all do dumb things. Sylvia didn't know about it until I confessed to it. I fell in love with Katie Malloch up in Montreal. She's a broadcaster.* We fell in love and had an affair. She followed me to Texas [for cutting horse contests].† Sylvia wasn't amused by that and God knows I don't blame her. This wasn't just a case of Ian out philandering about with the boys. There was a distinction there. She turned a

---

* Katie Malloch began her broadcast career with CBC Montreal in 1975 and currently co-hosts CBC Radio 2's *Tonic*.
† Ian and Tom Russell later wrote "Navajo Rug" which references "Katie" in its chorus.

blind eye to all that stuff. She was very understanding. I had done that kind of stuff throughout our marriage. Ronnie Hawkins, Gordon Lightfoot, we were all philandering. That doesn't excuse it but we'd end up coming home at night. There was no AIDS then. AIDS changed all that. But Katie and I fell for each other. She's a great lady and I still see her from time to time with her husband. But that affair lasted quite a while. It was in that limbo period after the TV show ended. Sylvia and I had broken up. I confessed to Sylvia about our love affair and she was pretty pissed about it. That was kind of the last straw for her. I should have kept my big mouth shut. But that's what happened."

"What it came down to," confirms Sylvia, "was that he finally got involved with someone that he said he was in love with, so I said, 'Okay. Fine. That's it.' Although six months later he denied he said he was in love with her, but that's another story. When he informed me he was in love with someone else, he then asked if I wanted him to move out. I told him I wanted him to stay until after Christmas, mainly for Clay, and after that he could move out to the farm, which is what he did."

Sylvia was booked to open for John Denver at the annual CNE in Toronto on August 24, but the breakup had recently happened and she was shattered. "She called me up tearfully wanting to pull out of the show because they had just split up," recalls Larry LeBlanc. In the end, she went ahead and performed. Ian attended her show.

The legal separation was not public knowledge at the time although insiders certainly knew. "I kept their split-up out of the papers for two or three years," reveals Larry. "It finally came out in a *Toronto Star* article. The reason we did that was because we didn't want any pressures on Clay. He was still in public school at that point and they were having troubles with him. I'm not sure but I don't think he took the breakup well. He worshipped his father in those days. Ian had a man's man thing about him, a real charisma. Clay was with Sylvia when Ian was carousing around downtown with Hawkins and Lightfoot, that whole crowd."

In the eventual divorce decree two years later, Ian retained sole ownership of his Newtonville farm property (expanded after the purchase of a neighbouring farm in the early '70s) while Sylvia kept the Rosedale home. "Ian got off easy," stresses Sylvia. "I got the house, true, but I paid him for his half of the house. I didn't claim on the farm because I never thought it was mine in any way. It was unfortunate that the lawyer I hired had a strong sentimental attachment to Ian & Sylvia and thought that we would get back together, so in the final analysis he wasn't working in my best interests. I just wanted it to be clean and over. No, I didn't claim on the farm, but I told him, and I'm sure he'll remember, that at some point I'm going to ask you for a real big favour and I want you to remember this. I haven't asked for that favour yet. But I would have been perfectly within my rights to claim on the farm."

Fortunately, due to the farsightedness of financial advisers in Albert Grossman's office, their songwriting and publishing had always been kept separate. "Our publishing was in good shape thanks to David Braun, the lawyer," Ian confirms. "She had her publishing and I had mine." This allowed each to retain an income stream without any issues over who had claims to what portions of the writing and publishing. "That made things easier all around," states Sylvia. Ian did not contest custody of Clay but retained visitation rights. "I had custody of Clay," states Sylvia. "He really wanted to move out west and do the ranch thing so there was no way we could ship Clay back and forth on weekends." As for child support, Sylvia was granted a monthly sum. "Well, yes, I was, but I didn't have it," she admits. "The deal that was worked out was for child support and it wasn't enough considering how much it cost to raise a child. Part of the agreement also was that I had to keep a full-time nanny* and that alone would have cost whatever Ian paid in child support. So, yes, I was dependent on child support but no, it wasn't adequate. The nanny was something he insisted on in the settlement because of me being a performer and possibly being away; he wanted Clay to have someone there full time. It was tough all around and an 18 ¼ per cent mortgage on this house wasn't easy either. That was pretty tight for me."

Both regard the divorce settlement as generally amicable. "Part of it was that the financial agreement was not acrimonious because that had always been separate," states Sylvia. As for Ian's assessment, "She took the house and I took the farm. That's all there was to it. It was nothing like my second divorce. Holy shit!"† As for son Clay, who was eleven when the decree came down, "I consciously tried not to say anything negative about his dad when he was growing up," Sylvia admits. "We were quite determined that Clay should not become caught in the middle of a battle between his parents." Nonetheless, Clay did suffer as a result of the divorce. For years he had been caught between two divergent lifestyles: his father's farm with its freewheeling cowboy culture, and his mother's disciplined home regimen in the upper-crust urban enclave of Rosedale. It was bound to take its toll. "He later became a kind of Queen Street 'all-night hanger outer,'" Ian recalls. "He was in several bands. We let him drop out of school, which was really a stupid thing to do. I don't think he even finished Grade 10. We

---

* Hazel continued to work for Sylvia until Clay eventually moved out on his own.
† Ian's 2007 divorce from his second wife, Twylla, was bitter, acrimonious, and costly. The two have only recently resumed communicating.

should never have let him quit school. We should have hired tutors. He was a quiet little boy but he did become rebellious later on. It's turned out fine now but it was stupid to do."

"It wasn't a question of letting him quit school," counters Sylvia. "He wouldn't go to school. At one point I wanted to put him in a private school but Ian wouldn't allow it. One of them I was looking at was Upper Canada College. Clay didn't want to do that but I think it would have been very good for him at that point. He needed that structure and discipline. Clay ended up going to an alternative school, which was too free. I think he undoubtedly inherited that sense of rebellion from his father. Probably a lot of the tension between the two of them is because they are too much alike, although I think Clay is kinder and more patient than his father. Clay and his father have had an up and down relationship. It's probably the best now than it's ever been. It was pretty hard on Clay, his expectations of his dad and vice versa. It's a hard thing for me to touch on. Actually, what I think improved it was at that point when Clay was about seventeen or eighteen. Whenever they would have some kind of confrontation I was the one who was trying to pour oil on troubled waters, trying to do all this conciliatory stuff. But around the time when Clay was seventeen or eighteen I just told them both, 'Okay guys, I'm not getting in the middle anymore. You have to straighten out your own problems. Don't call me.' That, I think, changed their relationship. Clay's worked with Ian and with me as well as on his own. But he's not in music as a career although he's a very good guitar player and songwriter.* I think a lot of that has to do with him having famous parents and people's expectations of him. What he did do in music was so different and uniquely his." Today, Clay

---

* Clay Tyson played in avant garde band the Look People and later recorded a self-titled solo album.

Tyson owns and operates a bicycle shop in Toronto specializing in building customized bikes, a niche in which he has found both success in and satisfaction.

Does Sylvia have much need to contact Ian anymore? "No, not really. Less and less over time unless something comes up, like when he phoned me recently when they were trying to get clearances for certain songs for a compilation. He was asking me about Bearsville Records and some publishing thing he couldn't find any record of." As for their current relationship, "Ian and I get along fine now," says Sylvia. "I don't let him get away with as much as I used to. I tend to call him on stuff," she laughs. "When I was interviewed for that recent Bravo TV special on Ian,* they interviewed us together and then separately. When I came back after my interview, Ian said to me, 'I hope you didn't say anything bad about me.' And I replied, 'Well, it can't all be sunshine and roses, can it?'"

Following a pleasant lunch together in Toronto in September 2009, as Ian was getting out of the car back at his hotel he commented to me, "I never should have left that woman."

★ *Songs from the Gravel Road*, featuring Ian performing with Sylvia, Gordon Lightfoot, Corb Lund, David Wilcox, and John Hiatt, was broadcast in Canada on Bravo TV in January 2010 and is now available on DVD.

8

I'M BOUND FOR MOVIN' ON

"People don't seem to realize that we've been apart far longer than we were together," Sylvia points out, regarding the enduring legacy of Ian & Sylvia. "Clay was eleven when we split up and he's in his mid forties now. Ian and I have both been solo artists for a very long time. People still get all misty-eyed, though, when you mention Ian & Sylvia," she confirms. Nonetheless, the elephant in the room remains. It invariably comes up in every interview with either of them, without exception. Inevitably, the question of an Ian & Sylvia reunion will rear its head. Both have learned over the years to deal with the unyielding hope that the two folk era heroes will get back together onstage. "That's not something I spend a lot of time thinking about," she laughs. "If I did it would be pretty dismal."

Following their separation, Ian continued on as Sylvia's record producer for her second Capitol Records release. In the fall of 1975, at Thunder Sound in Toronto again, she cut *Cool Wind from the North* with many of the same players who'd recorded with Ian serving double duty (Red Shea, Pee Wee Charles, Myrna Lorrie). While not as much of a breakthrough as *Woman's World*, Sylvia's second album, released in mid 1976, was once again a consistent effort, proving she was certainly comfortable in the country music genre. "River Road," later a hit for American country/pop star Crystal Gayle, was a semi-autobiographical look back at her Chatham childhood, the highlight of the album, and a staple of Sylvia's concerts. She later developed a one-woman show and an album, *River Road and Other Stories* (Salt Records) in 2000, drawn from childhood reflections and autobiographical songs. "Despite the autobiographical aspect of it, the show is really about song-writing," she clarified that year. "I'm quite proud of the production because I've never put those songs together like this before." Initially backed by a live band, Sylvia later opted for pre-recorded music for economic reasons, singing and playing guitar or button accordion to the tracks. For someone who rarely spoke onstage, being able to pull off an entire show alone was quite a feat. "I couldn't believe it when she called me up and told me she had figured out how she could do a one-woman show," laughs Larry LeBlanc. "I said to her, 'Sylvia, you do realize that you will be all alone onstage, don't you?' But she had it all worked out and it was amazing." Reviews were glowing. Notes long-time friend and former bandmate Joan Besen, later of award-winning country group Prairie Oyster, "Sylvia's whole performing career is a triumph of someone overcoming stage fright. She is very shy."

In August 1975 Sylvia appeared onstage alongside Canada's renowned opera contralto Maureen Forrester and beloved Québécoise chanteuse Pauline Julien in a CBC television special entitled *Three Women* featuring songs from all three, individually and collectively. She also began a stint that year as host of CBC Radio's folk 'n' roots music – based series *Touch the Earth*, a gig she held for five years. The weekly series became popular with the artsy crowd, casting Sylvia into a milieu whose waters could sometimes be quite turbulent for those who didn't know their stuff. Sylvia, however, was comfortable discussing art, literature, and world music with ease. She could walk the walk and talk the talk. She even numbered among her close friends well-known divorcé Prime Minister Pierre Elliott Trudeau. "We were simply friends," she reveals, "who occasionally had dinner together." Sylvia followed *Touch the Earth* with a spot as host of CBC TV's *Heartland* in 1980 and *Country in My Soul* from 1981 to '83. All this media work put Sylvia front and centre for many Canadians who had no idea that she was a multi-faceted individual. "Sylvia is fearless," boasts Larry. "She's the most adventuresome and bravest person I know. I'm well aware of her shyness but she is very inspirational." What will come as a surprise to Ian & Sylvia fans is that for three years Sylvia was a writer on CBC TV's mid '80s after-school pop-music fluff show *Video Hits*, hosted by Samantha Taylor during the big hair and Wham period.

Throughout this hectic period, Sylvia maintained a prolific songwriting output and when Capitol Records dropped her she simply set up her own label, Salt Records, and released two albums, *Satin on Stone* in 1978 and *Sugar for Sugar, Salt for Salt* the next year. "Although she would never say it, I think it was always a source of frustration for her that her contributions to Ian & Sylvia weren't appreciated or understood," Joan Besen stresses. "She had to deal with Ian being regarded as the driving force in the duo as if she didn't contribute anything. It was difficult for her being perceived not as a songwriter when she wrote 'You Were On My Mind' and so many other great songs." Adds Larry LeBlanc, "She is one of the foremost songwriters of our generation, not just in Canada but anywhere. But because Ian wrote the big ones – 'Four Strong

Winds' and 'Some Day Soon' – Sylvia's songwriting gets over-shadowed. Not enough people have recorded her songs. Ian & Sylvia never pushed their publishing catalogue."

To promote her albums, Sylvia assembled a backing band under the name Foxfire before picking up the unused Great Speckled Bird moniker. "For awhile there was no Great Speckled Bird after Ian and I split up," she explains, "but there was a keyboard player who had worked with us who had appropriated the name and was using it in sleazy bars. He had his own personal problems and the work was deteriorating. So I phoned Ian and told him what was happening. The name was going down the drain and I told him I didn't want to see that happen. It was being used under questionable cir-cumstances. He wasn't using the name so I asked him if I could and he had no problem with that. At least the association with one of us was still there and there was a quality associated with that name. For all of our differences, Ian and I have always maintained a pretty civilized approach to that kind of stuff. I would never have considered using the name without at least talking with him first."

She recalls a humorous incident related to her resurrecting the band name. "There was a club owner in, I think, Regina, who called me over after our set. He was chuckling to himself as he told me about a guy at the back of the club who asked him, "'Is that Sylvia Tyson?' 'Yeah.' "And that's the Great Speckled Bird?' 'Yeah.' And then this guy said, 'Those women take everything, don't they!'" The resurrected Great Speckled Bird became the backing band on *Country in My Soul*. "We backed up everyone from Doc Watson to the latest Nashville stars of the day on that show," boasts Joan Besen. "We expanded to a nine-piece band for the show. It was a great experience." Once the television show ended its run, Sylvia played less often and the band members drifted on to other gigs.

Among Sylvia's early band members was a young Hamilton-based guitarist, Daniel Lanois, who would go on to produce mega-star albums for U2, Bob Dylan, Emmylou Harris, and Neil Young, among others, as well as to pursue his own musical career. One characteristic of her bands was that she always had a female keyboard player. "Part of that was company on the road," observes Larry. "Her band became her family." Joan Besen joined on keyboards in 1978 and she and Sylvia instantly bonded. "I was a single parent," states Joan, "and it was hard for me as a single mom to leave Sonny at home. That's why I only pursued a career around Toronto. But Sylvia let me bring him with me on the road. I paid his expenses. She knew what it was like to have a child and be a working musician. That's why we were able to connect beyond the music. She understood. I don't think anybody else would have allowed me to do that but she'd been through it herself."

In latter years Sylvia reconnected with several of her earlier folk era friends, including Suze Rotolo, Mary Martin, and Carolyn Hester, who had lost touch with Sylvia after moving to California in 1972. However, the two were reunited at the World Folk Music Association concert in Washington, D.C. "Fate brought us together for that show and that was just so much fun," smiles Carolyn. "We ended up sharing a dressing room together and I was thrilled to see how beautiful she was still looking and how great she sounded and the dignity with which she carried herself. She was about to go on and her hair needed brushing. She was sitting at the dressing table so I grabbed the brush and said I'd brush her hair. She said, 'Oh good.' So as I was brushing her hair I had this overwhelming thought, 'I'm brushing Sylvia Tyson's hair!'" "If Sylvia is your friend she stays your friend," stresses Joan Besen. "She keeps friends. Career is not the primary driving force with her. Relationships are important to Sylvia."

Meantime, as Sylvia's star rose and she blossomed as a media celebrity in the latter '70s, Ian's career bottomed out. Following his abrupt departure from *The Ian Tyson Show*, he continued to tour and perform in Toronto clubs, where he was still a major draw at places like the Horseshoe Tavern on Yonge Street. "My tours were hot," he recalls, "even though I wasn't on TV, because they were rerunning it. Toronto was damn near a hot country town by then and I was making $6,000 a week. That went on for awhile." He took a half-hearted shot at establishing himself in Nashville,* before returning home, tail between his legs. "Nashville was a drug period for me. Not hard drugs but tranquilizers." Too proud to play the Nashville social scene and too insecure to push himself forward, he returned to Newtonville and signed a distribution deal with Boot Records, Stompin' Tom Connors's label. Stompin' Tom owed much of his early career success to Ian's patronage. *One Jump Ahead of the Devil* was financed by Ian and friend George Skelton and was recorded in Toronto, Nashville, and Edmonton. Released in 1978, it sold moderately well and spawned country hits "Half a Mile of Hell" and "What Does She See." "Unfortunately," Ian laments, "with the classic Tyson timing, in 1979 the goddamn music industry bottomed out, not just country but pop, too."

By then Ian had already pulled up stakes for Alberta, taking a job on a friend's ranch in Pincher Creek and moving into a tiny cabin on the property. "When I left Toronto nobody waved good-bye," he remembers. "But I couldn't get work down there in Toronto or in Nashville for some reason. I guess they figured I wasn't worth anything because I'd left the TV show. It was just a bad time and nobody knew what was going on. My green card was gone so I couldn't stay down in the States. The cutting horse

---

* Ian was granted temporary rights to cross the border before his previous conviction was ultimately expunged.

thing was just starting to take off in Texas. Land was cheap. Who knows what might have happened if I had applied Neil Young's royalties down there instead of Canada." He describes his time at the cabin as "just a two-year party." Clay came out for visits but as friends noted it was not the place for an impressionable young boy who idolized his father to see him there with other women. During the period, Ian had abandoned both performing and songwriting. "I'm tired of being a third-rate Canadian legend," he groused at the time of his move west. Then, in 1978, Canadian singer/songwriter and rock 'n' roll iconoclast Neil Young, long an Ian & Sylvia admirer, recorded "Four Strong Winds" on his platinum-selling *Comes a Time* country-folk album. The royalty cheque arrived in Ian's mailbox the next year, giving him enough for a down payment on the T-Bar-Y ranch in Longview, Alberta. "I remember very clearly when Neil Young recorded that song," says Ian. "It might have been Ben Keith who contacted me to tell me Neil had recorded it [Ben plays on the track]. Neil was big then. I was working the honky-tonks five or six nights a week at the time."

In 1980, John Brunton's Insight Productions was at work on a three-part history of Canadian pop music for CBC entitled *Heart of Gold*. Larry LeBlanc was the researcher for the series (which was narrated by acclaimed Canadian actor Donald Sutherland). As they waded through some thirty years of video tape and clips it became glaringly obvious that there was precious little on Ian & Sylvia. The decision was made to try to coax the two back together before the cameras. Larry contacted Sylvia and she was agreeable; the X factor was Ian. The argument was put forth that omitting Ian & Sylvia from the series was tantamount to an egregious disservice not only to their legacy but also to a proper documenting of Canadian music history. To everyone's astonishment, Ian, too, was agreeable to a one-off reunion before cameras – not before a live audience. No money was involved other than expenses. Ian flew to Toronto for the taping, which was set up in the basement of the old Masonic Temple (the one-time Rockpile concert venue) on Davenport Road. What appears on the show to be a live concert setting was, in fact, Ian & Sylvia performing "Four Strong Winds" to a small crew and John Brunton. Larry chose not to attend. "I was just too close to them and it would be like seeing your divorced parents getting back together. I also felt that if there were any issues between them that a neutral body, John Brunton, would be better at settling them rather than a familiar face."

By the early '80s Ian was holding down a regular gig at the Ranchman's Club in Calgary and taking home decent money, used to maintain his ranch and horse and cattle stock. He wasn't thinking in terms of a music career. At the Ranchman's, Ian met a teenage spitfire working as a waitress in the adjoining café. Despite her tender age, Twylla Biblow was hard to ignore. Pound for pound she was a match for Ian's temperament. The two took up together, much to the consternation of those who regarded the twenty-seven-year spread in age off-putting, and married in 1986. Their daughter, Adelita, was born the following year.

Having settled down to the cowboy lifestyle, financed in part by performances in Alberta clubs, Ian found a sense of content-ment he'd been missing for many years. He was living his dream. The serenity manifested itself in a surge of creativity but not the kind he'd experienced in the past. Ian wasn't looking to write the next country chart hit nor even a pop hit. No, his muse took him back to the old cowboy songs of his youth; the songs that first ignited in him his love for the Old West, a way of life that in reality no longer existed. What better way than to preserve that bygone way of life than to immortalize it in song? Friends recall how Ian would glow with an inner joy when he sang the old western songs. "During my time on the TV show, CTV were trying to market Ian as a mainstream pop star, basically," notes David Wilcox. "But at night when he'd had a few drinks or after a show he would sing those cowboy songs and that was my favourite thing about him, seeing and hearing him so soulfully doing those old songs."

Old Corrals and Sagebrush became the first in a series of albums dedicated to the lifestyle and stories of the Old West. Recorded on his own and licensed to Columbia Records, this was not country music in the sense of what was coming out of Nashville at the time. This was western music, cowboy ballads and Mexicali-flavoured melodies, all sung by someone with sincerity and integrity, whose heart was forever in the Old West. Sales were modest – Ian was not recording this body of songs for commercial appeal. He had struck a vein but it had yet to yield gold. *Ian Tyson* followed but wasn't on par with its predecessor. The third one was the charm.

With 1987's *Cowboyography*, Ian hit his stride, and at age fifty-three experienced a career renaissance that continues to carry him to this day. *Cowboyography* sold platinum in Canada, notching up over 130,000 copies and earning Ian a Juno award for best male country singer the following year, as well as CCMA (Canadian Country Music Association) awards for best album and best single for "Navajo Rug." At the time of the album's release, Ian remarked that he didn't care how many it sold as long as the real working cowboys heard it. *Cowboyography* was produced by Adrian Chornowol and released in Canada by the independent Edmonton label Stony Plain and distributed in the U.S. by Vanguard Records under the ownership of the Welk Group. Besides including one of Ian's most popular post–Ian & Sylvia songs, "Navajo Rug," the album revived "Summer Wages" and "Old Cheyenne" amongst a collection of superb compositions, revealing he had lost none of his songwriting craft and possessed an innate understanding of western culture, not just Canadian western culture. "The cowboy culture is vertical, north and south," he stresses. "It does not recognize the Medicine Line, the political boundaries." Ian Tyson was back, and on his own terms. "Ian's become a western cowboy culture historian with all his books on that way of life," says his friend singer/songwriter Corb Lund.

Hand in hand with the revival of his recording career, Ian discovered the annual cowboy poetry get-together held in tiny Elko, Nevada. Hal Cannon had started the event in 1984. For Ian it was an epiphany. "Elko saved me," he insists. "None of those buckaroos down in Elko knew who Ian & Sylvia were and couldn't have cared less but they loved those cowboy songs. I had a whole new start, a clean slate, and it was wonderful. I knew I could bring a whole new music to that part of the world and I did. I had a great band and we blew the place apart. It was a rebirth for me. Hal Cannon says that I changed western music. I really didn't discover who I was until *Cowboyography*."

Ian had found his niche and followed the acclaim rightly accorded *Cowboyography* with *I Outgrew the Wagon* (1989, boldly including a country remake of "Four Strong Winds"), *And Stood There Amazed* (1991), and *Eighteen Inches of Rain* (1994). As troubadour of the western cowboy culture, Ian was able to distance himself from the Ian & Sylvia legacy with his reinvention as the premier cowboy songwriter. "I think Sylvia got a little jealous that I had this renaissance, this whole new career with the Elko thing and the cowboy music," he muses. "But I never planned it. Like every other goddamn thing in my life, it just happened. When I started out I was probably the only songwriter in that genre.

Now there are plenty." As word of the annual Elko gathering spread, attendance also began to outgrow the wagon. "When the Ian & Sylvia freaks started coming around, the old folkies, I resented it because I had moved on. I don't resent it now. I understand it. What they're coming to see now is the legend, the persona. It doesn't matter if I sing or not. They come for the stories and to see Ian Tyson."

"The whole thing about the last man standing or the lion in winter, take your pick, it's true of Ian's image nowadays," states Larry LeBlanc. "He has somehow created this coalition of fans anywhere between eighteen and eighty who regard him as cool. It all gelled with *Cowboyography*. That was the crossroads. It redefined him and, more importantly, it sold big numbers. It went platinum and for a Canadian country album that's phenomenal." "Ian's solo career has been more prominent than mine," Sylvia acknowledges, "and a lot of that is that I haven't pursued a concert career. He's built up his audience over time. But I know I could still draw people as Sylvia Tyson if I were to put together a concert tour. I haven't really actively gone after that. It has a lot to do with the fact that I've never been someone who has to perform to feel complete. So I'm not dependent on that legacy. I don't have to go out every night and play 'Four Strong Winds.'"

That legacy surfaced once again when Sylvia, her former *Video Hits* and *Country in My Soul* producer Sandra Faire, and Sylvia's then-manager Alan Kates produced *Four Strong Winds: Ian & Sylvia and Friends* for a CBC TV special in October 1986. The concept behind the special was to stage a reunion concert in August before a live audience, initially to be held at the Filene Center at Wolf Trap National Park for the Performing Arts in Vienna, Virginia, on Tuesday, August 5. However, it was instead moved to the Kingswood Music Theatre at Canada's Wonderland (a theme park in suburban Toronto) and booked for August 18. Sylvia served as the executive producer of the one-hour special edited from the concert event, which aired on CBC in October. "I had been working with Sandra at that point and we had the idea for the reunion," Sylvia explains. "Ian and I had tossed it around but not seriously. Sandra and I basically put our heads together and decided to do it, so I approached Ian about it. He wasn't that keen until we told him how much we were going to pay him." Interviewed at the time, Ian stated, "It's Sylvia's baby and she wants to do it. I have mixed feelings about it."

Although the production was fraught with problems from the get-go, in the end it came across to television viewers like a family reunion. This was still months away from *Cowboyography* so Ian's star had not yet risen phoenix-like. Nonetheless, he agreed to the reunion not out of sentimentality but largely for the hefty five-figure cheque. He came in for a week of rehearsals and also helped publicize the event. He was even effusive in the interview sequences on the television special although, in typical Ian Tyson fashion, he later disparaged the show. He even took a shot at the sound system for the live concert, commenting to the crowd that it was "an authentic recreation of a 1962 sound system, folks." Larry LeBlanc served as public relations consultant for the production. "We had a lot of time together and I don't think I've ever laughed as much as I did with them," he recalls. "It was a very family atmosphere backstage, very easy-going. It was like attending a class reunion."

The "friends" included Judy Collins, Murray McLauchlan, Emmylou Harris, Linda Ronstadt (who was not at the live concert but had a separately filmed performance), and Gordon Lightfoot. Old running buddies Peter, Paul & Mary and Bob Dylan provided pre-recorded greetings, although nailing Bob down turned into a study in patience and determination. "We went through hell getting that video tribute from him," sighs Sylvia. "We had been trying for six months with his manager to get it. He kept telling us, 'Yes, yes, Bob will do it.' But after six months we were getting frantic. So Bob was doing a concert somewhere and he was · coming through the parking lot and they grabbed a video camera and got him to do it by a truck or something. It was very strange but typical of Bob." Equally elusive was Gordon Lightfoot, who couldn't give Sylvia a definitive answer as to whether he would appear for the live concert. There was some concern whether he could perform at all, given his poor health in recent months. In the end Gordon came through after steady badgering by Sylvia to make up his mind. His appearance, strolling out neatly attired in a white suit to join Ian & Sylvia on "Early Morning Rain," earned the greatest applause of all the guests. "Gordon held off until the last minute," notes Sylvia. "He hadn't been performing a lot and was undecided about appearing. So we had Murray McLauchlan prepared to do more. Finally I called Gordon and said that we couldn't keep hanging on like this because we had to publicize the show and he replied, 'Okay, you can publicize that I'll be there.' He had been very ill and I think people were shocked when they saw him looking gaunt." Adds Larry, "Then he gets onstage and we couldn't get him off. He was only supposed to do two songs but ended up doing four or five numbers. He hadn't performed in a few years and was obviously enjoying himself." Of note is the fact that the musical arrangement for "Early Morning Rain" on the show, played by Sylvia's backing band, included the contentious minor chord. "That minor chord still irritates Gordon," smiles Sylvia.

Opening with "You Were On My Mind," Sylvia looked radiant in a shimmering silver sequined dress, while Ian looked tall and handsome, a cowboy hat perched on his head. "Ian and Sandra Faire feuded over Ian's cowboy hat," chuckles Larry. "She wanted him to pull it up so the camera could see his face. But at that point Ian had the cheque in his pocket and didn't give a shit." What's surprising beyond the fact that the two were appearing together onstage were the frequent warm glances and smiles exchanged between them, something more often absent in the old days. "It was a polite relationship," remarks Sylvia on the cordiality between them on the show. They followed with "Lovin' Sound" before Judy Collins appeared to duet with Ian & Sylvia on "Some Day Soon." Judy then performed a solo version of Joni Mitchell's "Both Sides Now." *Toronto Star* music critic Peter Goddard remarked, "A glossy Judy Collins's glossy version of 'Some Day Soon' may look good on film. It sure sounded soppy live." Sylvia then dusted off her autoharp for "When First Unto This Country," off their debut album. Emmylou Harris, Nashville's darling of country roots music, joined Sylvia for "River Road," then, with Ian, the three sang "Summer Wages." Afterwards, Emmylou performed a solo version of Jesse Winchester's "My Songbird," backed only by Albert Lee from her Hot Band on mandolin. Canadian singer/songwriter Murray McLauchlan then came out for "Nova Scotia Farewell," never one of Ian's favourites back in the day, though always an audience winner. "I remember coming off stage having sung that song with Ian and Murray McLauchlan," laughs Sylvia, "and Ian saying, 'Now I'll never have to ever sing that fucking song again as long as I live!'"

Unable to attend the live taping due to a touring conflict, dedicated Ian & Sylvia fan Linda Ronstadt flew in on Friday to tape her duet with them on Steve Gillette and Tom Campbell's delicate "Darcy Farrow," filmed at CBC's studio on Sumach Street in Toronto. "I remember," says Larry LeBlanc, "the director was Peter

Mann, who used to be in the '60s band Sugar Shoppe and later put together the Nylons. So there he is going over the vocals with Ian & Sylvia and Linda Ronstadt and arranging their harmonies, telling them, 'No, no, a little more Linda here, and Sylvia, you hang back there. . . . ' It was amazing to watch. Linda Ronstadt just worships Ian & Sylvia."

Ian & Sylvia then closed the show with the inevitable "Four Strong Winds," joined on the chorus near the end by their guests. "Ian had been playing 'Four Strong Winds' on his own for years and his phrasing had changed," notes Sylvia. "He didn't sing it the way he used to so I had to watch him to make sure our phrasing matched. I found it's easier for us to do the older stuff that neither Ian nor I have been doing in the interim because the approach to it remains the same. The arrangements haven't changed, whereas with something like 'Four Strong Winds,' Ian's been doing it and has his own way of doing it now. The adjustment is a lot greater. There was a fair bit of rehearsing for that one at the old CBC Sumach studio."

Serving double duty as producer and performer prevented Sylvia from enjoying the reunion and guests. "In the end I didn't really get the chance to relish the moment because I had so much on my plate that night. I was very focused precisely on what I had to do next, so there wasn't really any sense of the reunion in that way because I had so much else to think about." Serving as host, Sylvia appeared nervous but not distractingly so. Reviewing the live concert, Peter Goddard wrote, "So, we've had it wrong all along. It's Sylvia Tyson who's the tough one, not Ian. He's the romantic, the buckaroo balladeer living in the new west, lost in the old. She, on the other hand, was insistent enough to corral him one more time – along with a number of their buddies – for last night's Ian & Sylvia reunion in the Kingswood

Music Theatre. By the time the Tysons had finally parted ways in 1975, it had been forgotten what brought them together – and to their early audiences – in the first place. If nothing else, they gave us a sharp reminder last night, rummaging around in their bag of vintage folk tunes for several Appalachian bluegrass pieces and an a cappella version of 'The Texas Rangers' [omitted from the television show] with its high, arching melody line and aching intervals."

The television broadcast was promoted heavily by CBC and drew a healthy audience share from those still keen on seeing the two together once again. Sylvia had accurately gauged the nostalgic mood of the public for a reunion but there were no plans or even discussion to take it any further. "Those Ian & Sylvia revivals we did were awful," Ian now claims. "I must admit I was a different Ian Tyson then but the one we did at Wonderland in Ontario wasn't rehearsed properly and I thought it was terrible. Those kinds of things don't really work." (That sound heard was that of a door closing firmly behind him.)

Both resumed their separate lives and careers. Returning to CTV, Ian took on hosting duties for an Edmonton-based television show entitled *Sun Country*. He continued to record and release albums at regular intervals for the next twenty-two years and to enjoy an unprecedented career revival. For someone who once said he didn't understand how anyone could reinvent themselves, here he was, the perfect example of an artist who had redefined and retooled his image in the eyes of the public. However, for those who looked deeper, Ian had always embraced the cowboy lifestyle in attitude and song. But now he was more uncompromising about it. "Unfortunately," laments friend Tom Russell, "since Ian got into the cowboy thing, he won't go back and re-record or play any of those great earlier songs. 'I was a folkie then,' he'll say. 'And now I'm doing this.' But those songs – like 'Four Rode By' or 'Red Velvet' – are by and large still strong today. Every Ian & Sylvia album had three or four or five gems on it." Ian prefers to not revisit the past. He's not interested in riding on old coattails. In 1989 Ian was inducted into the Canadian Country Music Hall of Fame and in 1995 he received the Order of Canada, the country's highest civilian award. Among a long list of honours he has recieved are the Prairie Music and Western Music Hall of Fame awards and the Alberta Order of Excellence.

But while Ian's songwriting, like fine wine, only appears to get better with age (his most recent album, 2008's *Yellowhead to Yellowstone and Other Love Stories*, is a shining example of a songwriter still very much in his prime), his voice has not. The combination of damage from straining his vocal cords over a bad PA system and the after effects of a virus have left his once rich baritone voice raw and grainy. Ian calls it his new voice and has not shied away from performing since his vocal chords were ravaged. Still, sales of his most recent album, the one with the new voice, were disappointing for him. "It's getting better, the old voice," he insists. "It'll never be the same, though." Nor has it slowed down his touring schedule either. Divorced from Twylla (the terms of which left him deeply embittered) and estranged from Adelita,* he continues to operate the T-Bar-Y ranch in Longview by himself and tour a good portion of the year. "Sylvia was kind of there for me when I went through my recent divorce," Ian acknowledges. As for the past, "the 'what if' with Ian & Sylvia," he muses, "is 'What if we had had a real producer?' If we had had a decent producer who knows what might have happened?"

---

* They have recently reconnected and re-established their relationship.

Sylvia kept a lower profile in the latter '80s, reappearing in 1993 as a member of Quartette alongside Colleen Peterson, Cindy Church, and Caitlin Hanford, all noteworthy singers and song-writers in their own right. Initially a one-off union, the vocal quartet has remained together blending blues, gospel, folk, coun-try, jazz, and pop to create an appealingly unique sound. To date, Quartette* have released six well-received albums and continue to perform sporadically. "It was good for Sylvia because it took the focus off her directly and shared the responsibilities," sug-gests Larry LeBlanc. All four contribute songs to the group, taking pressure off Sylvia to have to come up with a full album's worth of songs.

In addition to her work with Quartette, Sylvia has been active behind the scenes in the Canadian music business. She was a found-ing member of the Canadian Songwriters Hall of Fame in 1998 and currently serves as its president. Sylvia has been a driving force behind this worthy organization. Each year they host a gala to honour Canadian songwriters. "Sylvia has done so many things to keep the wheels of Canadian music rolling," acknowledges Joan Besen. "She is very dedicated to that and it's all voluntary. She is very committed to encouraging young songwriters and recogniz-ing songwriting talent." In 1995, Sylvia received the Order of Canada and she was inducted into the Canadian Country Music Hall of Fame in 2003.

In 1992, CARAS (the Canadian Academy of Recording Arts and Sciences) acknowledged Ian & Sylvia's groundbreaking achievements by honouring them with induction into the Canadian Music Hall of Fame. At the Juno awards ceremony held that year at Toronto's O'Keefe Centre, Blue Rodeo, Molly

---

* In 1996 Gwen Swick replaced Colleen Peterson, who died of cancer that year.

Johnson, 54–40's Neil Osborne, and the Skydiggers' Andy Maize performed a rocked-up medley of Ian & Sylvia songs while the two watched from the front row. Blue Rodeo's Jim Cuddy recalls, "We didn't think that tribute went that well. We're glad we got to do 'Four Strong Winds' again later for them. Those moments are difficult when you're playing their songs to someone and they're sitting right there in front of you. So that was a bit of a blur for us. Afterwards we didn't think that song came across that well and they didn't look like they were too pleased. Who knows what was going on at the time." In fact, the two were delighted and Ian got a kick out of host, SCTV star Rick Moranis's request at the close of the ceremonies that Ian please move his horse so Tom Cochrane, the big winner that night, could pull a U-Haul up to the door. "That award would never have happened without Peter Steinmetz, who was on the board of CARAS at that point," insists Sylvia. "It had to do with a conversation I had with Peter in an elevator. He said to me, 'You and Ian never won a Juno,' and I told him, 'There were no Junos back then.' From that he got the idea that we should be in the Canadian Music Hall of Fame and put it forward. It likely wouldn't have happened otherwise."

Vancouver's Greystone Books published Ian's autobiography, *I Never Sold My Saddle*, in 1994, which he wrote in collaboration with Canadian musicologist Colin Escott. Much of the book focused on his life in the West, lamenting the changes that have taken place that threaten the old way of life. One critic regarded it as nothing less than the manifesto of the Alberta-based right-wing Reform Party in its political tone. "It took me until I was forty-five years old to become political," Ian smirks. "And now I'm considered an environmental radical. Go figure." Ian & Sylvia's career received limited coverage in the book, suggesting that it was not a topic high on Ian's list of priorities.* One journalist recalled at the time mentioning Ian & Sylvia during a telephone interview, only to have the sometimes cantankerous Ian hang up on him.

Two years later CARAS spearheaded the compilation and release of the four-CD box set *Oh What a Feeling: A Vital Collection of Canadian Music*, with all proceeds going to several charities. As associate producer on the project, Larry LeBlanc was among those asked to choose the selections and provide liner notes. While the songs that spanned the four disks focused mostly on the latter '60s onward, there was one exception. "When we did the *Oh What a Feeling* box set," he explains, "there was only one earlier track included and that was 'Four Strong Winds.' You don't have a Canadian music scene without Ian & Sylvia, and by the same token, Paul Anka. Both are just as important but Ian & Sylvia eclipse Paul because they stayed here. Paul went down to the States and stayed. Ian & Sylvia proved you could go to the United States and work but still come back to Canada and live here. In their peak they were among the top-four folk music acts of that time." Vanguard Records agreed and in 2001 released a four-CD box set that gathered together all seven Ian & Sylvia albums on the label, despite the fact that almost all of them remained in print. In the new millennium Ian & Sylvia's music is even easier to obtain than in the previous four decades, and in a variety of releases and compilations (including their two Newport Folk Festival appearances), testament to the timeless quality of the music.

And still the accolades continued. In 2005, CBC Radio ran a series entitled *50 Essential Canadian Popular Songs* in which listeners voted on a series of songs nominated by a panel of experts and

---

* In 2010 Random House (Canada) published Ian's second autobiography, *The Long Trail: My Life in the West*. Sylvia's first work of fiction, *Joyner's Dream*, was published by Harper Collins Books in 2011.

media personalities. The winner, hands down by a wide margin, was "Four Strong Winds." The runners-up were, at number 2, "If I Had $1,000,000" by the Barenaked Ladies; number 3, Neil Young's "Heart of Gold"; number 4, "Northwest Passage" by Stan Rogers; number 5, the Guess Who's Vietnam War–era anti-America rant "American Woman"; number 6, the immortal "Canadian Railroad Trilogy" by Gordon Lightfoot; number 7, Joni Mitchell's "Both Sides Now"; number 8, Leonard Cohen with "Suzanne"; number 9, Joni Mitchell again with "Big Yellow Taxi"; and number 10, Gordon Lightfoot once more with "Early Morning Rain." Impressive company, indeed. "'Four Strong Winds' deserves to be number 1," acknowledges Gordon Lightfoot. "Rightly so. I'm up in there somewhere but I'm glad their song is number 1. It should be. I'm just glad it's them and not me." Comments Ian, "That blew my mind. I think a big part of that was the fact that I did a very emotional version of that song at the Mayerthorpe Mountie killings memorial service, which was huge and televised. I don't think I ever sang it as well before or since."

In 2006, the Mariposa Folk Festival Hall of Fame inducted Ian & Sylvia at a celebratory event held at Hugh's Room in west Toronto. The Hall of Fame had been established the previous year with inductees Edgar Cowan, Ruth Jones McVeigh and her late husband Dr. Crawford "Casey" Jones, Sid Dolgay of the Travellers, and Pete McGarvey, all of them instrumental in creating that first festival in 1961. The second year recognized Ian & Sylvia for their pivotal role over the years, and also inducted Bohemian Embassy founder Don Cullen. At the induction ceremony, several artists, including the Good Brothers, Blue Rodeo's Greg Keelor, Margaret Good, and former Great Speckled Bird member David Wilcox, performed Ian & Sylvia songs. The real treat came when Ian & Sylvia themselves got up to perform together. Host Nancy White termed it "Canada's version of a reunion of the Beatles!" The two sang three songs: "When First Unto This Country," "Four Strong Winds," and "Texas Rangers." There had been no formal rehearsal beforehand. "That was a surprise to everybody," smiles Sylvia. "It was fun, too," adds Ian.

That set the stage for the Mariposa Folk Festival's fiftieth anniversary in the summer of 2010.

SOME DAY SOON

It was Sunday afternoon July 11, 2010, the final day of the fiftieth anniversary of the Mariposa Folk Festival, the granddaddy
of all Canadian music gatherings, and word was out in the backstage area: Ian Tyson was in a foul mood. He'd just returned from
taking part in one of the many afternoon songwriter workshops
scattered about the outdoor festival site, nestled along the shores
of Orillia's Lake Couchiching in the heart of Ontario's cottage
country about an hour or so north of Toronto. Billed as "Whiskey,
Wood, and Wire" and held on the Estelle Klein Stage, the workshop was hosted by recent Juno award–winning singer/songwriter
David Francey. As Ian strode purposefully through the backstage
area a festival volunteer approached him, proffering a Mariposa
2010 poster for him to sign, only to be rebuffed with a brusque
"Nope!" Arriving at his trailer, Ian mounted the steps and closed
the door. Luthier John Marr of MacKenzie & Marr Guitars managed a hasty photo op with Ian holding their signature Ian Tyson
acoustic model before being ushered out of the trailer. A handful

of fans gathering by the steps were informed that Mr. Tyson was not seeing anyone at the moment.

Forty-nine years earlier on a warm August evening, Ian & Sylvia were the penultimate act on the closing night of the first Mariposa Folk Festival, their status as the king and queen of the nascent Toronto folk music scene overshadowed only by the Travellers, a quartet of left-leaning Toronto folkies modelled after the Weavers, whose "This Land Is Your Land," altered to reflect Canada's geography, had become somewhat of a national anthem. Ian was still two years away from writing his own Canadian anthem, "Four Strong Winds." Largely forgotten in the intervening decades, the Travellers chose to remain in Canada; Ian & Sylvia sought a wider audience and the recording opportunities that at that time only a move to the United States could offer.

Much had been made of the celebratory nature of the anniversary event in pre-publicity and promotion as well as throughout the festival site, peaking with an onstage tribute to many of the surviving founders, sandwiched between sets early Sunday evening. Included were Ruth Jones McVeigh who, along with her late husband Crawford "Casey" Jones, was the Festival's founder; Sid Dolgay of the Travellers; and Don Cullen, who operated the Bohemian Embassy coffeehouse. Edgar Cowan, who produced the first show, and Ted Schafer, who served as master of ceremonies, were conspicuous by their absence from the tribute. So, too, were Ian and Sylvia, who chose to remain in their individual trailers. There was an important distinction to be made between the now geriatric founders being assisted to the stage by crew members and the two performers who were still recording, writing, and treading the boards.

The Mariposa Folk Festival had suffered through a rough history since its glorious debut. Following its second year, the town of Orillia banned further festivals, and the organization, now under the direction of Estelle Klein, bounced from location to location (including a spell at Toronto's Harbourfront) until making a return to Orillia's Tudhope Park alongside Lake Couchiching in 2000, where it has remained ever since. Over the decades the festival has witnessed appearances by the likes of Joni Mitchell, Neil Young, Gordon Lightfoot, Leonard Cohen, Bruce Cockburn, James Taylor, Daniel Lanois, Bonnie Raitt, and Loreena McKennitt. Even Bob Dylan visited in 1972 and sat among the audience.

The 2010 festival site resembled one of those travelling Renaissance Festivals that set up each summer at locations across the continent, with various new age hippy-dippy craft tents, organic food vendors, roaming jugglers, straw under foot, and colourfully and ornately adorned patrons skewed heavily towards the baby boomer demographic. As one backstager wryly commented, there were more grey ponytails than at the Kentucky Derby. And plenty of balding pates, too. Throughout the day the spectre of rain hung over the festival site, with the sun peeking through a low cloud covering. Known as the Gordon Lightfoot curse, named for the last time he appeared at the festival amid a torrential downpour, the clouds finally burst forth around 5:00 p.m., to deliver a heavy dousing before the sun emerged once again. Much of the site was now mucky, despite the covering of straw.

Ever since the roster of artists had been announced the previous fall, speculation ran rampant that there would be an Ian & Sylvia reunion. Both deflected any such fanciful conjecture right up to the day of their appearance. Perhaps that explained Ian's temperament on the Sunday. "I think there's a plan afoot to get us to perform together at the fiftieth anniversary of Mariposa but I don't think that'll pan out," Sylvia contended back in September of 2009. Nevertheless, there was no doubting the nostalgic direction of this

year's festival, with Gordon Lightfoot as closing-night headliner
and Ian, Sylvia, and Murray McLauchlan in support. Of the four,
only the Tysons had appeared at the inaugural festival back in 1961
(Gordon made his Mariposa debut the following year). Bonnie
Dobson, the only other surviving original still performing, had
offered to make the trek from her home in the U.K. on her own
dime to perform, but details could not be worked out in time. Thus
it seemed only fitting that Ian & Sylvia reunite onstage for old
time's sake. If only it were that simple. Despite persistent rumours
to the contrary, neither had spoken to the other regarding performing together, right up to Sunday afternoon. Nonetheless, it was the
one topic on everyone's mind at the festival, on both sides of the
stage: would Ian & Sylvia give everyone their "Mitch & Mickey
moment."* One backstage jokester went around telling people Ian
and Sylvia were going to renew their wedding vows onstage.

"The anticipation is in the air," enthused popular CBC Radio
host and festival master of ceremonies Shelagh Rogers backstage.
"Everyone is hoping for it. There has been so much anticipation
about will they or won't they. But I do think it's going to happen.
When it does happen it will be devastating but in a good way.
There won't be a dry eye anywhere. Together and separately
they've written anthems for our country so it will be pride and
goose bumps. It'll be marvellous. Even thinking about it gives
me goose bumps. They are two artists who defined Canadian
music and are hugely respected." A couple of years earlier,
Shelagh's daily CBC Radio show *Sounds Like Canada* had declared
"Four Strong Winds" the ultimate Canadian song, far surpassing
stiff competition from Gordon Lightfoot, Leonard Cohen, and
Neil Young.

---

* The Ian & Sylvia-like characters whose reunion is much anticipated throughout Christopher Guest's folk music lampoon *A Mighty Wind*.

Jim Cuddy and Greg Keelor of Canadian country-rock band Blue Rodeo were the special surprise guests on the Sunday evening show but were not immune to the wave of Ian & Sylvia nostalgia engulfing the festival. Blue Rodeo had been part of a tribute to Ian & Sylvia back in 1992 on the occasion of the duo's induction into the Canadian Music Hall of Fame.* "When Greg and I started Blue Rodeo," says Jim, "we sort of rejected a lot of the rock band stuff and just went with acoustic guitars and we were influenced by Ian Tyson. But there was no record label interest. However, by the time we got going with the band, Ian was one of the first western endorsers of Blue Rodeo. And I don't know if he even knows this or not. That was in the days when our success was still regarded with suspicion in country music circles. We played the Canadian Country Music Awards in Calgary. Everyone clapped politely but Ian stood up and then everyone stood up. We'd never met him but his endorsement meant a lot to us. It got us accepted in country music circles. Subsequent to that we've met him and gotten to know him and he's a wonderful man." As for all the buzz about a reunion, "I think that rumour will exist as long as they're both still playing," Jim acknowledges. "I think everyone is hoping for it. But I also like them both as individual artists."

The day before, Sylvia's vocal group Quartette had performed on the Estelle Klein stage and member Caitlin Hanford was still on site Sunday for an afternoon song-circle appearance. She, too, was hoping to witness a bit of Canadian music history take place. "I think that it's really special that Ian and Sylvia are on the same show together and I'm hoping to hear them do something. Oh, it would be just fantastic. I'm kind of hoping they do 'Four Strong

---

* CARAS (the Canadian Academy of Recording Arts & Sciences) selects inductees each year although no such Hall of Fame exists in any physical sense. It is merely ceremonial.

Winds' but who knows. It would be great if they did. Maybe they'll do 'A Kiss at the End of the Rainbow' from *A Mighty Wind* with Mitch & Mickey. But whatever they do I'm just thrilled that they're both here. I've admired their work for so long. I grew up on an island near Seattle and used to hang out with the hippies down the street from me and they had an Ian & Sylvia album and they'd listen to it over and over. I had no idea that years later I would end up moving to Canada and being in a band with Sylvia."

Not everyone was in tune with the persistent reunion buzz. When a young female volunteer working as security for the backstage area was asked if Sylvia had arrived, she replied, "Who's Sylvia?" only to be castigated by her baby boomer colleague.

One possible obstacle to any potential reunion was the state of Ian's voice. Two years earlier he had startled concert goers and record buyers with a vocal sound that was part whisper and part grainy croak, the result of his catching a virus, coupled with oversinging in an effort to come to terms with a bad PA mix at an outdoor event. "I played the Havelock Jamboree, a big outdoor show in Ontario," Ian explains. "I fought the sound system and I lost. I knew I'd hurt my voice and it was recovering slowly when I was hit with a bad virus which seemed to last forever. My old voice isn't coming back, the doctors told me, so I've had to get used to this new one." The loss of his distinctive rich baritone made news across the country and sales of his subsequent album, *Yellowhead to Yellowstone*, languished, a point not lost on Ian who would announce a song with, "Here's one from an album that's hard to find." Privately he lamented the lack of radio airplay and the fickle nature of the music business. Sylvia's voice showed no signs of wear and tear over the years. Then again, she also didn't perform as much as Ian, who continued to tour regularly. Could they still pull out their signature vocal blend or would Ian sound like a croaking frog next to her? Although his voice had been improving he was nonetheless sensitive about it.

Sylvia's solo set followed the fiftieth anniversary onstage tribute. The contrast couldn't have been more startling, and perhaps it was intentional. Dressed to kill in an elegant black and silver outfit and high-heeled boots, she looked every inch the country music queen she has become. "I don't think Sylvia has looked or sounded more beautiful," gushed Shelagh Rogers. "Simply gorgeous." Canadian music royalty, indeed. At sixty-nine, her voice had lost none of its timbre, although the once ever-present vibrato has toned down over the years. She played many of her favourites that had defined her solo career post–Ian & Sylvia, including "River Road," "The Night the Chinese Restaurant Burned Down," "Spring of '45," picking up her button accordion for "Pepere's Mill" (written with legendary Canadian songbird Lucille Starr). It was at that moment that Ian, having left the festival site not long after his afternoon workshop and recently returned, emerged from his trailer and ambled over to the side of the stage and stood on the stairs to watch Sylvia. He remained there for the duration of her well-received set. More stooped over than in recent years, Ian's walk was a bit laboured and it was obvious he was showing his seventy-six years. He was, however, in an improved disposition, evidenced by his choosing to take in his former partner's set, something no one would have bet on witnessing earlier in the day. As Sylvia closed with "You Were On My Mind" everyone in the audience watched the wings to see if Ian would emerge and join her. He didn't, but as Sylvia descended the stairs from the stage he was there to greet her with a warm hug and a "Well done, my dear!"

By that point, the subject of their joining one another on stage had yet to be broached between them. But as the two embraced they quietly chatted. Asked immediately afterwards what the topic of conversation might have been, Sylvia responded, "Well, I just spoke with Ian about my possibly coming up and doing 'Four Strong Winds' with him and he was favourable to it."

Ian's solo set was up next. He had enjoyed a career rejuvenation in recent years, redefining himself on a series of albums as the lone voice of the Old West with songs like "M.C. Horses," "Springtime in Alberta," "The Gift," "Navajo Rug," "Jerry Ambler," and "Jaquima to Freno." His only nod to his earlier career was to play "Some Day Soon" and "Summer Wages" in his concerts. If the calls for an encore went long enough he'd favour audiences with "Four Strong Winds" but it was never a guarantee with Ian. Sylvia had managed to steer clear of the Ian & Sylvia legacy in her own solo career. "Up until a few years ago in my shows I didn't do any Ian & Sylvia songs," she admits. "I did my songs from then, like 'You Were On My Mind,' but only recently did I start doing 'Four Strong Winds' as part of an encore, and the whole house goes all misty-eyed."

While there is much to be gained in the short term by currying fan favour and catering to their nostalgic expectations, any artist who has ever gone off on a solo career knows there is a price to be paid when you accede to joining up with your former partners for a trawl through your old hits. While offering a good time for the artists and audience in the moment, it nonetheless marks a step backwards, a concession that perhaps your former association may still eclipse your individual efforts since. Hence many artists resist such overtures from ex-associates or fan demands. The wisdom is that as soon as you take a step backwards, you're finished. Still, there are those artists who have managed to balance their past association with their present career, Paul McCartney for one. But does anyone really buy a high-priced McCartney concert ticket with the great anticipation of hearing him launch into his most recently recorded material or are his concert goers waiting all night for the Beatles and Wings numbers? In the case of Ian & Sylvia, both have sought to distance themselves from their collective past in the intervening decades. Yet it still haunts them. I once told Ian after a concert in which he did not perform "Four Strong Winds" that everyone was waiting all evening for that number. "I know," he retorted.

Backed by bass and lead guitar, with Ian on rhythm and occasional picking, Ian's set was plagued by continual sound problems. Nonetheless, he managed to delight the crowd with songs and stories. Midway through he told the audience, "They say I played here fifty years ago. I couldn't have been here fifty years ago. I'd have been only three years old! Must be a typo. It was only thirty years ago." As his set neared its close someone in the audience called out, "How about 'Four Strong Winds' with Sylvia?" Ian ignored him. However, once the inevitable call for an encore came, his guitarist began playing the familiar opening notes to that song. That's all anyone in the audience needed as their cue to rise to their feet, cheering. Remarking how he couldn't remember this old song and needed some help, Sylvia then emerged from the wings to Ian's left as he looked to his right for her. The audience yelled out, "She's over there!" as Ian turned to catch Sylvia at the far microphone. Smiling, he then launched into the verses with Sylvia joining on the choruses. It was clear that this was an unrehearsed moment. There were some pitch issues but none of that mattered to the audience who swayed en masse to the rhythm of the music, singing along teary-eyed. Sylvia moved to centre stage where she joined Ian for the final verse. As the song concluded she planted a kiss on his cheek. It was, indeed, a rare and special moment in Canadian music history. The dream nurtured in the hearts of those four thousand or so had been fulfilled. It was left to the guys from

Blue Rodeo and Gordon Lightfoot to follow. But in the hearts of many of those in attendance, the show had reached its peak at that moment.

"I'm just glad it's over," commented Sylvia afterwards, smiling. "There was so much expectation." As for Ian, he conceded, "Well, that's what everybody fuckin' wanted!" before complaining about the bad sound mix. "The sound was terrible. I mean why come down here and work your ass off all afternoon getting it right and then they fuck up the sound on you that night. It was total shit. I thought we did okay but it was so disappointing, the sound." And having his former partner join him onstage? "It was great. But she sings it in a different key now."

Reflecting on their Mariposa moment a few days later, Sylvia remained judicious. "With that kind of thing, I'm well aware of the effect that it has on the people who see it. But when you're doing it you're just doing it. You're not thinking about the effect you're having or the legacy or any of that. You're concentrating specifically on what you're doing onstage at that moment. I'm pleased that people were pleased but it was not as big a deal for me as it was for them. It was no big emotional moment for me. When you're in the middle of it you don't get a sense of the moment."

Was she aware of the expectation amongst the crowd? "Certainly. The big question on everybody's mind was 'Will they or won't they?' The truth is it wasn't exactly planned, although it was anticipated. The anticipation was palpable. We could have gotten away without doing it but there would have been a lot of disappointed people. Ian is less concerned about that than I am." She confirmed that there had been no discussion of a reunion until just prior to Ian's set. "I came down the stairs and said to Ian, 'I think we have to do it.'" She was unaware that Ian had been enjoying her set from the wings.

"I know he was self-conscious about his voice," Sylvia concludes. "Personally, I think his voice has come back a long way towards him sounding like his old self again. But I think it worked. It wouldn't have mattered to the crowd, though. They were all singing along anyway."

While perhaps not fulfilling everyone's dreams of a full set of Ian & Sylvia favourites, the fact that they did unite to perform their best-known and most beloved song was enough for everyone to go home satisfied. Certainly history was made that evening, but perhaps more than those in the audience realized, because any further Ian & Sylvia reunions are not likely to take place. In the euphoric aftermath of their brief Mariposa reunion there was plenty of speculation and conjecture that the two might tour together, performing separately before uniting for an emotion-filled closing set. The reality is that such a dream tour, as successful and warmly received as it would no doubt be, is not in the cards, nor is it something either would ever consider. As Sir Paul McCartney used to say when the inevitable Beatles reunion question was posed, "You can't reheat a soufflé."

Both Ian and Sylvia hold fond memories of those days together and the music they created, but neither is keen to become dependent on reliving it night after night. Audiences continue to come out to see them separately, though in their hearts they remain ever hopeful of hearing an Ian & Sylvia song. "Although they may have followed our careers ever since," opines Sylvia, "and bought our solo records, they still cleave to those original Ian & Sylvia songs. Their first connection with Ian and me was through those songs and I thank God for that. 'You Were On My Mind' has paid the bills so many times for me over the years. Those old songs that they are coming to hear allow you to play them your new songs. It's how they hear your new songs."

"We had a damn good run," muses Ian, reflecting on Ian & Sylvia's legacy, "and recorded some pretty fine music." That music has stood the test of time and will go on to outlive both of them.

"The music we made together still holds up for me," affirms Sylvia. "All of it. I make no apologies for it. I can listen to certain other music of that era that doesn't hold up today and has become dated. The stuff we did seems to me to be more classic. I'm very proud of that music. It was great music then and it's still great music and that's the bottom line for me."

ACKNOWLEDGEMENTS

I would like to extend my sincerest gratitude to Ian Tyson and Sylvia Tyson for their time, cooperation, and support of this book. This has been a dream project for me. Extra special thanks to Peter O'Brien (*Omaha Rainbow*) for his Ian Tyson interview, Edgar Cowan for his detailed journals, Holger Petersen (Stony Plain Records) for his 1972 Ian & Sylvia interview and support, and Larry LeBlanc for resources and input. Thank you to Joan Besen for lighting the initial spark that got this project started. Thanks to everyone who agreed to be interviewed and whose names appear throughout the book. Additional thanks to Gordon Lightfoot, Anne Leibold, Eric Weissberg, Barnes Newbury, Barry Ballard, Richie Unterberger, Carny Corbett, Russell deCarle, Dick Weissman, Bob Mersereau, Alana Levandoski, the Blue Sky Motel and Cathy at Heidi's Restaurant in Longview, Alberta, the staff at the King Eddy Hotel in Toronto, Jeff Bishop at the Sound Exchange Winnipeg for the albums, Mike Hill at the Mariposa Folk Festival, the Manitoba Arts Council, and to my friend Kara Wright for getting me to LAX airport on time to make it to Mariposa.

To my editor Philip Rappaport at M&S, thank you for your advice, encouragement, counsel, and feedback. And to my agent David Johnston, thank you for steering the ship in the right direction.

Between the researching and writing of this book, Ben Keith and Suze Rotolo passed away. I consider myself honoured to have met and interviewed both these outstanding individuals. Their recollections and insights enrich this book.

As always, an extra special thank you to my wife Harriett for her endless support, encouragement, and patience (even when my office is a disaster area).

John Einarson, Winnipeg, 2011

INDEX

Notes: A page number followed by the lowercase letter *n* indicates a footnote. In subheadings, I&S stands for Ian & Sylvia, and Bird stands for Great Speckled Bird. The Tysons are indexed both separately (under Tyson, primarily for their personal life) and together (as Ian & Sylvia, primarily for their professional life)